F   IEU

GAIUS JULIUS CAESAR was born in 100 B.C. into an ancient patrician family. He was an adolescent during the period of the proscription of Marius (his father's brother-in-law), the dictatorship of Sulla and the early career of Pompey. His family were traditionally against the patrician senatorial oligarchy and Caesar followed suit. He was imprisoned for a short time by Sulla, but managed to maintain good relations with the nobles for ten years after his release; he was even co-opted into the college of priests (73 B.C.). However he came out openly for Pompey in 71 B.C., and Caesar, Pompey and Crassus (whom the senate had also alienated) formed the 'first triumvirate'. For the next nine years Caesar was away on campaigns, returning in 60 B.C. from his service as governor of Further Spain to be elected consul. He was then created governor of Transalpine Gaul, a task which was to occupy him for nine years. He had left the two triumvirs to safeguard his interests in Rome but they had many differences and met in Luca (56 B.C.) in an attempt to solve them. Pompey was appointed sole consul in 52 B.C. after the death of Crassus, which resulted in civil war and the defeat of the Pompeian faction in Spain (45 B.C.). Caesar came back to Rome as dictator. He tried to improve conditions for the Roman citizen and increase the honesty and efficiency of the government. His dictatorship was declared perpetual in February 44 B.C., but his many bitter enemies hatched a conspiracy and assassinated him in March 44 B.C.

S. A. HANDFORD was born at Manchester in 1898 and educated at Bradford Grammar School and at Balliol College, Oxford, where he took a 'double first' in Classics. He was a Lecturer in Swansea, and Lecturer and Reader at King's College, London. He published several books on classical subjects, and translated Caesar, Sallust and Aesop for the Penguin Classics. He died in October 1978.

JANE GARDNER was born in 1934, and has degrees in Classics from Glasgow and Oxford Universities. She is a Lecturer in Classics and Curator of the Ure Museum at Reading University. Her publications include an edition, with W. F. Bolton, of Ben Jonson's *Catiline* (1973), *Leadership and the Cult of the Personality* (1974), and a translation of Caesar's *The Civil War* for the Penguin Classics.

CAESAR
THE CONQUEST
OF GAUL

TRANSLATED BY
S. A. HANDFORD

REVISED WITH A NEW INTRODUCTION
BY
JANE F. GARDNER

PENGUIN BOOKS

Penguin Books Ltd, Harmondsworth, Middlesex, England
Penguin Books, 625 Madison Avenue, New York, New York 10022, U.S.A.
Penguin Books Australia Ltd, Ringwood, Victoria, Australia
Penguin Books Canada Ltd, 2801 John Street, Markham, Ontario, Canada L3R 1B4
Penguin Books (N.Z.) Ltd, 182–190 Wairau Road, Auckland 10, New Zealand

—

This translation first published 1951
Reprinted 1953, 1956, 1958, 1960, 1963, 1965, 1967, 1970, 1972, 1974,
1976, 1978, 1979, 1980, 1981
Revised with a new introduction 1982

—

Copyright the Estate of S. A. Handford, 1951
Introduction and revisions copyright © Jane F. Gardner, 1982
All rights reserved

—

Filmset, printed and bound in Great Britain by
Hazell Watson & Viney Ltd, Aylesbury, Bucks
Set in VIP Plantin

CONTENTS

CAESAR THE CONQUEST OF GAUL

INTRODUCTION

1 Roman politics in the late Republic

Gaius Julius Caesar spent nine years – almost a sixth of his entire life and more than a third of his life as a member of the Senate – away from Rome, campaigning in Gaul. Half-way through, the military command he held was extended for a further five-year period. Political necessity, rather than military or than his personal irreplaceability in command, required that he continue in post. His victories had already been awarded public thanksgivings of unprecedented length in Rome; nevertheless, to resume private status would have meant political suicide – at the least, exile.

Politics at Rome was personal and factional, its significant operation confined within the membership of the Senate. Constitutionally, Rome was a Republic, with the legislative and electoral sovereignty vested in popular assemblies. In practice, control of government was in the hands of the Senate, itself made up of past and present holders of public office, and the effective policy-making body, although technically it was merely advisory to the magistrates. Before the birth of Caesar, there had been two major developments which had fundamentally changed the character of Roman politics. The Gracchi had shown that the sovereign power of the people could be used to break the Senate's *de facto* control of government. However, they had no armed power with which to defend themselves against the senators' reaction. Marius' military innovations produced an army for whom soldiering was a means of earning a livelihood and – in the absence of a service gratuities commission – its commander the person to whom the soldiers looked to secure some provision for them on demobilization. Both became factors in the internal power struggles in the Senate. The tribunate was used as a means of proposing or blocking legislation whose 'popular' provisions often were – or could be alleged to be – a mere bait for the electorate and a cover for ulterior personal power-seeking. The acquisition of a military command brought with it the opportunity to gain wealth, patronage, electoral support and armed power. Sulla, who himself seized power by force of arms after a civil war, attempted to forestall any repetition of such events by a programme of legislation which regulated the *cursus honorum* – the sequence of magisterial offices – expanded the judicial system and put it under exclusive senatorial control, and imposed restrictions on the powers of the tribunes. Within less than a decade, virtually his entire construction had been either dismantled or ignored.

One of the prime agents in this was Pompey, whose own consulship in 70 B.C. flouted Sullan regulations – he was below the legal minimum age and had held none of the qualifying offices. A few years later, he gained in rapid succession, through tribunician legislation, two military commands – that against the pirates in 67, followed the next year by a command in Asia Minor for the pursuit of the war against Mithridates.

Meanwhile, his former consular colleague and rival, Crassus, made various attempts to strengthen his own position at Rome and there are good grounds for believing that Caesar was one of the rising politicians to whom he lent support. By family connection (he was a nephew by marriage of Marius), as well it would seem as by personal bent, Caesar favoured the 'popular' line in politics. He had backed Pompey's rescinding of Sullan measures and supported the proposal to give him the Asiatic command. Cicero hints very strongly that he and Crassus were intended to be the chief beneficiaries of an agrarian commission which, if set up, would have created a group of officials holding military commands and with vast powers of patronage through the acquisition and distribution of land. His name was also linked with the failed *popularis* Catiline, whom Cicero has deluded subsequent generations into regarding as little better than a psychopath.

By 62 B.C., however, Caesar had had little success in his political ventures, though his career had advanced as far as the praetorship. As well as the matters already mentioned, he had in the mid sixties sponsored a series of abortive prosecutions against persons involved in the violence associated with the overthrow of Saturninus and with the Sullan proscriptions. His aim is uncertain but may have been to try to alert the Romans to the danger of leaving unresolved the question of the permissibility of the procedures by which, since the Gracchi, summary force had on several occasions been used by the State to deal with political opposition.

In 62 B.C. Pompey returned from the East and to general surprise disbanded his armies and returned to private life. With his troops, however, he found that he also gave up his influence with the Senate. Delays and excuses were interposed to the ratification of his Eastern settlement and the provision of land grants for his veterans. Cicero had hoped that political strife at Rome might be terminated by securing cooperation and recognition of common interest, a 'harmony of the orders', between the ruling élite, the Senate, and the non-senatorial wealthy class, the 'equestrian' order (or 'knights'), with Pompey as the leader and rallying-point acceptable to both.

This idea presented no real contribution to solving the political problems of the day; it was merely an attempt to shore up the *status quo*. In any case, the Senate failed to carry out its role. Instead, it alienated not only Pompey but also Crassus and Caesar. Crassus was rebuffed when he supported the request of a company of tax farmers for the remission of part of their contracted price for the taxes of Asia – this also alienated the equestrians. Caesar, on his return in 60 B.C. from service as Governor in Further Spain, wanted a triumph for his victories over certain Spanish tribes. He also wanted to be consul in 59 B.C. However, in order to retain his military command until he held his triumph, he had to remain outside the city. Accordingly, he requested exemption from the regulation requiring consular candidates to appear in person. His request was blocked by a filibuster. In the end, he gave up his triumph and secured election as consul – possibly with some help from Crassus and Pompey. The three men, somewhere about this time, formed an unofficial coalition, known to modern historians as the 'first triumvirate', for mutual self-help:

As consul, Caesar secured the immediate wants of Pompey and Crassus and provided for himself as well. The Senate had tried to block his further advancement, before the election, by assigning as provinces for the consuls of 59 trivial responsibilities in Italy – the supervision of forests and cattle pastures. Caesar used a tribune to put through the popular assembly a law giving him Cisalpine Gaul and Illyricum for five years. When the Governor of Transalpine Gaul died suddenly, the Senate assigned that province to him as well, partly perhaps in order to save themselves the humiliation of seeing it awarded to him in any case by a popular assembly.

His consulship in itself gave grounds for apprehension of what might happen when he should return from his Gallic command. He had used Gracchan methods to by-pass senatorial opposition; he had intimidated the opposition by the threat of armed force (from veterans supplied by Pompey); and he had carried through legislation in defiance of his consular colleague's attempt to block business (by the technical device of announcement that he was 'watching for omens').

By 56 B.C. the triumvirate seemed to be in danger of collapse and Caesar's interests threatened. Publius Clodius Pulcher, both as tribune in 58 B.C. and subsequently, when he began to terrorize Rome with an armed gang, had been stirring up public feeling against the triumvirs and specifically against Pompey – it was suspected, with the encouragement of one of the others. Pompey in 57 B.C. secured a five-year commission to control the corn supply, but relations between him and Crassus were damaged by their rivalry to secure a military command for the restoration of the king of Egypt. Eventually, Pompey even alleged that he was in danger of his life at the hands of agents of Crassus. Meanwhile, Lucius Domitius Ahenobarbus, a member of the senatorial opposition to the triumvirs, was announcing his own candidature for the consular elections for 55 and his intention of securing Caesar's recall from Gaul.

Return from Gaul would mean a return to private status (since Caesar was not eligible for re-election as consul for several more years) and, inevitably, prosecution on one of a number of possible charges arising out of his conduct as pro-consul, and a 'rigged' trial. Caesar held meetings with the other two triumvirs within his Cisalpine province in the spring of 56, as a result of which a law, jointly sponsored by both, was passed in 55 extending Caesar's command for a further five years. Pompey and Crassus secured for themselves consulships for 55 and the passage of a tribunician law assigning them provinces – Syria for Crassus, for a war against the

Parthians, and both Spains to Pompey, for five years, with the additional proviso that Pompey could govern *in absentia* and so remain near Rome.

However, the deaths of Julia (Caesar's daughter and Pompey's wife) in 54 and Crassus in 53 drastically weakened the ties between Pompey and Caesar; and then, after several years of public rioting, disorder and violence, Pompey was commissioned by the Senate to restore order and made sole consul in 52 B.C. One of his first acts as consul was to secure the renewal of his provincial command for a further five years, without making a corresponding provision for Caesar.

Pompey was now torn two ways – between loyalty to his partner, Caesar, on the one hand, and, on the other, the allurements of the power and recognition now offered by the formerly hostile senators, at the price of abandoning Caesar. The temptation to break his promises to Caesar must have been great. These promises, however, ought to be kept – if not from a sense of honour, at least from the consideration that Caesar, with his seasoned army in Gaul, was in a position to fight for his claims.

It was necessary for Caesar that when he gave up his Gallic command he should immediately take on the consulship and so be immune from prosecution. To achieve this, it was necessary that no successor to his command should be appointed by the Senate until he became consul-elect, and that he should be able to stand as candidate *in absentia*. Pompey had already secured the latter privilege for Caesar by a law. As consul, however, he passed a law insisting on personal candidature, then subsequently added a clause exempting Caesar; he also made into law a senatorial decree of the previous year, requiring the lapse of a five-year interval between the holding of the office of praetor or consul and the tenure of a provincial command. This made available for assign-ment a number of ex-magistrates of more than five years' standing who had not held a province (Cicero was among those affected and was despatched, much against his will, to Cilicia). However, this law, unlike the Sempronian law it superseded, was not immune from tribunician veto, and Pompey himself, both in 51 B.C. and again in 50, helped to block discussion of a successor to Caesar. Thus he did his best, in his vacillating way, to ride both horses.

In December 50 the consul Marcellus put separately to the Senate the two questions whether a successor should be sent to replace Caesar and whether Pompey should be required to resign his command. The first was carried, the second rejected. The tribune Curio countered with the proposal that *both* Caesar and Pompey should resign. This motion was overwhelmingly carried – and promptly vetoed by another tribune. Marcellus tried again on the following day and, being vetoed by Curio, declared a state of emergency and called upon Pompey to save the State, authorizing him to command the two legions in Italy (VIII.54-5) and raise additional levies. Pompey accepted the commission since the decision had, in effect, been made for him.

Although Pompey was ostensibly the representative of the Senate and constitutionality, the civil war that followed was essentially a conflict between two powerful individuals, each with a strong personal following. The same is true of the further civil fighting after Caesar's death. Public order and efficient government were restored only when the leader of one faction emerged with such overwhelming strength as to compel obedience. That was Caesar's great-nephew, the future emperor Augustus.

2 *Gaul and its inhabitants*

The Gaul which Caesar conquered included France, except the southern part which was already a Roman province, southern Holland, Belgium, Germany west of the Rhine and most of Switzerland. Its inhabitants he regards – with some oversimplification – as forming three distinct groups (I.1). The ethnic relationships between these are uncertain; however, they form part of a much larger grouping of barbarian peoples, linked together by some degree of racial as of cultural similarity, covering western and central Europe as far as the Danube and extending beyond into Britain, Ireland and even Turkey. To these, and more particularly to those in north-western Europe, Greek and Roman writers applied more or less interchangeably the names of 'Celts' and 'Gauls'.

Caesar's tripartite division records the effects of successive waves of migration into the area of his conquest. These folk movements had been going on at least since the fourth century B.C., when a group penetrating Italy had actually sacked Rome in 390 B.C., and the north of the Italian peninsula – later the province of Cisalpine Gaul – had received settlements; and they were still going on. In Britain, the archaeological record reflects invasion and settlement of the south-east by Belgic people in the first half of the first century B.C. and perhaps even some refugees from Caesar's activities in Gaul. Native hillforts are found to have been established or improved, presumably to meet the invasions, and their situations form a defensive arc complementary to the distribution of finds of Gallo-Belgic coins. There are also signs of intensified trading between Britain and the mainland, both that of the Veneti with the tin-producing south-west and of the Morini and Menapii with the south-east. In northern Italy, the movements of Germanic tribes – the Cimbri and the Teutoni – at the end of the second century B.C. had given the Romans a bad scare. And, as Caesar tells us, further movements, this time on the part of the Helvetii and of the Germanic Suebi, were occasioning disturbance to the neighbours of the Transalpine province and concern to the Romans, when he entered on his command.

Contact with Mediterranean civilizations, in particular with the Greeks through the cities of the Provençal strip and with the Romans, left its mark on the development of Gallic culture and civilization. Trade spread up through the great river valley of the Rhône as early as the sixth century B.C. The Greek foundation Massilia (Marseille), established about 600 B.C., became an important trading centre, through which passed Greek exports and also Etruscan. The latter also came via the Alpine passes. The Gallic products exported in return were probably similar in range to those Strabo lists as coming from Britain – 'corn, cattle, gold, silver, iron . . . together with hides, slaves and hunting dogs' (IV.5.2). Caesar notes the skill of the native iron and copper miners (III.21; cf. VII.22); metals from Britain also reached the Mediterranean via Gaul.

One Mediterranean product of which the Gauls were passionately fond was wine. 'Therefore many Italian merchants with their usual love of lucre look on the Gallic love of wine as their treasure trove'

(Diodorus Siculus V.26.3). He tells us that the wine was imported by boat on the navigable rivers and by waggon across the plains, and fetched enormous prices; a Gaul would barter a slave for a jar of wine. Finds of imported artefacts seem to bear this out. The most common imported vessels found in Gaulish graves are the large bronze beaked flagons of Etruscan make in the period 550 to 400 B.C., and later imitated by Gaulish craftsmen. Large Etruscan wine jars are also found, and Athenian black- and red-figure cups. In Caesar's time, the vine was not yet cultivated in the Transalpine province.

As early as the third century B.C. the Gauls were producing their own coinages, in imitation of Greek types. Distinctive Gallic decorative art appears, already full-blown and highly developed, in the mid fifth century. This early style appears not as a gradual development from earlier native art but as a sudden efflorescence drawing heavily on foreign influences, particularly Greek, or Greco-Etruscan, and eastern. Motifs were not simply copied, but rather modified, adapted and elaborated. From Greek art certain plant forms in particular were taken over, especially palmette and lotus-flower shapes. The fantastic animals and masks of frequent occurrence may owe something to Scythian art, or were perhaps mediated through Etruscan work. In its later phases, Celtic art becomes more stylized and less obviously connected with its alien models. There is increasing use and elaboration of certain types of motif and ornament. Characteristic are the three- and four-cornered whirligigs linked by spirals, motifs running out into symmetrically patterned tendrils and compass-based designs. As with the coinage, decorative art in Gaul shows a fondness for natural motifs (on the Greek coin models, of course, those most commonly offered were horses and human heads) and a predilection for turning them into decorative patterns.

Urban civilization was already considerably developed by Caesar's time. There were many walled towns, connected by good roads and river bridges. Metalwork was skilled and of a high standard. Many peoples even produced their own currency. Settled agriculture, particularly corn-growing, was widespread. Political development varied in degree. Those areas most directly in contact with the Province show most signs of being influenced by Roman political institutions. The Celtic tribes in particular, and especially three important sections singled out for mention by Caesar – the Arverni, the Aedui and the Helvetii – had already abandoned hereditary kingship and instead had magistrates, annually elected and answerable to councils, and public codes of law. The tribes further away, the northern Celts, the Aremorican tribes and the Belgae, both those on the mainland and those in Britain, still retained kingship. The Germanic tribes beyond the Rhine, according to Caesar, were still pastoral, without settled agriculture, accepted a centralized authority only in time of war, and positively rejected what they regarded as the enervating luxuries offered by traders (as did the Nervii – II.15).

Of these groups the first, i.e. primarily the Celtic peoples, were already evolving out of the old tribal system into that of the primitive state, a type of government familiar to the Romans and with which they could deal by familiar methods. Treaties and promises of friendship already existed between some of them and the Romans. However, these governments were still far from stable. Caesar himself comments (II.1) on the commonness of usurpation of monarchy. In the context, he appears to be referring to the Belgae, but in his narrative elsewhere we find monarchic ambitions imputed to the Helvetian Orgetorix (I.2), the Aeduan Dumnorix (I.9ff.) and hinted at in Vercingetorix (VII.4, 20), while the anxiety shown in the treatment of suspected usurpers is reminiscent of Livy's descriptions of the hypersensitive reactions of citizens of the infant Roman republic.

This political instability is linked by Caesar with an instability in character. There are frequent references, direct and indirect, to the Gallic character scattered through the first seven books. They are impulsive, emotional, easily swayed, fickle, loving change, credulous, prone to panic, scatter-brained. Hirtius, in the eighth book, also comments on their volatile nature (VIII.13). In chapter 25 he says that the Treveri, neighbouring the Germans and sharing their ferocity, could be controlled only by armed force.

Caesar was not the first ancient author to write about the Gallic temperament. Like his younger contemporaries, the geographer Strabo and the historian Diodorus Siculus, he drew some of his information about the ethnology and habits of the Gauls from the

Histories of Posidonius, written in the first half of the first century B.C. The two later authors' descriptions of the Gauls include some comments on their character and disposition, probably also drawn from Posidonius. Strabo's account, in particular, resembles Caesar's (Strabo IV.iv. 2, 4). The whole race, he says, is madly keen on war, brave and impetuous and easily outwitted. Because of their frankness and straightforwardness their sympathies are easily roused to war in support of friends who think themselves wronged.

In the first six books, although Caesar repeatedly characterizes the Gauls as a whole, with no distinction of race or tribe, nearly all the contexts in which his remarks occur relate to the peoples remote from the Province and not forming part of the pre-existing system of alliances and friendship with the Romans – the Belgae, the Aremorican tribes and the Aquitanians. It is noteworthy that several times (especially II.1, III.10, IV.5, IV.13) these references are made in the context of a situation where Caesar's forces have been or are about to be extending their operations beyond the territory already held, and a long way out of the Province. It might be suspected that Caesar is trying to counter possible attacks on himself for having carried his offensive, on several occasions, beyond what might be regarded as strictly necessary for the safeguarding of the Province.

In VII.42 we find, for the first time since II.1, his comments on the Gallic temperament applied to a Celtic people – in this instance, the Aedui. In both passages, anger against the Romans is being whipped up by agitators with ulterior personal motives. Thus personal and political instability are linked to reinforce the theme of the need for military action.

3 The course of the war

It is not likely that when Caesar entered upon his provincial command he entertained the intention of conquering the whole of Gaul; had that been so he would hardly in going first to Transalpine Gaul in 58 B.C. have left three of his legions in northern Italy. The province he had chosen for himself was Cisalpine Gaul and Illyricum, firstly for its political value, since it kept him close to

Italy, secondly because it nevertheless offered scope for military success in operations against the tribes bordering the north-east frontier. That his first intention was an Illyrian campaign is indicated by his having based the three legions in Aquileia. After the campaigning season of 57, he set out on a reconnaissance trip to Illyria (III.7.1). He is perhaps attempting, at this point, to give the impression that he had still intended an Illyrian campaign in 56, had the Venetic revolt not intervened; but, as we shall see, there are grounds for suspecting that, while not ruled out for the future, this was not then his first priority. That Caesar himself had been instrumental in having Ariovistus declared 'Friend of the Roman People' in 59 B.C. suggests that he had hoped to delay the possible eruption of trouble for Rome's clients beyond the frontier of the Transalpine province. Events, however, moved otherwise.

Campaigns beyond the frontier of a province needed justification, and this Caesar is at pains to provide for those of 58. The Helvetii had wronged Rome's allies (I.11, 14); they were a threat to the Province (I.10, 30) – the latter not very plausible geographically; and they had committed as yet unavenged injuries on the Romans (I.7, 12, 13, 30). Since Ariovistus was actually a 'Friend' the case against him is harder to establish. In the end, Caesar lays most stress on the 'German menace' (spec. I.33, 40) and on Ariovistus' truculence. Yet, why *not* pursue the implications of 'Friendship' along the lines Ariovistus is made to suggest in I.44? The answer Caesar provides for his Roman audience (I.45 – composed, let us remember, probably no earlier than 52 B.C.) is that Rome had the prior claim to the area, should she choose to exercise it.

As Caesar represents the matter, the Helvetic invasion had nothing to do with the Aedui, but originated in the personal treasonable ambitions of Dumnorix and Orgetorix. Yet the unmasking of Orgetorix apparently leaves Dumnorix's position among the Aedui unaffected, while not leading, either, to the abandonment of the Helvetic invasion. One may suspect that the Aedui, finding themselves 'warned off' Ariovistus by the Romans in 59 rather than given any practical help against him, themselves invited the Helvetii to come in, on the pretence of merely passing through Celtic territory, to help them wage war on Ariovistus, thus forcing Caesar to take sides in a war between two of Rome's allies.

In the second year, it is difficult to discern whether Caesar is reacting to events, as he seems to be trying to suggest in II.1ff., or had himself deliberately created provocation to the Belgae in order to justify further campaigning. His legions had wintered at Besançon, well outside the Province, but strategically justifiable to guard against renewed hostilities by the Suebi. However, the effect, intentional or otherwise, was to provoke the Belgae, whose bravery, ferocity – and connections with some Germanic tribes – are stressed (II.3ff.). In passing we are told that the peaceful submission of the Aremorican tribes had been achieved (II.34), but not why Roman troops had been sent there.

Caesar is at pains to imply that, as far as he was concerned, Gaul was pacified by the end of the campaigning season of 57 and Illyria was his next objective (II.34, III.7). Most of the legions had wintered in Central Gaul, plausibly enough, in view of the recent fighting with the Belgae; but in which direction had he intended moving them in the campaigning season of 56? Events in Rome menaced his continued tenure of his command (see §1 above) and Illyria could hardly be represented as an urgent priority. In the event, suppression of the Venetic revolt kept him in Gaul in 56, but there is reason to believe that he had intended to invade Britain in that year. Strabo (IV.iv.1) says the reason for the Venetic revolt was to hinder Caesar's voyage to Britain, and protect their trade there. An expedition to Britain could hardly be represented as an urgent necessity either. Caesar piles up rather too many, not all mutually compatible, excuses for his invasion at the end of the 55 campaigning season (IV.20). Again, as with the expedition across the Rhine in that year, Caesar justifies the extension of his field of operations by representing it as a punitive expedition, and by alleging the need to overawe the dubiously loyal, volatile (IV.13) Gauls.

The publicity value of the British expeditions was enormous, their political value for Rome negligible. Caesar, said Tacitus (*Agricola* 13) had merely pointed the way to Britain, not acquired it.

The major revolts in Gaul that occupied the rest of Caesar's time there go some way to justify his frequently repeated statement about the insecurity of the conquest. In the end, Gaul *was* pacified and Caesar had the credit of adding a large new province to the Roman empire. Nothing succeeds like success; but it does not necessarily follow that the ultimate conquest proves Caesar's consistent brilliance as a strategist and tactician. According to one military historian, Caesar's great gift – apart from the invaluable ability to get the best out of his men – was his swiftness to react to and extricate himself from the consequence of his own errors.

4 Caesar the man

Caesar was from a patrician family said first to have come to Rome from Alba Longa when the latter was destroyed by the Roman king Tullus Hostilius. The family claimed descent through Iulus (otherwise Ascanius) the son of Aeneas the Trojan, who was the son of Venus herself. Thus, they were descended both from a god and from the ancestor of the founder of Rome, though when Caesar was born it was a considerable time since any of the family had risen beyond the praetorship.

Caesar referred to his family's legendary descent in his funeral speech for his aunt Julia, wife of Marius. Both his father and his uncle had supported Marius, and the family was therefore regarded as belonging to the *populares* ('radicals' or 'demagogues', depending on one's political sympathies) and was viewed with suspicion by the *optimates* (the 'good men') – upholders of the senatorial oligarchy's entrenched power and privilege.

Caesar himself was at one stage in danger of losing his life during the dictatorship of Sulla, because of his Marian connection and his own early marriage to a daughter of Cinna, but influential friends persuaded the dictator to spare him. For the next ten years or so he was quiet, and was sufficiently well regarded by the patrician nobles to be co-opted in 73 B.C. into the college of priests.

Within two years, however, he openly showed himself a supporter of popular measures, backing Pompey's work in undoing the Sullan constitution. From then right down to the Civil War Caesar is consistently found supporting popular legislation and reforms. As dictator his legislation, in marked contrast to that of Sulla, was directed towards bettering the conditions of Roman citizens and the inhabitants of the empire as a whole, rather than to strengthening the power and prosperity of the noble few.

At the same time, his career is marked by evident and strong ambition, and more than once he showed himself ready to ignore constitutional restrictions in order to achieve his aims. His *dignitas* – the status and prestige within the state which he felt his due – was of prime importance to him, rather than the actual power involved in being dictator. Personal survival, against Pompey and his senatorial enemies, was his reason for fighting the Civil War; and there are no good grounds for believing the hostile tradition that alleges that after the Civil War he aimed at establishing himself as an actual king. In his own time, his enemies put about the story that he wanted to make himself a king – even a Hellenistic-type king, worshipped with divine honours. This has been taken seriously by some modern historians.

Certainly, extravagant honours, divine and secular, were heaped upon him, by senatorial decree – quasi-regal dress, a golden throne in the Senate house, his image on coins, a statue in the temple of Quirinus, etc. Many of these appear to have proceeded from the fearful adulation of a subservient Senate; some may have arisen from the misguided enthusiasm of his supporters. We do not know whether Caesar himself actually inspired any of these, or even what his attitude to them was, but it is doubtful whether he would value such tangible trivialities when he had achieved the intangible, weighty realities of power and status.

Much of our evidence for the period of his dictatorship stems from a hostile tradition ready to put an adverse interpretation on his every passing remark and action, and to detect tyrannical arrogance and contempt for the Senate. This is the construction put on his appointment of Caninius to fill the vacancy caused by the sudden death of a consul on the last day of his term of office, although Caesar may have been behaving merely with excessive punctiliousness (admittedly, piquant, in view of his past record) in fulfilling the requirements of the constitution. On a certain occasion, he failed to rise to receive the Senate when they came to inform him of their latest honorific decrees; however, one version of the story says that he stayed seated because of a sudden attack of faintness (often the forewarning of one of his epileptic fits).

Certainly, he sometimes met opposition with impatience. In 49 B.C. he gained access to the State treasury only by using physical force against the tribune who tried to bar his way. In 44 B.C. he used the popular assembly to have two tribunes deposed. The tribunes had summarily arrested and committed for trial two persons, one who had put a diadem on the head of Caesar's statue in the forum and one who had saluted Caesar as king when he was riding in procession from the celebration of the Alban festival. Caesar did nothing initially, but when the tribunes then proceeded to publish an edict complaining that they had no freedom of speech, he had them deposed. Certainly his forbearance at their earlier, rather officious, behaviour is as noteworthy as his subsequent loss of patience is understandable.

The most notorious of his remarks, and the one which seems to have been interpreted to add most weight to the allegation that he felt nothing but scorn for the constitution and perhaps even wanted to overthrow the Republic, was the pronouncement that Sulla was a dunce for having resigned the dictatorship. This is ambiguous and of course could be interpreted as meaning that Caesar valued autocratic power for its own sake and was determined to hang on to it, but it could equally bear the meaning that Sulla had not retained the dictatorship long enough for the effective restoration of public order or, perhaps, that he had short-sightedly failed to see that his attempts to patch up the constitution could not of themselves compel people to behave constitutionally.

In fact, Caesar's relations with the Senate do not suggest that he contemplated scrapping the machinery of the Republic. He consulted it constantly on the minutest details of public business. Naturally, he was in a position to exercise a great deal of patronage. During the Civil War, so far as we can tell from Dio's account, Caesar personally appointed all, or the most important magistrates for 47 and 46 B.C. The Senate voted this power to him for the appointment of the magistrates for 45, but for 44 he accepted only the appointment of the consuls. In the last year of his life, when the magistrates were appointed for three years in advance, in the prospect of Caesar's departure for a Parthian campaign, he chose only half, under a tribunician bill. Naturally, his personal commendation of candidates would carry considerable weight, but this in itself was merely an extension of the Republican practice of personal canvass by distinguished citizens in support of candidates.

His enrolments of new senators were, of course, interpreted as displaying his contempt for the Senate, in turning it into a body of compliant placemen. The ranks of the Senate had been severely depleted by the Civil War. Hostile tradition stresses the alleged ignoble origins of the new senators he enrolled – centurions, scribes, sons of freedmen, newly enfranchised aliens, etc. A popular jingle equated new Gaulish senators with the trouser-wearing captives from Caesar's triumphs. In fact, only a very few Roman citizens from the provinces are attested in the Senate at this time (though the evidence is, admittedly, sparse), and these are from the more Romanized provinces. The newly won Gallic territory is not represented, while some of the inhabitants of the Transalpine province were by this time second- or third-generation Roman citizens. Senior centurions could be persons of quite high social standing – in the following century, we find such men moving into an equestrian career in public service. Scribes and the sons of freedmen could also be men of high social standing. Moreover, the needs of the government of Rome itself and of the provinces produced an automatic increase in the numbers of the Senate, since the number of annually elected quaestors, the office which, since Sulla's day, gave automatic entry to the Senate, was raised to forty in 44 B.C. Such care to preserve the effective strength of the Senate hardly seems to display contempt for it.

It is fairly certain that Caesar intended to retain power indefinitely. His acceptance of the title *dictator perpetuus* indicates as much. This is not to say that he had any intention of converting his dictatorship into a monarchy. His dictatorship had been conferred on him by the vote of the Roman people, who were still the constitutional sovereign and could revoke it. There is no positive evidence that he had considered removing his power from popular control, or making provision for a successor to himself. The incident at the festival of the Lupercalia, when he put aside a crown offered to him by Mark Antony *might* have been intended by Caesar as a way of sounding public opinion – which proved hostile to kingship; equally, it might have been intended to demonstrate that he did not want the title of king; or the initiative might have been entirely Mark Antony's. A rumour was put about by his enemies, that the keeper of the Sibylline books (a collection supposedly of very ancient oracles) was going to find an oracle saying that the Romans would need a king to defeat the Parthians.

Likewise, Octavian, the person who on Caesar's death emerged as his testamentary heir, and who, some months after, gained recognition as his adopted son, allegedly under the terms of his will, had not during Caesar's lifetime been built up to any position of prestige and influence such that his acceptance as Caesar's political heir and the heir to his constitutional powers would have been necessary to prevent a civil war. It does not seem that Caesar contemplated founding a dynasty. In any case, even Octavian's personal inheritance might well have been altered had Caesar lived a little longer, for Caesar had a young wife and his will envisaged the possibility of begetting sons.

After the Civil War, Caesar lived for less than a year. His dictatorship was not characterized by proscriptions and confiscations of property. Instead, he introduced legislation to benefit Roman citizens and provincials, to increase the efficiency and honesty of government, and to accelerate the Romanization of the provinces. It has been said that Caesar's rule marks the move from the old conception of the empire as a rich field for exploitation by the Romans, and especially the Roman ruling classes, to that of the empire as a community, to which the Roman government had responsibilities.

In February 44 Caesar's dictatorship, which had previously been bestowed for only ten years, was declared perpetual. Only death could now remove him from power. A conspiracy was hatched, of rather mixed motivation. Some resented his autocracy and the loss of the freedom to conduct politics in the old way; some of his own partisans felt they had a grievance in that they had not received the advancement they had hoped for; some few idealists perhaps really thought they were striking a blow to end corrupt politics and establish a Republic characterized by public order, efficient government and a concern for the public good rather than personal or factional interest. On 15 March, 44 B.C., Caesar was assassinated.

5 Caesar as author

Caesar's *Gallic War* is divided into eight books, of which only the first seven, taking the narrative down to the autumn of 52 B.C., were written by Caesar. The eighth was added, shortly after Caesar's death, by his friend Aulus Hirtius, who had served with him. Whether Caesar himself had intended to add an account of the relatively unimportant minor campaigns of 51 we do not know. Probably all seven were written together, in the winter of 52–51, and they were perhaps intended as an aid to his canvass for the consulship. His *Civil War* falls into three books, covering the period from the beginning of 49 down to the beginning of the Alexandrian War in the autumn of 48 B.C. The rest of the Civil War is covered in three separate works by other hands, the *Alexandrian War*, the *African War* and the *Spanish War*, of which the first may again be by Hirtius. The *Civil War* itself is apparently unfinished, but whether it was actually written during the Civil War, as self-justifying propaganda, or in the short time after his return to Rome, we do not know.

The *Gallic War* and the *Civil War* are Caesar's only surviving works. He called both 'Commentaries', and as the word originally meant something like 'memoirs' or 'reports', his intention may have been to suggest that these were unvarnished, objective *reportage*. The title also incidentally disclaims for them the status of literary works; rather they are source material for working up into a historical narrative conformable to current ideas on literature. Cicero, however, writing in 46 B.C., and echoed by Hirtius in his preface to Book VIII of the *Gallic War*, says in the *Brutus* (262):

They are like nude figures, upright and beautiful, stripped of all ornament of style as if they had removed a garment. His aim was to provide source material for others who might wish to write history, and perhaps he has gratified the insensitive, who may wish to use their curling-tongs on his work; but men of good sense he has deterred from writing.

That is, these bald 'reports' are so elegantly and lucidly written that they compel our admiration even without the addition of further ornament.

Nevertheless, the *Civil War* bears many signs of being intended as propaganda; and, as has been suggested in §3 above, the *Gallic War* is perhaps not altogether a straightforward account of events. Moreover, certain matters – the part played by personal ambition in determining Caesar's course of action, and the large personal fortunes that he and some of his associates made from his conquests – are discreetly unmentioned while he sometimes seems to dissimulate his real intentions to conceal their relative failure – see, for example, the narrative of the Gergovia campaign. In particular, no indication is given that the expeditions into Germany and Britain achieved no lasting result. However, even if a judicious subtraction is made for possible distortion of his own and others' motives, the body of fact that is left is invaluable. The *Gallic War* is our only direct source on the history and institutions of the Gauls in that period, and it is also the only narrative actually written by a great general of antiquity about his own campaigns.

Like all Romans engaged in public life Caesar had from time to time to practise the art of oratory. Quintilian, in his treatise on rhetorical training written in the first century A.D., went so far as to say that, had Caesar been able to devote himself to forensic oratory, he and he alone of his time could have rivalled Cicero (*Institutio oratoria* X.i.114). Among the qualities he ascribes to him are elegance of language, something by which Caesar himself set great store. He went so far as to write a work in two volumes, dedicated to Cicero, called *De Analogia* (*On Selection of Words*). From such references as survive, it seems that Caesar advocated that the orator should, on the one hand, avoid the use of foreign coinages and colloquialisms; on the other, he should avoid bizarre and unfamiliar words. His aim should be a lucid, pure Latinity. Caesar's own Commentaries go a long way to fulfil this aim. They are simply written, without being dull or repetitive.

Other lost works of which we hear include *Anticato*, an answer to Cicero's eulogy of M. Porcius Cato, which appears to have been somewhat ungenerous in spirit and to have done the dictator little credit. He also wrote a work on astronomy, perhaps connected with his reform of the calendar, and a poem called *The Journey*, allegedly written on a journey to Spain, which took twenty-four days. Six lines survive of his poetry – hexameters which lament the lack of 'comic force' of the dramatist Terence but praise him specifically as a lover of 'pure speech'.

6 Preface to the second edition

S. A. Handford's accurate and elegant translation has been retained, with certain alterations in arrangement. The traditional order of the text has been restored, along with its conventional division into books and sections. A translation has been supplied of the preface to Book VIII and sections 48.10–11 and 50–5 of that book, omitted by Handford. Parts of the text which he presented as footnotes have been restored to an integral place in the text.

The glossary has been completely re-done and now contains more than twice as many items as the original. There are a few additional notes and also a few changes to some of Handford's more tendentious judgements. The editor has also seized the opportunity, in writing a new introduction, of being tendentious herself.

More maps have been supplied, and there is a special appendix listing the differences between the Latin text used by Handford (the Teubner edition) and the one most commonly used and accessible in Britain, the Oxford Classical Text.

SUGGESTIONS
FOR FURTHER READING

Badian, Ernst, *Roman Imperialism in the Late Republic*, Blackwell (Oxford, 1968), Cornell University Press (1968).

Balsdon, J. P. V. Dacre, *Julius Caesar and Rome*, Penguin (Harmondsworth, 1971).

Crawford, Michael H., *The Roman Republic*, Fontana (London, 1978), Harvester Press (Hassocks, 1978), Humanities Press (New Jersey, 1978).

Cunliffe, Barry, *The Celtic World*, Bodley Head (London, 1979), McGraw-Hill (New York, 1979).

Cunliffe, Barry, *Iron Age Communities in Britain*, Routledge and Kegan Paul (London, 1974).

Dillon, Myles and Chadwick, Nora, *The Celtic Realms*, Weidenfeld and Nicolson (London, 1967).

Fuller, Major-Gen. J. F. C., *Julius Caesar: Man, Soldier and Tyrant*, Eyre and Spottiswoode (London, 1965).

Gelzer, Matthias, *Caesar: Politician and Statesman*, Blackwell (Oxford, 1968), Harvard University Press (1968).

Piggott, Stuart, *The Druids*, Thames and Hudson (London, 1968), Praeger (New York, 1968), Penguin (Harmondsworth, 1974).

Powell, T. G. E., *The Celts*, Thames and Hudson (2nd ed., London, 1979), Praeger (New York, 1979).

Todd, Malcolm, *Roman Britain 55 B.C. - A.D. 400*, Fontana (London, 1981).

Wiseman, Anne and Peter, *Julius Caesar: The Battle for Gaul*, Chatto and Windus (London, 1980).

Greece and Rome, vol. IV, no. 1 (March 1957), Oxford University Press: a commemorative volume of essays on the bimillennium of Caesar's death.

BOOK I
THE EXPULSION OF INTRUDERS

1 Repulse of the Helvetii (58 B.C.)

1. Gaul comprises three areas, inhabited respectively by the Belgae, the Aquitani, and a people who call themselves Celts, though we call them Gauls. All of these have different languages, customs, and laws. The Celts are separated from the Aquitani by the river Garonne, from the Belgae by the Marne and Seine. The Belgae are the bravest of the three peoples, being farthest removed from the highly developed civilization of the Roman Province, least often visited by merchants with enervating luxuries for sale, and nearest to the Germans across the Rhine, with whom they are continually at war. For the same reason the Helvetii are braver than the rest of the Celts; they are in almost daily conflict with the Germans, either trying to keep them out of Switzerland or themselves invading Germany. The region occupied by the Celts, which has one frontier facing north, is bounded by the Rhône, the Garonne, the Atlantic Ocean, and the country of the Belgae; the part of it inhabited by the Sequani and the Helvetii also touches the Rhine. The Belgic territory, facing north and east, runs from the northern frontier of the Celts to the lower Rhine. Aquitania is bounded by the Garonne, the Pyrenees, and the part of the Atlantic coast nearest Spain; it faces north-west.

2. The foremost man among the Helvetii, in rank and wealth, was Orgetorix. In the consulship of Marcus Messala and Marcus Piso (61 B.C.) he was induced by the hope of obtaining royal power to organize a conspiracy of noblemen, and persuaded his country-men to emigrate *en masse*,[1] telling them that they were the best fighters in Gaul and could very easily conquer the whole country. They listened the more readily to his proposal because their territory is completely hemmed in by natural barriers – on one side by the Rhine, a very broad and deep river, which is the frontier

between them and the Germans; on another side by the high mountain range of the Jura, between them and the Sequani; on a third, by the Lake of Geneva and the Rhône, which form the boundary between the Helvetii and the Roman Province. These obstacles restricted their movement and made it more difficult to attack their neighbours; and as they are a warlike people they greatly resented this restraint. Considering their large population, military prestige, and reputation for bravery, they felt that their territory – only two hundred and twenty miles long, one hundred and sixty-five wide – was unduly small.

3. Impelled by this feeling and by the influence of Orgetorix, they determined to prepare for emigration by buying up all the draught cattle and wagons they could, sowing as much land as possible in order to secure an adequate supply of corn for the journey, and establishing peaceful and friendly relations with their neighbours. They thought that two years would suffice for completing these preparations, and passed a formal resolution fixing their departure for the third year. Orgetorix was put in charge of the arrangements and undertook a mission to the neighbouring peoples, in the course of which he persuaded a Sequanian named Casticus, whose father Catamantaloedis had been king of his tribe for many years and had been honoured by the Senate with the title of 'Friend of the Roman People', to seize the royal power which his father had held before him. He also induced the Aeduan Dumnorix, Diviciacus' brother, who at that time held the chief magistracy of his tribe and enjoyed great popularity, to make a similar attempt, and gave him his daughter in marriage. Orgetorix convinced them that these schemes were quite easy of achievement by telling them that he intended to usurp the sovereignty of his own state, which he said was beyond question the most powerful in Gaul, and that he would use his wealth and military strength to secure them the possession of their thrones. His arguments proved effective. The three men swore an oath of mutual loyalty, hoping that once they had made themselves kings the great power of the warlike peoples they ruled would enable them to get control of all Gaul.

4. The intrigue was revealed to the Helvetii by informers, and in accordance with the national custom Orgetorix was summoned

to stand his trial in chains. Since condemnation would mean death at the stake, he collected all his slaves, numbering some ten thousand, from his various estates, and brought them to the place of trial on the day appointed for the hearing, together with all his numerous retainers and debtor-bondsmen. By means of their protection he escaped trial. His countrymen were angered by this behaviour and attempted to assert their rights by armed force. But while the magistrates were calling up a large body of men from the countryside, Orgetorix died – perhaps, as the Helvetii believe, by his own hand.

5. The Helvetii, however, did not relax their efforts to carry out their intended migration. As soon as they considered themselves ready, they burnt all their twelve towns and four hundred villages, as well as the isolated buildings belonging to private individuals, and also the whole of their grain, except what they intended to carry with them; for they thought that, if there was no possibility of returning home, they would be more willing to face all the perils that awaited them. Every man was directed to take with him from home three months' supply of flour for his own use. They persuaded their neighbours the Rauraci, Tulingi, and Latovici to follow their example – to burn their towns and villages and go with them – and were joined also by the Boii, who formerly lived on the other side of the Rhine, but had recently migrated into Austria and attacked the town of Noreia.

6. There were only two routes by which the Helvetii could leave their country. One led between the Jura mountains and the Rhône[2] through the land of the Sequani, and was so narrow and difficult that wagons could scarcely pass along it in single file; and a high mountain overhung it, so that a mere handful of men could easily make it impassable. The other route, leading through the Roman Province, was much easier and more convenient; for the Rhône, which forms the frontier between the Helvetii and the Allobroges, who had recently [61 B.C.] been subdued by Rome, is fordable at several places. The frontier town of the Allobroges, nearest to Switzerland and connected with it by a bridge, is Geneva. The Helvetii thought that they could either induce the Allobroges to let them pass through, as they were believed to be still unfriendly towards the Romans, or compel them by force to do so. When

everything was ready for their departure, they fixed a day for a general muster on the bank of the Rhône – the 28th of March in the consulship of Lucius Piso and Aulus Gabinius (58 B.C.).

7. When Caesar was informed that they were attempting to pass through the Province, he left Rome at once and travelled post-haste to the neighbourhood of Geneva. As there was only one legion stationed in Gaul, he ordered as many fresh troops as possible to be raised throughout the Province, and had the bridge at Geneva destroyed. On hearing of his arrival the Helvetii sent an embassy, composed of their most illustrious citizens and headed by Nammeius and Verucloetius, to say that they intended to march through the Province because there was no other route open to them. They promised to do no harm and asked for his consent. As Caesar remembered that the consul Lucius Cassius had been killed by the Helvetii, and his army routed and sent under the yoke[3] (107 B.C.), he was not disposed to grant their request. If people so hostile to Rome were permitted to go through the Province, he did not think they were likely to refrain from damage to persons and property. However, to gain time for the assembly of the troops he had ordered to be levied, he told the envoys that he would consider the matter at leisure: if they wished to present their request again, they were to return on the 13th of April.

8. In the meantime he employed the legion he had with him, and the troops that had been raised in the Province, to fortify the bank of the Rhône for a distance of eighteen miles between the Lake of Geneva and the Jura, the frontier between the Helvetii and the Sequani. This was effected by means of a rampart sixteen feet high with a trench running parallel. He then placed redoubts at intervals along the fortification and garrisoned them with pickets, so that he could stop the Helvetii more easily, should they attempt to force a passage. When on the appointed day the envoys returned, he told them that it would be contrary to precedent and the traditions of the Roman state to allow anyone to march through the Province, and that if they tried to use force he would stop them. Disappointed of this hope, some of the Helvetii endeavoured – generally, though not always, by night – to get across by lashing boats together and making a number of rafts, others by wading through the shallowest places. But the Roman troops always

hastened up to the danger-points, and aided by the fortifications drove them back with volleys of missiles and forced them to abandon their attempts.

9. There remained only the route through the land of the Sequani, which was so narrow that it could not be used without their consent. Being unable to obtain permission by their own efforts, the Helvetii sent an embassy to Dumnorix the Aeduan, hoping by his intercession to gain what they desired. Dumnorix's popularity and open-handedness had won him great influence among the Sequani, and he was well-disposed towards the Helvetii because he had married a woman of their country, a daughter of Orgetorix. His ambition for kingly power made him favour political change, and he wanted to lay as many tribes as possible under obligations to himself. Accordingly he undertook the commission, induced the Sequani to let the Helvetii go through, and arranged an exchange of hostages between them. The Helvetii undertook to pass through without harming anyone or doing any damage; the Sequani, to let them travel without interference.

10. Caesar was informed that the Helvetii intended to cross the territories of the Sequani and the Aedui and to enter the country of the Santoni, which is not far from that of the Tolosates, a tribe living in the Roman Province.[4] He saw that it would be very dangerous to the Province to have a warlike people, hostile to Rome, established close to its rich cornlands, which were without any natural defences. Accordingly, leaving Titus Labienus, one of his generals, in charge of the fortifications he had constructed, he marched at top speed into northern Italy, enrolled two new legions there, sent for the three which were in winter quarters near Aquileia, and hastened back with all five by the shortest route over the Alps into Gaul. An attempt was made to hinder his march by the Ceutrones, Graioceli, and Caturiges, who seized some commanding heights. Beating them off in several engagements, Caesar marched in six days from Ocelum, the westernmost town in the Alpine district of Italy, into the territory of the Vocontii in the Province, and then continued through the country of the Allobroges into that of the Segusiavi, the first people on the west bank of the Rhône who live beyond the Provincial frontier.

11. By this time the Helvetii had marched through the pass and

across the country of the Sequani, and had reached that of the Aedui, whose land they were pillaging. Unable to protect themselves or their property, the Aedui sent to ask Caesar for help, pleading that they had always been loyal to Rome, and that it was not right to allow their land to be ravaged almost under the eyes of his army, their children carried off into slavery, and their towns taken by storm. At the same time the Ambarri, who had ties of friendship and kindred with the Aedui, informed Caesar that their fields too had been pillaged, and that it was almost more than they could do to repel the Helvetii's assaults upon their towns. The Allobroges also, who had villages and estates beyond the Rhône, came fleeing for refuge and said that they had been robbed of everything but the bare soil of their country. These complaints convinced Caesar that he must act immediately: if he delayed, his allies would have all their property destroyed and the Helvetii get clear away to the country of the Santoni.

12. There is a river called the Saône, which flows through the territories of the Aedui and the Sequani into the Rhône with an extremely sluggish current, so that the eye cannot tell in which direction it is going. The Helvetii were crossing this river on rafts and small boats tied together. On learning from his patrols that they had got three quarters of their forces across, but that the remaining quarter was still on the east bank, Caesar left camp with three legions some time after midnight and came into contact with the division that had not yet crossed. Attacking them unexpectedly when they were hampered by baggage, he destroyed a large number, and the rest took to flight and hid in the neighbouring woods. The troops in this division formed one of the four clans into which the Helvetian people was divided, known as the Tigurini. Fifty years earlier, the men of this clan had left home independently of the others, and after the battle in which the consul Cassius was killed had sent his army under the yoke. Thus, whether by accident or by divine providence, the section of the Helvetii that had inflicted a signal defeat upon Rome was the first to suffer for it. In thus punishing the Tigurini Caesar avenged a private injury as well as that done to his country; for a general named Lucius Piso, grandfather of the Lucius Piso who was Caesar's father-in-law, had been killed in the same battle as Cassius.

13. After this success Caesar wanted to pursue the remaining forces of the Helvetii. He therefore built a bridge over the Saône and led his army across. Alarmed by his unexpected arrival and seeing that he had effected in one day the crossing which they had the greatest difficulty in accomplishing in twenty days, they sent an embassy to him headed by Divico, who had been their commander in the campaign against Cassius. He told Caesar that if Rome made peace with the Helvetii they would go and remain wherever Caesar chose to settle them. If, however, he persisted in making war upon them, he would do well to remember the Romans' previous reverse and the traditional bravery of the Helvetii. He had made a surprise attack on one clan at a moment when their comrades who had crossed the river could not come to their help; but he should not on that account exaggerate his own prowess or despise them. They had learned from their fathers and ancestors to fight like brave men, and not to rely on trickery or stratagem. So let him beware; or it might be that the place where they stood would become famous in future ages as the scene of a Roman disaster and the destruction of a Roman army.

14. Caesar replied that he had no hesitation about the action he should take, especially as he had not forgotten the Roman reverse to which the envoys referred, a misfortune that he resented all the more because it was undeserved. If the Romans at that time had been conscious of any act of oppression, it would have been easy to take precautions; they were caught off their guard because they knew they had done nothing to justify apprehension and thought it undignified to fear without cause. Even if he were willing to forget this old affront, could he banish the recollection of their fresh insults – their attempt to force a passage through the Province in defiance of his prohibition, and their attacks upon the Aedui, the Ambarri, and the Allobroges? 'The victory of which you boast so arrogantly,' he said, 'and the surprisingly long time during which you have escaped punishment, are both due to the same cause. When the gods intend to make a man pay for his crimes, they generally allow him to enjoy moments of success and a long period of impunity, so that he may feel his reverse of fortune, when it eventually comes, all the more keenly. However, if you will give hostages as a guarantee that you mean to carry out your

undertakings, and will recompense the Aedui and the Allobroges for the injury you have done to them and their allies, I am willing to make peace with you.'

Divico replied that it was the traditional custom of the Helvetii to demand hostages of others, but never to give them – as the Romans had good cause to know. With this rejoinder he departed.

15. The next day the Helvetii quitted their encampment. Caesar did the same, sending ahead, to discover in what direction they were marching, his entire force of four thousand cavalry, raised from various parts of the Province and from the Aedui and their allies. These pursued the Helvetian rearguard too eagerly, and engaging their cavalry on unfavourable ground suffered a few casualties. The Helvetii were elated at repulsing such a large force with only five hundred horsemen, and with increased boldness halted several times and challenged the Romans with their rear-guard. Caesar would not allow his men to fight them, and contented himself for the moment with preventing them from foraging, looting, and ravaging the country. So the two armies marched for about a fortnight, the enemy's rear and the Roman vanguard being never more than five or six miles apart.

16. Meanwhile Caesar was daily demanding from the Aedui the grain which, as he reminded them, their government had promised. For on account of the cold climate the standing corn was still unripe, and there was not even a sufficient supply of hay. Some grain that Caesar had brought up the Saône was of little use at the moment because the Helvetii had diverged from the river, and he did not want to lose contact with them. The Aedui kept putting him off from day to day, saying that the grain was being collected, was in transit, was on the point of arriving, and so forth. When he saw that there was going to be no end to this procrastination, and the day on which the soldiers' rations were due was approaching, he summoned the numerous Aeduan chiefs who were in the camp, including Diviciacus and Liscus, their chief magistrate – the Vergobret, as the Aedui call him – an annually elected officer holding power of life and death over his countrymen. Caesar reprimanded them severely for failing to help him at such a critical moment, when the enemy was at hand and it was impossible either to buy corn or to get it from the fields. He pointed out that it was

largely in response to their entreaties that he had undertaken the campaign, and in still stronger terms than he had yet used accused them of betraying him by this neglect.

17. His remarks at last induced Liscus to drop concealment and speak out. 'There are a number of private individuals in our state,' he said, 'who have great influence over the masses, and are more powerful than the magistrates themselves. It is these who, by criminal and seditious talk, work on the fears of the people to prevent them from bringing in the grain that is due. They argue that if the Aedui are no longer able to maintain their supremacy in Gaul, it is better to have Gauls as masters than Romans, and say they are certain that, if you defeat the Helvetii, you mean to rob the Aedui of their liberty along with all the rest of the Gauls. These men also keep the enemy informed of your plans and of all that goes on in the camp, and I have no power to control them. Indeed – in case you wonder why I have waited to be compelled before revealing these facts – I realize I am running a very grave risk in doing so. That is why I held my tongue as long as I could.'

18. Caesar perceived that Liscus' remarks alluded to Diviciacus' brother Dumnorix, and as he did not want the matter discussed with a number of others present, he promptly dismissed the assembly, telling Liscus to stay behind. When they were alone he questioned him about what he had said in the meeting, and Liscus now spoke with greater freedom and confidence. On putting the same questions to others in private, Caesar found that his report was true. It was indeed Dumnorix that he had referred to, a man of boundless daring, extremely popular with the masses on account of his liberality, and an ardent revolutionary. For many years he had bought at a cheap price the right of collecting the river-tolls and other taxes of the Aedui, because when he made a bid at the auction not a soul dared bid against him. In this way he had made a fortune and amassed large resources to expend in bribery. He maintained at his own expense a considerable force of cavalry, which he kept in attendance upon him, and his power was not confined to his own country, but extended over the neighbouring tribes. To increase it he had arranged a marriage for his mother with a nobleman of very great influence among the Bituriges; his own wife was a Helvetian and he had married his half-sister and

other female relations to members of other tribes. On account of his matrimonial connection he was a keen partisan of the Helvetii, and he had his own reasons for hating Caesar and the Romans, because their arrival in Gaul had decreased his power and restored his brother Diviciacus to his former position of honour and influence. If disaster should befall the Romans, he felt sure that with the aid of the Helvetii the throne was within his grasp, whereas a Roman conquest of Gaul would mean that he could not hope even to retain his present standing, much less make himself king.[5] Caesar also learnt in the course of his enquiries that, in the cavalry reverse a few days before, it was Dumnorix and the Aeduan horsemen under his command – sent to Caesar's aid by the tribal authorities – who had been the first to turn tail, and so made the rest of the cavalry lose their nerve.

19. The suspicions aroused by these revelations were confirmed by certain indubitable facts. Dumnorix had secured a passage for the Helvetii through the territory of the Sequani, and arranged an exchange of hostages between them. He had done this not merely without the authority of Caesar or the Aeduan government, but actually without their knowledge; and he was denounced by the chief magistrate of his tribe. Caesar therefore decided that he had good grounds for either punishing him himself or calling on his fellow tribesmen to do so. The one objection to this course was that he knew Dumnorix's brother Diviciacus to be an enthusiastic supporter of Roman interests, a very good friend to him personally, and a man of exceptional loyalty, fair-mindedness, and moderation; and there was reason to fear that he would be much displeased if his brother were executed. Accordingly, before taking any action he sent for Diviciacus, and dismissing the ordinary interpreters talked to him with the assistance of Gaius Valerius Troucillus, a prominent man in the Province of Gaul and an intimate friend of his own, in whom he had entire confidence. He reminded Divicia-cus of what he himself had heard said about Dumnorix in the meeting, informed him of what had been stated in his private interviews with various persons, and earnestly begged him not to take offence, but to consent to his either hearing the case himself and passing judgement on Dumnorix, or else instructing the Aeduan state to do so.

20. Bursting into tears, Diviciacus embraced Caesar and besought him not to deal too severely with his brother. 'I know,' he said, 'that the allegations against him are true, and no one regrets it more than I do. For when I had great power at home and in the rest of Gaul, while he was too young to have much influence it was I that raised him to greatness; and the resources and strength that he thus acquired he is now using, not only to weaken my position, but to bring me near to ruin. Nevertheless, he is my brother; and apart from my own feelings, I cannot afford to be indifferent to public opinion. If you take severe measures against him, everyone will think – in view of my friendly relations with you – that I desired it, and I shall become very unpopular throughout Gaul.' He was continuing to plead at some length, with tears in his eyes, when Caesar grasped his hand, reassured him, and bade him say no more. 'So high is my regard for you,' he said, 'that, since you wish it and beg me so earnestly, I will both overlook the injury to Roman interests and swallow my own indignation.' He then summoned Dumnorix and in his brother's presence stated his reasons for complaint about his conduct, mentioning the information he had received and the charges made against him by his own government. He warned him to avoid henceforth giving any cause for suspicion; what was past, he would overlook for his brother's sake. However, he placed Dumnorix under surveillance in order to ascertain what he was doing and whom he talked with.

21. That same day the patrols brought word that the Helvetii had stopped at the foot of a hill eight miles from Caesar's camp, whereupon he sent a party to reconnoitre the hill and find out what the ascent was like on the farther side. They reported that it was quite easy. Shortly after midnight he explained his plans to Labienus, his second-in-command, and detailed him to climb to the summit with two legions, taking as guides the men who had reconnoitred the ground. In the early hours of the morning Caesar himself marched towards the enemy, following the route by which they had proceeded, and sending all the cavalry in front. They were preceded by a patrol under command of Publius Considius, who was reputed a first-class soldier, and had served under Sulla and later under Crassus.

22. At daybreak Labienus was actually in possession of the summit, while Caesar was not more than a mile and a half from the enemy's camp; and he learned afterwards from prisoners that neither his own approach nor that of Labienus had been observed. But suddenly Considius galloped up and said that the hill Labienus had been sent to occupy was held by the enemy; he knew this, he said, because he had recognized their Gallic arms and the crests of their helmets. Accordingly Caesar withdrew to a hill close by and formed his line of battle. Labienus had been instructed not to engage until Caesar's force was seen close to the enemy's camp, so that they might be attacked on all sides at once. After occupying the hill, therefore, he was waiting for Caesar to appear, without offering battle. It was only quite late in the day that Caesar learned the truth from his patrols – that it was the Romans who were in possession of the hill, that the Helvetii had moved camp, and that Considius had lost his head and reported that he had seen what was not there to be seen. During that day Caesar followed the enemy at the usual interval and pitched his camp three miles from theirs.

23. Next day, as the distribution of rations was due in two days' time and he was only seventeen miles from Bibracte, by far the largest and richest town of the Aedui, he thought it advisable to secure his food supply, and therefore diverged from the route that the Helvetii were following and marched towards the town. His movements were reported to the enemy by some runaway slaves of Lucius Aemilius, the commander of Caesar's Gallic cavalry. The Helvetii perhaps thought that we were breaking contact with them out of fear, especially as we had declined an engagement the day before, although we had the advantage of position; or it may be they were confident of being able to cut us off from access to supplies. In any case they changed their plan, altered the direction of their march, and began to hang upon our rear and harass it.

24. Observing this, Caesar withdrew to a hill close at hand and sent out his cavalry to meet the enemy's attack. In the meantime he formed up his four veteran legions in three lines half-way up the hill, and posted the two recently levied in Italy on the summit with all the auxiliaries, so that the whole of the hillside above him was occupied with troops. The baggage and packs he ordered to be collected in one place, and defence works to be dug round them by

the veterans posted in the top line. The Helvetii, who were following us with the whole of their transport, now parked it all together, and, after repulsing our cavalry with a battle line drawn up in very close order, formed a phalanx[6] and climbed towards our first line.

25. Caesar had all the horses – starting with his own – sent away out of sight, so that everyone might stand in equal danger and no one have any chance of flight. Then he addressed the men and joined battle. By throwing down spears from their commanding position the troops easily broke the enemy's phalanx, and then drew their swords and charged. The Gauls were much hampered in action because a single spear often pierced more than one of their overlapping shields and pinned them together; and, as the iron bent, they could not pull them out. With their left arms thus encumbered it was impossible for them to fight properly, and many, after repeated attempts to jerk their arms free, preferred to drop the shields and fight unprotected. At length, exhausted by wounds, they began to fall back towards a hill about a mile away. They had gained the hill, and our men were approaching to dislodge them, when the fifteen thousand Boii and Tulingi who protected the rear of their column suddenly marched up, attacked us on the right flank,[7] and surrounded us. Thereupon the Helvetii who had retreated to the hill began to press forward again and renew the battle. We changed front and advanced in two divisions – the first and second lines to oppose the Helvetii whom we had already once defeated and driven back, the third to withstand the newly arrived troops.

26. This double battle was long and fiercely fought. When they could no longer sustain the Roman charges, the Helvetii resumed their retreat up the hill, while the Boii and Tulingi retired to the laager where the baggage was stacked, to continue the struggle – for throughout this battle, which lasted from midday till evening, not a single man of them was seen in flight. At the laager fighting actually continued until late at night, for the enemy had made a barricade of the wagons, and rained down missiles on all who approached; some also wounded our men with spears and javelins discharged low down between the wagons and between the wheels. After a long struggle we captured the laager and the baggage it

contained, and also Orgetorix's daughter and one of his sons. About a hundred and thirty thousand Helvetii who survived the battle marched without halting all that night, and arrived after three days in the country of the Lingones. We had not been able to pursue immediately because we spent these days in attending to the wounded and burying the dead. But Caesar sent a letter and a message to the Lingones warning them not to supply the Helvetii with grain or aid them in any way, on pain of being treated as enemies, and three days later he started in pursuit with the whole army.

27. The Helvetii were compelled by want of all kinds of supplies to send envoys offering surrender. These met Caesar on the march, prostrated themselves before him, and with tears of supplication besought him to grant them peace. Caesar commanded that the Helvetii should stay where they were until he arrived. They obeyed, and on reaching the place he required them to give hostages and to surrender their arms and the slaves who had deserted to them. While these were being searched for and collected, six thousand men of the clan known as the Verbigeni quitted the encampment in the early hours of the night and set out for the German frontier on the Rhine. Either they were afraid that they would be massacred when once they had given up their arms, or they hoped to escape punishment altogether, thinking that they could get away unobserved in such a large crowd of prisoners, and that the Romans might never learn of their departure.

28. But Caesar heard of it, and sent word to the tribes through whose territory the fugitives were passing that they were to hunt them down and bring them back, or he would hold them responsible. When they were brought back he put them to death; but all the rest were allowed to surrender after handing over the hostages, deserters, and arms. The Helvetii, together with the Tulingi, Latovici and Rauraci, were bidden to return to their own country; and as all their produce was gone, so that they had nothing at home to live on, Caesar directed the Allobroges to supply them with grain, and ordered the Helvetii themselves to rebuild the towns and villages they had burnt. His chief reason for doing this was that he did not want the country they had abandoned to remain uninhabited, lest the Germans across the Rhine might be

induced by its fertility to migrate into Switzerland, and so become near neighbours of the Roman Province, and especially of the Allobroges. The Boii were given a home in the country of the Aedui, who asked Caesar to consent to this arrangement because the Boii were known as a people of exceptional bravery. The Aedui assigned them land, and later admitted them to equality of rights and liberties with themselves.

29. Some documents found in the Helvetian camp were brought to Caesar. They were written in Greek characters, and contained a register of the names of all the emigrants capable of bearing arms, and also, under separate heads, the numbers of old men, women, and children. The grand total was 368,000, comprising 263,000 Helvetii, 36,000 Tulingi, 14,000 Latovici, 23,000 Rauraci, and 32,000 Boii; and the list of men fit for military service contained 92,000 names. By Caesar's orders a census was taken of those who returned home, and the number was found to be 110,000.

2 Expulsion of Ariovistus from Gaul (58 B.C.)

30. On the conclusion of the Helvetian campaign the leading men of tribes in almost every part of Gaul came to offer Caesar congratulations. They realized, they said, that although his motive in fighting the Helvetii was to punish them for their past injuries to Rome, what had happened was just as much to the advantage of Gaul as of the Romans; for the intention of the Helvetii, in abandoning their home at a time when they enjoyed great prosperity, was to make war on all Gaul and become masters of it, and so to have the whole country from which to select the district they thought most fertile and convenient for settlement, and to compel the other tribes to pay tribute. The deputies asked Caesar to let them fix a day for convening a pan-Gallic assembly, saying that there were certain requests they would like to submit to him when they were all agreed about them. With Caesar's consent they appointed a date for this assembly, and swore to one another not to disclose its proceedings without its express authority.

31. When the assembly had met and concluded its business, the same chieftains who had been with Caesar before returned and

asked leave to interview him privately in a place secluded from observation, in order to discuss a matter that concerned not only their own interest, but that of the whole country. When the interview was granted they all prostrated themselves before him with tears in their eyes. They explained that they were very anxious to prevent what they said from being disclosed; this was just as important to them as obtaining the request they had come to make, because its disclosure would bring the most cruel punishment upon them. Their spokesman was the Aeduan Diviciacus.

The Gauls, he said, were divided into two parties, one dominated by the Aedui, the other by the Arverni. After a fierce struggle for supremacy, lasting many years, the Arverni and Sequani hired some German mercenaries to help them [70–65 B.C.]. A first contingent of about fifteen thousand had crossed the Rhine; but when the uncivilized barbarians had acquired a taste for residence in Gaul, with its good land and high standard of life, more were brought over, and there were at present about a hundred and twenty thousand of them in the country. The Aedui and their satellite tribes had fought the Germans more than once, and had suffered disastrous defeats, by which they lost all their noblest citizens, councillors, and knighthood. These calamities had broken the supremacy which they formerly maintained in Gaul by their own prowess and by the ties of hospitality and friendship that united them with the Romans; and they had been forced to surrender their most distinguished citizens as hostages to the Sequani, and to bind themselves by oath not to attempt to recover them and not to solicit the aid of Rome, but to submit for ever without demur to the sovereign power of their conquerors.

'I myself,' he said, 'am the only man of the whole Aeduan nation who could not be prevailed upon to swear this oath or to give my children as hostages. That was why I fled from my country and went to Rome to claim assistance from the Senate – because I alone was not restrained either by an oath or by the surrender of hostages.'

But a worse fate, he went on to say, had befallen the victorious Sequani than the conquered Aedui. For the German king Ariovistus had settled in their territory and seized a third of their land – the best in all Gaul. And now he was bidding them evacuate another third, because a few months previously he had been joined by twenty-four thousand men of the Harudes, and must find them a home to settle in. In a few years' time the whole population of Gaul would be expatriated and all the Germans would migrate across the Rhine; for there was no comparison between the soil of Germany and that of Gaul, or between their respective standards of living. After a single victory over the united Gallic forces at Admagetobriga [61 B.C.], Ariovistus had shown himself an arrogant and cruel tyrant, demanding the children of every man of rank as hostages, and making an example of them by the infliction of all manner of torture, if the least indication of his will and pleasure was not instantly complied with. The man was an ill-tempered, headstrong savage and it was impossible to endure his tyranny any longer. Unless Caesar and the Romans would help them, the Gauls must all do as the Helvetii had done – leave their homes, seek other dwelling-places out of reach of the Germans, and take their chance of whatever fortune might befall them.

'If my words come to the ears of Ariovistus,' he concluded, 'I do not doubt that he will inflict the most inhuman punishment on all the hostages he has in his power. But your great prestige, the recent victory of your army, and the terror of the Roman name, could deter him from bringing fresh German hordes across and protect all Gaul from his depredations.'

32. When Diviciacus had finished his speech, the whole deputation began with many tears to implore Caesar's aid. He noticed, however, that the Sequanian representatives did not follow the example of all the rest, but hung their heads in dejection with their eyes fixed on the ground. In astonishment he asked them the reason for this behaviour, but without making any reply they maintained their attitude of silent dejection. After he had questioned them repeatedly without being able to get a word out of them, Diviciacus spoke again. The lot of the Sequani, he explained, was even more grievous and miserable than that of the rest, because they alone dared not, even in secret, complain or beg for relief. They stood in terror of Ariovistus' cruelty, even when he was far away, just as much as if they were in his presence; for while the others could at any rate flee away out of his reach, the Sequani,

having admitted him into their midst and allowed all their towns to fall into his power, must submit to any atrocities he chose to commit against them.

33. On receiving this information Caesar reassured the Gauls and promised to attend to the matter, adding that he had great hopes that the privilege he had secured for Ariovistus, as well as the weight of his authority, would induce him to cease his oppression. He then dismissed the meeting. In addition to what he had been told, many other considerations convinced him that this problem must be faced and some action taken. The most important was the fact that the Aedui, who had frequently been styled by the Senate 'Brothers and Kinsmen of the Roman People', were enslaved and held subject by the Germans, and that Aeduan hostages were in the hands of Ariovistus and the Sequani, which, considering the mighty power of Rome, Caesar regarded as a disgrace to himself and his country. Furthermore, if the Germans gradually formed a habit of crossing the Rhine and entering Gaul in large numbers, he saw how dangerous it would be for the Romans. If these fierce barbarians occupied the whole of Gaul, the temptation would be too strong for them: they would cross the frontier into the Province, as the Cimbri and Teutoni had done before them [109–101 B.C.], and march on Italy, for the Roman Province lay just across the Rhône from the territory of the Sequani. This danger, he considered, must be provided against immediately. Moreover, Ariovistus personally had behaved with quite intolerable arrogance and pride.

34. Accordingly Caesar decided to send envoys requiring him to select for a conference some place lying between their present positions, as he wished to discuss business of state of the highest importance to them both. To this delegation Ariovistus replied: 'If I wanted anything from Caesar, I should go to him; so if he wants anything of me, he must come to me.' He added that he dared not come without the protection of his army into the part of Gaul occupied by Caesar, and that to concentrate his forces would mean making elaborate and troublesome arrangements for provisioning them. He could not imagine what business Caesar, or the Romans at all for that matter, had in the part of Gaul which was his by right of conquest.

35. At this Caesar sent a second embassy to remind Ariovistus of the important privilege conferred upon him by himself and the Roman government, when during Caesar's consulship [59 B.C.] he received from the Senate the titles of 'King' and 'Friend'. Since his way of showing his gratitude was to refuse an invitation to a conference for the discussion of matters affecting their common interest, the envoys were instructed to deliver him an ultimatum: first, he was not to bring any more large bodies of men across the Rhine into Gaul; secondly, he was to restore the Aeduan hostages he held, and to authorize the Sequani to restore those whom they held; finally, he was not to oppress the Aedui or to make war on them or their allies. On these conditions Caesar and the Roman government would maintain cordial and friendly relations with him. If these demands were refused, then, in accordance with a decree of the Senate passed in the consulship of Marcus Messala and Marcus Piso [61 B.C.], directing all governors of the Province of Gaul to do everything consistent with the public interest to protect the Aedui and other Roman allies, Caesar would not fail to punish his ill-treatment of them.

36. In reply Ariovistus said that it was the recognized custom of war for victors to rule the vanquished in any way they pleased, and that the Romans acted on this principle by governing their conquered subjects, not according to the dictates of any third party, but at their own discretion. Since he did not dictate to them how they were to exercise their rights, he ought not to be interfered with in the exercise of his. It was because the Aedui had tried the fortune of war, and were the losers in the fight, that they had to pay him tribute; and Caesar was doing him a serious wrong in coming to Gaul and causing him a loss of revenue. He would not return the hostages to the Aedui, but would refrain from making any wanton attack upon them or their allies, if they kept their agreement and paid the tributes regularly every year; if they did not, the title of 'Brothers of the Roman People' would not save them from the consequences. 'I am not impressed,' he concluded, 'by Caesar's threat to punish my "oppression" of these people. No one has ever fought me without bringing destruction upon himself. Let him attack whenever he pleases. He will discover what German valour is capable of. We have never known defeat, we have had

superb training in arms, and for fourteen years have never sheltered beneath a roof.'

37. At the very moment when this message was being reported to Caesar, delegations arrived from the Aedui and the Treveri. The Aedui came to complain that the Harudes, who had lately crossed into Gaul, were ravaging their territory, and that even the surrender of hostages had failed to induce Ariovistus to leave them in peace. The Treveri stated that a hundred clans of the Suebi had encamped on the bank of the Rhine and were trying to cross under the command of Nasua and his brother Cimberius. Caesar was much perturbed by this news, and decided that he must act immediately, lest, if this fresh horde of Suebi joined forces with Ariovistus' veteran troops, it might become more difficult to resist them. Accordingly, he arranged for a supply of grain as quickly as he could, and advanced at top speed towards Ariovistus.

38. After three days' march it was reported that the German was hastening with all his forces to occupy Besançon, the largest town of the Sequani, and had already advanced three days' journey beyond his own frontier. Caesar felt that he must take energetic measures to prevent the fall of this town, for it contained an abundance of military stores of every kind, and its natural defences were so strong that it offered every facility for protracting hostilities. The river Doubs forms an almost complete and perfect circle round it; the gap left unprotected is little more than five hundred yards wide, and is blocked by a high hill so completely that the spurs at its base run right down to the river bank on either side. This hill was girt by a wall which gave it the strength of a citadel and joined it with the town. Caesar hastened there by forced marches continued day and night, occupied the town, and placed a garrison in it.

39. During the few days that they spent near Besançon to lay in a stock of corn and other provisions, the soldiers began to question the Gauls and merchants there, who talked about the enormous stature, incredible courage, and splendid military training of the Germans. Some affirmed that on many occasions when they had met them in battle, the very expression on their faces and the fierce glance of their eyes were more than they could endure. This gossip threw all ranks into a sudden panic

that completely unnerved them. It began with the military tribunes, the prefects of the auxiliary troops, and the men with little experience of war who had followed Caesar from Rome in order to cultivate his friendship. Most of these alleged some urgent reason or other for leaving camp, and asked Caesar's permission to go. Some stayed out of shame and a desire to avoid the suspicion of cowardice. But they were unable to hide their feelings, and at times could not help shedding tears; skulking in their tents, they bemoaned their fate or joined their friends in lamenting the peril that threatened them all alike. All over the camp men were signing and sealing their wills. The talk of these frightened people gradually affected even seasoned campaigners, including some centurions and cavalry officers. Those who wished to be thought less timid than the rest said that it was not the enemy they feared, but the narrow defiles through which they had to pass and the great forests that lay between them and Ariovistus, or pretended to be afraid that it would prove impossible to maintain an adequate supply of corn. Some even went so far as to tell Caesar that when he gave the command to strike camp and advance, the soldiers would be too panic-stricken to obey.

40. Observing this state of affairs, Caesar summoned the centurions of every grade to a council, and began by severely reprimanding them for presuming to inquire or conjecture where he was leading them, or with what object. At the time of his consulship, he said, Ariovistus had sought the friendship of Rome with great eagerness; and what reason was there for thinking that he would so light-heartedly refuse to carry out his obligations? For his own part, he was convinced that when the king was acquainted with his demands and saw the fairness of the terms proposed, he would not reject the friendship offered by the Roman government and by himself. If, however, a mad impulse should lead him to make war, what reason had they after all for being afraid? Both their own courage and his careful attention to his duties gave good grounds for confidence.

'Our countrymen faced this enemy,' he continued, 'in our fathers' time, when Gaius Marius won a victory over the Cimbri and Teutoni by which, as all agreed, the whole army earned as much glory as its commander. They faced them again more recently in Italy, when they defeated the rebellious slaves,[8] aided though these were to some extent by the military training and discipline that they had acquired from their Roman masters. This shows what a great advantage resolute courage is: for a long time the Romans had an unreasoning fear of the slaves while they were still unarmed, yet afterwards defeated them when they were not only armed but flushed with victory. Moreover these Germans are the same men whom the Helvetii have often met in battle; not only in Switzerland but also in Germany, and have generally beaten; yet the Helvetii were not a match for our army.

'If anyone is alarmed by the fact that the Germans have defeated the Gauls and put them to flight, he should inquire into the circumstances of that defeat. He will find that it happened at a time when the Gauls were exhausted by a long war. Ariovistus had remained for many months under cover of his camp and the surrounding marshes, so that they had no chance of fighting him, and then he attacked suddenly, when in despair of bringing him to battle they had broken up into scattered groups. Thus his victory resulted from his cunning strategy rather than the bravery of his troops. The employment of such strategy was possible against inexperienced natives, but even Ariovistus can have no hope of being able to trick our armies by such means.' He went on to say that those who tried to disguise their cowardice by pretending to be anxious about the corn supply or the difficulties of the route were acting presumptuously: it was plain that they either lacked confidence in their general's sense of duty or else meant to dictate to him. He was attending to these matters. Corn was being supplied by the Sequani, Leuci, and Lingones, and the harvest was already ripe in the fields; and as to the route, they would soon be in a position to judge for themselves. The suggestion that the men would not obey orders to advance did not trouble him at all; for he knew that in all cases in which an army had refused obedience, it was either because their generals had been unsuccessful and were regarded as unlucky, or because they were proved dishonest by the discovery of some misconduct. His own integrity was attested by his whole life; his power of commanding success, by the campaign against the Helvetii. Therefore he was going to do that very night what he had at first intended to defer till later: he would move camp in the early hours of the morning, so as to find out with the least possible delay whether their sense of honour and duty or their fear was the stronger. If no one else would follow him, he would go all the same, accompanied only by the 10th legion; of its loyalty he had no doubt, and it should serve as his bodyguard. (Caesar placed the highest confidence in this legion for its bravery and had shown it particular favour.)

41. This address had a dramatic effect on all ranks, and inspired them with the utmost enthusiasm and eagerness for action. First of all, the men of the 10th commissioned their military tribunes to thank Caesar for his high opinion of them, and to assure him that they were ready to take the field at any moment. Then the other legions prevailed on their tribunes and first grade centurions to make their peace with him, professing that they had never entertained doubts or fears, and had never imagined that it was for them to direct the campaign, which they realized was their commander's business. Accepting their excuses, Caesar told Diviciacus to study the available routes, because he trusted him more than any of the other Gauls, and was advised by him to make a detour of some fifty miles, which would enable them to march through open country. Starting in the small hours, as he had said he would, he marched without interruption for six days, and was then informed by his patrols that Ariovistus' forces were twenty-three miles away.

42. Hearing that Caesar had moved nearer, Ariovistus sent a message saying that he had no objection to arranging the interview previously requested, as he thought he could now do so without risk. Caesar did not reject his offer, thinking that Ariovistus was now coming to his senses again, since he undertook of his own accord to do what he had refused before when asked. He hoped too that the recollection of the great favours the king had received from himself and the Roman government would make him abandon his stubborn attitude, when he heard what was required of him. The interview was arranged for the fifth day following, and in the meantime messengers kept going to and fro between them. Ariovistus insisted that Caesar should not bring any infantry to the conference; he was afraid, he said, of being caught in a trap. Each

of them must come with a mounted escort only; otherwise he
would not come at all. As Caesar did not want to give him an
excuse for cancelling the meeting, yet dared not entrust his safety
to the Gallic cavalry, he decided that his best course would be to
take away all their horses and mount upon them the infantrymen
of the 10th legion, in whom he had such complete confidence, and
thus have an escort on whose devotion he could rely absolutely in
case of need. While this was being done one of the legionaries
made quite a witty remark. 'Caesar's being better than his word,'
he said. 'He promised to make the 10th his bodyguard, and now
he's knighting us.'

43. In an extensive plain⁹ there stood a fairly high mound of
earth, about equidistant from the camps of Caesar and Ariovistus.
Here they came, as agreed, to hold their conference. The mounted
legion that Caesar had brought was posted some three hundred
yards away from the mound, and Ariovistus' horsemen took up
their position at an equal distance. The king stipulated that they
should confer on horseback, each accompanied by ten men. On
reaching the place Caesar began by recalling the favours that he
himself and the Senate had conferred on Ariovistus – how he had
been honoured with the titles of 'King' and 'Friend', and had
received handsome presents – pointing out that very few princes
had been granted such distinctions, which were usually reserved
for those who had rendered important services to Rome.

'You would have had no right,' he said, 'to apply to the Senate
for any such favours; you owe them entirely to my kindness and
my generosity and that of the Senate. The friendship between my
country and the Aedui is of long standing and founded on solid
grounds. Resolutions of the Senate, expressed in most complimentary terms, have repeatedly been passed in their honour. They held
a position of supremacy in Gaul all along, even before they sought
our friendship; and since it has always been our policy to see that
our allies and friends, far from losing anything they had already,
should have their credit, honour and importance increased, how
can we allow them to be robbed of what they already had when
they became our friends?'

He then repeated the demands which he had instructed his
envoys to present – that Ariovistus should not make war on the

Aedui or their allies; that he should restore their hostages; and even if he could not send any of the Germans back home, he should at least not let any more cross the Rhine.

44. Ariovistus had little to say in reply to these demands, but spoke at length about his own merits. He had crossed the Rhine, he said, not of his own accord but in response to the invitation of the Gauls, and it had needed the prospect of a rich reward to induce him to leave his home and his relatives. The possessions he had in Gaul had been ceded to him by the Gauls themselves, and the hostages had been given voluntarily. As for the tribute he exacted, this was customarily regarded as the right of a victorious belligerent. He had not been the aggressor: the Gauls had attacked him, all their tribes having marched out and taken the field against him. He had completely routed their entire force in a single battle. If they wanted to try their luck again, he was quite ready for another fight; if they wanted peace, it was unfair for them to object to the tribute that they had hitherto paid without demur. The friendship of the Roman people ought to be a distinction and a protection to him, not an occasion of loss, and it was with this expectation that he had sought it. If through Roman interference his subjects were absolved from payment and withdrawn from his control, he would be just as ready to discard that friendship as he had been to seek it. The large numbers of Germans he was bringing into Gaul were brought to secure his safety, not for aggression; the proof of that was that he had not come till he was asked, and had fought only in self-defence. However, he had come there before the Romans, whose armies had never before marched beyond the frontier of the Province. What did Caesar mean by invading his dominions?

'This part of the country,' he said, 'is my province, just as the other part is yours. I could not expect you to let me make raids into your territory with impunity, and it is a gross injustice for you to interfere with me in the exercise of my lawful rights. You say that the Aedui have been called "Brothers" by the Roman Senate. Well, I may be a "Barbarian"; but I am not such a barbarian, and not so ignorant, as not to know that in the recent revolt of the Allobroges [61 B.C.] you got no help from the Aedui, and that they had to do without the benefit of your assistance in the war they have just fought with me and the Sequani. I suspect that this talk of friendship is just so much pretence, and that your object in keeping an army in Gaul is to crush me. Unless you take yourself off from this country, and your army with you, it won't be as a "Friend" that I shall treat you. In fact, if I killed you, there are plenty of nobles and politicians in Rome who would thank me for it; I know this, because they themselves commissioned their agents to tell me so. I could make them all my grateful friends by putting an end to you. But if you will go away and leave me in undisturbed possession of Gaul I will reward you handsomely, and whenever you want a war fought, I will see the job through for you, without your lifting a finger or running any risk.'

45. Caesar explained at some length why he could not think of abandoning his intention. It was contrary to his principles and to those of the Roman government to desert a loyal ally; and he could not admit that Gaul belonged to Ariovistus any more than to Rome. The Arverni and the Ruteni had been conquered by Quintus Fabius Maximus [121 B.C.], although the Roman people afterwards pardoned their hostility and refrained from annexing their land or exacting tribute from them. If priority of arrival was to be the criterion, the Romans' title to rule Gaul was unimpeachable. If they were to abide by the decision of the Senate, Gaul ought to be independent, since the Senate had determined that, although conquered, it should be allowed self-government.

46. While these questions were being argued, word was brought to Caesar that Ariovistus' horsemen were approaching nearer the mound, riding towards our soldiers, and throwing stones and javelins at them. Caesar broke off the conversation, went to his men, and forbade them to throw a single missile in retaliation. For although he knew that a legion of picked troops could engage cavalry without the slightest risk, he did not choose to give anyone the chance of saying, if the enemy were driven off, that he had broken his word by treacherously attacking them during a parley. When the news spread through the ranks of the army that Ariovistus had arrogantly warned the Romans off the whole of Gaul, and that his cavalry had interrupted the conference by attacking our troops, the men's enthusiasm and eagerness for battle knew no bounds.

47. The next day Ariovistus sent envoys to Caesar to say that he

wished to resume their interrupted discussion, and to ask him either to appoint a day for another personal interview, or, if he did not want to do that, to send an officer to represent him. Caesar did not see that anything was to be gained by a further interview, especially as on the previous day Ariovistus had been unable to restrain his men from attacking the Roman troops, and he thought it would be running a great risk to send a Roman officer and place him at the mercy of such savages. He decided that his best plan was to send Gaius Valerius Procillus, a young man of high character and liberal education, whose father Gaius Valerius Caburus had been granted Roman citizenship by Gaius Valerius Flaccus. Procillus was a man who could be trusted. His knowledge of the Gallic language would be useful, since by long practice Ariovistus had learnt to speak it fluently; and in his case the Germans would have no motive for foul play. With him he sent Marcus Metius, who was bound to Ariovistus by ties of hospitality, and their orders were to hear what the king had to say, and report to Caesar. But as soon as Ariovistus saw them at his camp headquarters, he shouted out in front of his whole army: 'What are you coming here for? To play the spy, I suppose?' And when they attempted to speak, he stopped them and had them put in chains.

48. On the same day he advanced and took up a position at the foot of a mountain six miles from Caesar's camp. The next day he marched his army past the camp and himself encamped two miles farther on, with the object of intercepting the convoys of grain and other supplies that were being sent up from the Sequani and the Aedui. On each of the five days following, Caesar led his troops out in front of his camp and kept them for some time in line of battle, so as to give Ariovistus the opportunity of fighting if he wanted to; but each day the king kept his main forces in camp, merely engaging in cavalry skirmishes.

The Germans were trained in the use of a special battle technique. They had a force of six thousand cavalry, each of whom had selected from the whole army, for his personal protection, one infantryman of outstanding courage and speed of foot. These accompanied the cavalry in battle and acted as support for them to fall back upon. In a critical situation they ran to the rescue and surrounded any cavalryman who had been unhorsed by a severe wound. They acquired such agility by practice, that in a long advance or a quick retreat they could hang on to the horses' manes and keep pace with them.

49. Caesar saw that the Germans were not going to come out of their camp, and since he could not afford to be cut off from supplies any longer, he chose a suitable site for a camp about a thousand yards beyond the enemy's position, and marched there in battle formation of three lines. The first and second lines were ordered to stand by under arms; the third, to make fortifications for the camp. The place being less than a mile away, Ariovistus sent some sixteen thousand light infantry and all his cavalry to overawe our soldiers and prevent them from continuing the work. Caesar, however, did not vary his original plan; the first two lines were told to drive off the enemy, while the third finished their task. When the entrenchments of the camp were completed, he left two legions and a detachment of auxiliaries to occupy it, and led the other four legions back to the large camp.

50. The next day he followed his usual routine by bringing the troops out of both camps, deploying them for action a short distance from the large camp, and offering battle. Finding that even then the enemy would not come out, he returned to camp about midday, whereupon Ariovistus at last sent a detachment to attack the small camp, and a hotly contested battle was kept up until evening. At sunset, after severe casualties had been sustained by both sides, Ariovistus retired. On inquiring from prisoners why he would not fight a general engagement, Caesar was told that the German matrons, who used to draw lots and employ other methods of divination to decide whether it was advisable to join battle, had pronounced that the Germans were not destined to win if they fought before the new moon.

51. Next day, leaving adequate garrisons in the two camps, Caesar posted all his auxiliaries in front of the small camp, where they would be visible to the enemy and give an impression of strength – since his regular infantry was numerically weak in comparison with the Germans. He then drew up the legions for action in three lines and advanced right up to Ariovistus' camp. The enemy was now compelled to lead his forces out, and drew up the various tribal contingents at equal intervals – Harudes,

Marcomanni, Triboci, Vangiones, Nemetes, Eudusii, and Suebi. So that there might be no hope of escaping by flight, they formed a barrier of carriages and wagons along the rear of their whole line, and in them placed their women, who as the men marched to battle stretched out their hands and implored them with tears not to let them be enslaved by the Romans.

52. Caesar placed each of his five generals ahead of a legion and detailed his quaestor to command the remaining legion, so that every soldier might know that there was a high officer in a position to observe the courage with which he conducted himself, and then led the right wing first into action, because he had noticed that the enemy's line was weakest on that side. Our troops attacked with such vigour when the signal was given, and the enemy also dashed forward so suddenly and swiftly, that there was no time to throw spears at them. So the men dropped their spears and fought hand to hand with their swords. By quickly adopting their usual phalanx formation the Germans were able to withstand the sword thrusts, but many of our soldiers actually threw themselves on the wall of shields confronting them, wrenched the shields out of the enemy's hands, and stabbed them from above. The Germans' left was thus routed, but their right began to press our troops hard by weight of numbers. Their perilous position attracted the attention of young Publius Crassus, who was in charge of the cavalry and better able to move about and see what was happening than those in the fighting line. He therefore sent up the third line to their relief.

53. This move turned the battle once more in our favour, and the enemy's whole army broke and fled without stopping until they came to the Rhine, some fifteen miles away.[10] A very few of the strongest tried to swim the river, and a few others saved themselves by finding boats – including Ariovistus, who had the luck to come across a small craft moored to the bank. All the rest were hunted down and killed by our cavalry. Ariovistus' two wives both perished in the flight – one a Suebic woman whom he had brought from Germany, the other a Norican whom his brother King Voccio sent to him while he was in Gaul; and of his two daughters, one was killed and the other captured. Valerius Procillus was being dragged along by his guards among the German fugitives, fettered with three chains, when Caesar himself, who was with the

pursuing cavalry, came up with him. This fortunate chance pleased Caesar as much as the actual victory, for the man whom it rescued from the enemy's clutches and restored to him was the worthiest in the whole Province, besides being his own friend and host; and his death, which Providence thus averted, would have marred the pleasure and rejoicing that attended so splendid a triumph. Procillus recounted how, before his very eyes, the German had three times cast lots to decide whether he should be burnt to death at once or reserved for execution later, and how he owed his life to the way the lots had fallen. Metius also was found and brought back to Caesar.

54. When the news of the battle reached the other side of the Rhine, the Suebi, who had advanced as far as the river bank, turned back homewards, and the Rhineland tribes, seeing what a panic they were in, pursued and killed a large number of them.

Caesar had completed two important campaigns in a single summer. He now took the army into winter quarters in the country of the Sequani[11] somewhat earlier than the usual time of year, and leaving Labienus in command started for northern Italy to hold the assizes.

BOOK II
THE CONQUEST OF THE
BELGIC TRIBES

1 Collapse of the Belgic coalition (57 B.C.)

1. While Caesar was in Italy, and the legions in their winter quarters, repeated rumours reached him, alleging what was confirmed by dispatches from Labienus – that all the Gallic tribes, whose territory, as said above, comprises a third of Gaul, were conspiring against the Romans and exchanging hostages. Their action was said to be due to two causes. In the first place, they were afraid that if all the rest of Gaul was subdued, our troops would advance against them. Secondly, they were instigated, from various motives, by a number of Celtic Gauls. Some of these were as much annoyed by the sight of a Roman army wintering in Gaul, and establishing itself there, as they had been by the continued presence of the Germans in the country; others, fickle and inconstant, merely hankered after a change of masters. There were also some adventurers who saw that under Roman rule they would not find it so easy to usurp thrones, as was commonly done in Gaul by powerful men, and by those who could afford to hire mercenaries.

2. These alarming reports induced Caesar to raise two new legions in Italy,[12] and to send them in the spring to Gaul under the command of Quintus Pedius, one of his generals. As soon as forage began to be plentiful he joined the army in person, and instructed the Senones and the other tribes whose territory bordered on that of the Belgae to find out what was going on among them and inform him. As their reports all agreed that troops were being levied and concentrated, he decided that he must take the offensive at once; and after arranging for a supply of grain he broke camp and in a fortnight was on the Belgic frontier.

3. On his arrival, which owing to the speed of his march was quite unexpected, the Remi, the nearest of the Belgae to Celtic

Gaul, sent Iccius and Andecombogius, the leading men of their tribe, to tell him that they placed themselves and all they possessed under the protection and at the disposal of the Roman people. They explained that they had taken no part in the conspiracy which the rest of the Belgae had planned against the Romans, and that they were ready to give hostages, to obey his orders, to admit him into their strongholds, and to furnish corn and other supplies. The remainder of the Belgae, they said, were up in arms, and had been joined by the Germans living on the Gallic side of the Rhine; and all of them were possessed by such fury that even the Suessiones – their own near kinsmen, who enjoyed the protection of the same laws as themselves, and obeyed the same king and the same magistrate – had refused to listen when they tried to deter them from joining the movement.

4. On being asked for the names of the tribes that had taken up arms, and particulars of their numbers and military strength, the envoys stated that most of the Belgae were descended from tribes which long ago came across the Rhine from Germany and settled in that part of Gaul on account of its fertility, expelling the former inhabitants. The Belgae, they said, were the only people who half a century earlier, when all the rest of Gaul was overrun by the Teutoni and the Cimbri, prevented the invaders from entering their territory – the recollection of which made them assume an air of much importance and pride themselves on their military power. Regarding their numbers the Remi professed to have detailed information, explaining that they were united with the various tribes by ties of blood and marriage, and knew the strength of the contingent that each had promised in the general council of the Belgae.[13] The most powerful of all, they said, were the Bellovaci, on account of their bravery, prestige, and large population; they could muster 100,000 troops, had promised 60,000 picked men, and claimed the direction of the whole campaign.

The Suessiones, near neighbours of the Remi themselves, had an extensive and very fertile territory. They had been ruled within living memory by Diviciacus, the most powerful king in Gaul, who controlled not only a large part of the Belgic country, but Britain as well. Their present king was Galba, to whom, as a just and able man, the supreme direction of the war was being entrusted by common consent; he possessed twelve strongholds, and undertook to furnish 50,000 troops. An equal number was promised by the Nervii, who were considered by the Belgae themselves to be their fiercest fighters, and lived farthest to the north. The Atrebates were to provide 15,000 men, the Ambiani 10,000, the Morini 25,000, the Menapii 9,000, the Caleti 10,000, the Veliocasses and the Viromandui 10,000 between them, and the Atuatuci 19,000; the Condrusi, Eburones, Caerosi, and Paemani (who are all known as German tribes) thought they could raise an army about 40,000 strong.

5. Caesar addressed the Remi in gracious and reassuring terms, telling them to send their whole council to him and to place the children of their leading citizens in his hands as hostages. These orders were carefully and punctually obeyed. He impressed upon Diviciacus the Aeduan the importance, alike for Rome and for the general safety of Gaul, of preventing the junction of the various enemy contingents, in order to avoid the necessity of fighting such powerful forces all at once. He explained that the best way of effecting this was for the Aedui to invade the land of the Bellovaci and start devastating it, and dismissed Diviciacus with orders to do so. When, however, he learnt from his patrols, and from the Remi, that the Belgae had already completed their concentration and were approaching, he hastily crossed the river Aisne, just within the borders of the Remi, and encamped. This movement enabled him to protect one side of his camp by the river and to secure his rear, and assured the safety of the convoys that were to be sent up by the Remi and others. The river was spanned by a bridge, at the head of which he placed a strong guard, leaving one of his generals, Quintus Titurius Sabinus, on the left bank with six cohorts. He ordered the camp to be made with a rampart twelve feet high and a trench eighteen feet wide.

6. Eight miles away was a town of the Remi called Bibrax, which the Belgae, directly they reached it, assaulted so violently that the garrison had difficulty in holding out to the end of the day. The Belgae have the same method of attacking a fortress as the rest of the Gauls. They begin by surrounding the whole circuit of the wall with a large number of men, and showering stones at it from all sides; when they have cleared it of defenders, they lock their

shields over their heads, advance close up, and undermine it. These tactics were easy to employ on the present occasion; for with such a large force hurling stones and javelins, no one could possibly stay on the wall. When night stopped the assault, Iccius, the governor of the town – a Roman nobleman, who was very influential with his countrymen and had been one of the envoys deputed to ask Caesar for peace – sent word that unless relieved he could not hold out longer.

7. Shortly after midnight, using as guides the men who had brought Iccius' message, Caesar sent some Numidians,[14] Cretan archers, and Balearic slingers to help him. Their arrival restored the morale of the Remi and filled them with fresh ardour for the defence of the town, while the enemy gave up hope of capturing it. Accordingly, after staying there a short time longer, the Belgae proceeded to ravage the countryside and to burn all the villages and homesteads within reach, and then marched their whole army towards Caesar's camp and themselves encamped barely two miles away. The smoke and flame of their watchfires showed that their camp stretched for about eight miles.

8. As the Belgic forces were very strong and had a great reputation for bravery, Caesar determined at first not to fight a general action, but he engaged every day in cavalry skirmishes, in order to discover what the enemy could really do, and how his own men stood up to them; and he soon found that his troops were as good as theirs. The ground in front of his camp was ideal for deploying the army for action. The low hill on which the camp stood was of just the right width, on the side facing the enemy, for the legions to occupy in battle formation; on each flank it descended steeply to the plain, while in front it formed a slight ridge and then sloped gently down. On either side of the hill Caesar had a trench dug, running for about six hundred and fifty yards at right angles to the line along which the troops would be drawn up, and placed redoubts and artillery at both ends of each trench, to prevent the enemy from using their numerical superiority to envelop his men from the flanks while they were fighting. He left the two newly enrolled legions in camp, to be used as reinforcements wherever they were needed, and drew up the other six in front in line of battle. The enemy also had marched out and deployed for action.

9. There was a small marsh between the two armies. The Belgae waited in the hope that our troops would try to cross it, and our men stood with weapons in their hands, ready to pounce upon them at a disadvantage if they attempted to cross first, while in the meantime a cavalry skirmish went on between the lines. Since neither side would make the first move, as soon as the cavalry fight ended in our favour Caesar led the infantry back into camp. The Belgae then marched straight from their battle position to the Aisne, which I have explained was in the rear of our camp. They found a ford and tried to get a part of their forces across, intending to storm a redoubt commanded by Sabinus and break down the bridge, or, failing this, to deprive us of a very useful source of supplies for the campaign by devastating the land of the Remi, and to cut our communications.

10. On being informed of this by Sabinus, Caesar crossed the bridge with all the cavalry, the light-armed Numidians, the slingers and the archers, and advanced against them. A fierce battle ensued. He attacked them in the river, which impeded their movements, and killed a large number. Others made a very daring attempt to cross over their dead bodies, but were driven back by a shower of missiles, while some of the firstcomers who had succeeded in getting across were rounded up and destroyed by the cavalry.

The Belgae now realized that their hope of crossing the river was as vain as their hope of capturing Bibrax had proved to be, and that the Romans would not advance into an unfavourable position to fight. Their own supply of grain, too, was running short. Summoning a council of war, therefore, they decided that the best course was for every man to return to his own home and wait to see whose territory the Romans invaded first; they would then rally from all parts to its defence, and would have the advantage of fighting in friendly country, where their home supplies of grain would be available. In addition to the other reasons, they were led to this decision by the knowledge that Diviciacus and his Aeduans were approaching the frontier of the Bellovaci, whose soldiers were so anxious to go to the help of their own people that they could not be induced to stay any longer where they were.

11. In pursuance of their resolve the Belgae left camp some time before midnight amid great uproar and confusion, without any

proper order or discipline, since every man wanted to reach home
quickly and tried to get the first place on the road. The result was
that their departure resembled a rout. The movement was immediately reported to Caesar by his scouts, but he was afraid at first that
an ambush was being laid, because the reason for their retreat was
not yet apparent, and therefore kept all his forces in camp. At
daybreak, however, the reports of his patrols satisfied him that the
enemy really were retreating, whereupon he sent forward the
generals Quintus Pedius and Lucius Aurunculeius Cotta, with all
the cavalry, to delay the march of their rearguard, and ordered
Labienus to follow in support with three legions. These troops
attacked their column from behind and pursued it for many miles,
killing a large number as they fled; for while the rearguard, with
which our men were actually in contact, halted and put up a gallant
resistance, all those in front, imagining that they were far enough
off to be safe, and not being under the immediate necessity of
defending themselves or under the control of anyone in authority,
broke their ranks directly they heard the shouting of the comba-
tants, and tried to escape. Thus our troops were able, without any
risk, to kill as many of them as there was time to kill. When
nightfall compelled them to stop, they returned to camp in
accordance with their orders.

2 Piecemeal conquest of the Belgic tribes (57 B.C.)

12. The next day, before the enemy could recover from their
panic, Caesar advanced into the country of the Suessiones, which
adjoined that of the Remi, and by a forced march reached the
fortress of Noviodunum. Being informed that it was not garrisoned, he tried to storm it directly he arrived, but the width of
the moat and the height of the wall enabled the few defenders
to repel his assault. After constructing a camp, therefore, he
formed a line of mantlets and set about the usual preparations
for a siege. But the next night, before his preparations were
completed, the whole fugitive army of the Suessiones came
crowding into the place. When they saw the mantlets rushed up
to the wall, earth shovelled into the moat, and siege towers

erected, they were alarmed by the impressive size of this apparatus, which had never before been seen or heard of in Gaul, and by the speed with which the Romans worked. They therefore sent envoys asking to be allowed to surrender – a request which Caesar granted on the intercession of the Remi, who pleaded for the lives of their kinsmen.

13. He took the leading men of the Suessiones as hostages, as well as two of King Galba's own sons, and accepted the surrender of the tribe after all the arms in the fortress had been handed over.

Caesar marched next against the Bellovaci, who retired with all their belongings into the fortress of Bratuspantium. When his army was about five miles off, all the older men came out, and signified by supplicatory gestures and cries that they placed themselves at his mercy and were not offering resistance. In the same way, when he marched close up to the fortress and began to make a camp, the women and children appeared on the wall with arms outstretched in their habitual manner of entreaty and begged for peace.

14. Their plea was supported by Diviciacus, who after the retreat of the Belgae had disbanded the Aeduan forces and returned to Caesar. He said that the Bellovaci had always lived under the friendly protection of the Aedui, until their leading men induced them to sever the connection and take up arms against Rome, by telling them that the Aedui were enslaved by Caesar and had to endure every kind of ill-usage and humiliation.

'The people responsible for the adoption of this policy,' he continued, 'have now realized what a calamity they have brought upon their country, and have fled to Britain. To the prayers of the Bellovaci we Aeduans add our own, begging you to treat them with your usual clemency and humanity. By so doing you will enhance our prestige with all the Belgic tribes – a matter of importance to us, because we always rely on their troops and resources to see us through any war in which we are involved.'

15. Caesar said that he would spare the Bellovaci and accept their submission out of respect for Diviciacus and the Aedui; but as the tribe was very influential among the Belgae, and had the largest population, he demanded six hundred hostages. When these had been handed over and all the arms in the fortress collected, he

marched into the country of the Ambiani, who at once surrendered unconditionally.

The Ambiani were neighbours of the Nervii, about whose character and habits Caesar made enquiries. He learnt that they did not admit traders into their country and would not allow the importation of wine or other luxuries, because they thought such things made men soft and took the edge off their courage; that they were a fierce, warlike people, who bitterly reproached the other Belgae for throwing away their inheritance of bravery by submitting to the Romans, and vowed that they would never ask for peace or accept it on any terms.

16. After three days' march through Nervian territory, Caesar learnt from prisoners that the river Sambre was not more than ten miles from the place where he was encamped, and that all the Nervian troops were posted on the farther side of it, awaiting the arrival of the Romans. Already with them in the field, he was told, were their neighbours the Atrebates and the Viromandui, whom they had persuaded to try the fortune of war along with them; and they were expecting to be joined by the forces of the Atuatuci, which were already on the way. They had hastily thrust their women, and all who were thought too young or too old to fight, into a place which marshes made inaccessible to an army.

17. On receiving this information Caesar sent forward a reconnoitring party, accompanied by some centurions to choose a good site for a camp. A large number of Gauls, including some of the Belgae who had surrendered, had attached themselves to Caesar and were marching with the troops. Some of these, as was afterwards ascertained from prisoners, had observed the order in which our army marched during the previous days, and at night made their way to the Nervii and explained to them that each legion was separated from the following one by a long baggage train, so that when the first reached camp the others would be far away; it would be quite easy to attack it while the men were still burdened with their packs, and when it was routed and its baggage plundered, the others would not dare to make a stand.

There was one thing that favoured the execution of the plan suggested by these deserters. The Nervii have virtually no cavalry. To this day they pay no attention to that arm, their whole strength consisting of infantry. So, long ago they devised a method of hindering their neighbours' cavalry when it made plundering raids into their territory. They cut off the tops of saplings, bent them over, and let a thick growth of side branches shoot out; in between them they planted briars and thorns, and thus made hedges like walls, which gave such protection that no one could even see through them, much less penetrate them. As these obstacles hindered the march of our column, the Nervii thought the proposed plan too good to leave untried.

18. At the place that the Romans had chosen for their camp a hill sloped down evenly from its summit to the Sambre. Opposite it, on the other side of the river, rose another hill with a similar gradient, on the lower slopes of which were some three hundred yards of open ground, while the upper part was covered by a wood which it was not easy to see into. In this wood the main part of the enemy's forces lay concealed, while on the open ground along the river bank a few pickets of cavalry were visible. The depth of the river was about three feet.

19. Caesar had sent his cavalry a little in advance and was following with the rest of his forces, but the column was formed up in a different manner from that which the Belgic deserters had described to the Nervii. In accordance with his usual practice when approaching an enemy, Caesar marched at the head of the column with six legions, unencumbered by heavy baggage; then came the transport of the entire army, protected by the two newly enrolled legions, which brought up the rear.

First of all, our cavalry crossed the river with the slingers and archers and engaged the enemy's horsemen. These kept on retiring into the wood where their comrades were and then reappearing to charge our troops, who dared not pursue them beyond the end of the open ground. Meanwhile the six legions that were the first to arrive measured out the ground and began to construct the camp. The Gauls concealed in the wood had already formed up in battle order and were waiting full of confidence. As soon as they caught sight of the head of the baggage train – the moment which they had agreed upon for starting the battle – they suddenly dashed out in full force and swooped down on our cavalry, which they easily routed. Then they ran down to the river at such an incredible speed that almost at the same moment they seemed to be at the edge of the wood, in the water and already upon us. With equal rapidity they climbed the hill towards our camp to attack the men who were busy entrenching it.

20. Caesar had everything to do at once – hoist the flag which was the signal for running to arms, recall the men from their work on the camp, fetch back those who had gone far afield in search of material for the rampart, form the battle line, address the men, and sound the trumpet signal for going into action. Much of this could not be done in the short time left available by the enemy's swift onset. But the situation was saved by two things – first, the knowledge and experience of the soldiers, whose training in earlier battles enabled them to decide for themselves what needed doing, without waiting to be told; secondly, the order which Caesar had issued to all his generals, not to leave the work, but to stay each with his own legion until the camp fortifications were completed. As the enemy was so close and advancing so swiftly, the generals did not wait for further orders but on their own responsibility took the measures they thought proper.

21. After giving the minimum of essential orders, Caesar hastened down to the battlefield to address the troops and happened to come first upon the 10th legion, to which he made only a short speech, urging them to live up to their tradition of bravery, to keep their nerve, and to meet the enemy's attack boldly. Then, as the Nervii were within range, he gave the signal for battle. On going to the other side of the field to address the troops there, he found them already in action. The soldiers were so pushed for time by the enemy's eagerness to fight that they could not even take the covers off their shields or put on helmets – not to speak of fixing on crests or decorations. Each man, on coming down from his work at the camp, went into action under the first standard he happened to see, so as not to waste time searching for his own unit.

22. The battlefront was not formed according to rules of military theory but as necessitated by the emergency and the sloping ground of the hillside. The legions were facing different ways and fighting separate actions, and thick hedges obstructed their view. The result was that Caesar could not fix upon definite points for stationing reserves or foresee what would be needed in each part of the field,

and unity of command was impossible. In such adverse circumstances there were naturally ups and downs of fortune.

23. The 9th and 10th legions were on the left, and discharged a
volley of spears at the Atrebates, who happened to be facing them.
Breathless and exhausted with running, and many of them now
wounded, the Atrebates were quickly driven down to the river,
and when they tried to cross it our soldiers with their swords
attacked them at a disadvantage and destroyed a large number.
Crossing the river themselves without hesitation and pushing
forward up the steep slope, they renewed the fight when the enemy
began to resist once more, and again put them to flight. Meanwhile
in another part of the field, on a front facing in a slightly different
direction, the 11th and 8th legions engaged the Viromandui, drove
them down the hill, and were now fighting right on the river banks.
By this time, however, the Roman camp was almost entirely
exposed in front and on the left, and the 12th and 7th legions,
which were posted fairly close together on the right, were attacked
by the whole force of the Nervii, led in a compact mass by their
commander-in-chief Boduognatus. Some of them began to surround the legions on their right flank, while the rest made for the
hilltop where the camp stood.

24. At the same time, the Roman cavalry and light-armed
troops, routed by the first attack, were in the act of retreating into
the camp, when they found themselves face to face with the Nervii
and took to flight again in a different direction. The servants, too,
who from the back gate on the summit of the hill had seen our
victorious troops cross the river, and had gone out to plunder, on
looking back and seeing the enemy in the camp immediately ran
for their lives. Meanwhile shouting and din arose from the drivers
coming up with the baggage, who rushed panic-stricken in every
direction. With the army were some auxiliary cavalry sent by the
Treveri, a people with a unique reputation for courage among the
Gauls. When these horsemen saw the Roman camp full of the
enemy, the legions hard pressed and almost surrounded, and the
non-combatants, cavalry, slingers, and Numidians scattered and
stampeding in every direction, they decided that our case was
desperate, and, riding off home in terror, reported that the Romans
were utterly defeated and their camp and baggage captured.

25. After addressing the 10th legion Caesar had gone to the right wing, where he found the troops in difficulties. The cohorts of the 12th legion were packed together so closely that the men were in one another's way and could not fight properly. All the centurions of the 4th cohort, as well as a standard-bearer, were killed, and the standard was lost; nearly all the centurions of the other cohorts were either killed or wounded, including the chief centurion Publius Sextius Baculus, a man of very great courage, who was so disabled by a number of severe wounds that he could no longer stand. The men's movements were slow, and some in the rear, feeling themselves abandoned, were retiring from the fight and trying to get out of range. Meanwhile the enemy maintained unceasing pressure up the hill in front, and were also closing in on both flanks. As the situation was critical and no reserves were available, Caesar snatched a shield from a soldier in the rear (he had not his own shield with him), made his way into the front line, addressed each centurion by name, and shouted encouragement to the rest of the troops, ordering them to push forward and open out their ranks, so that they could use their swords more easily. His coming gave them fresh heart and hope; each man wanted to do his best under the eyes of his commander-in-chief, however desperate the peril, and the enemy's assault was slowed down a little.

26. Noticing that the 7th legion, which stood close by, was likewise hard put to it, Caesar told the military tribunes to join the two legions gradually together and adopt a square formation, so that they could advance against the enemy in any direction. By this manoeuvre the soldiers were enabled to support one another, and were no longer afraid of being surrounded from behind, which encouraged them to put up a bolder resistance. Meanwhile the two legions which had acted as a guard to the baggage at the rear of the column, having received news of the battle, had quickened their pace, and now appeared on the hilltop, where the enemy could see them; and Labienus, who had captured the enemy's camp, and from the high ground on which it stood could see what was going on in ours, sent the 10th legion to the rescue. The men of the 10th, who could tell from the flight of the cavalry and the non-combatants how serious things were, and what peril threatened the camp, the

legions, and their commander-in-chief, strained every nerve to make the utmost speed.

27. Their arrival so completely changed the situation that even some of the Roman soldiers who had lain down, exhausted by wounds, got up and began to fight again, leaning on their shields. The non-combatants, observing the enemy's alarm, stood up to their attack, unarmed as they were; and the cavalry, anxious to wipe out the disgrace of their flight, scoured the whole battlefield and tried to outdo the legionaries in gallantry. But the enemy, even in their desperate plight, showed such bravery that when their front ranks had fallen those immediately behind stood on their prostrate bodies to fight and when these too fell and the corpses were piled high, the survivors still kept hurling javelins as though from the top of a mound, and flung back the spears intercepted by their shields. Such courage accounted for the extraordinary feats they had performed already. Only heroes could have made light of crossing a wide river, clambering up the steep banks, and launching themselves on such a difficult position.

28. So ended this battle, by which the tribe of the Nervii was almost annihilated and their name almost blotted out from the face of the earth. On hearing the news of it, their old men, who, as already said, had been sent away with the women and children into tidal creeks and marshes, decided that nothing could stop the victorious Romans or protect their conquered tribe, and with the consent of all the survivors they sent envoys to Caesar and surrendered. In describing the calamity that had befallen their state, they asserted that they had three councillors left out of six hundred, and scarcely five hundred men capable of bearing arms out of sixty thousand. Caesar, wishing to let it be seen that he showed mercy to unfortunate suppliants, took great care to protect them from harm, confirmed them in possession of their territories and towns, and commanded their neighbours to refrain from injuring their persons or property, and to make their dependants do likewise.

29. The Atuatuci who, as mentioned above, were coming in full force to help the Nervii, on hearing of their defeat turned back without halting and went home. Abandoning their other strongholds and fortified refuges, they collected all their possessions into

one town of great natural strength.[15] It was surrounded by very high and precipitous rocks, except at one point where there was a gently sloping approach not more than two hundred feet wide. This place the garrison had fortified with a double wall of great height, on top of which they now fixed heavy stones and beams sharpened to a point.

The Atuatuci were descended from the Cimbri and Teutoni, who on their march towards the Roman Province and Italy deposited on the left bank of the Rhine the cattle and baggage that they could not take with them, with six thousand men to guard it. After the destruction of their fellow countrymen [102–101 B.C.] these settlers struggled for many years with the neighbouring people, sometimes attacking them, at other times defending themselves against attack, until at length all the tribes made peace with them and allowed them to make their home in the district where they now live.

30. On the arrival of the Roman army the Atuatuci at first made a series of sorties from their fortress and engaged in skirmishes; but when they found themselves enclosed by an earthwork twelve feet high, with a circuit of five miles and redoubts at frequent intervals, they stayed inside. The Romans formed a line of mantlets and constructed a siege terrace. When they began to erect a siege tower at some distance, the defenders on the wall at first made abusive remarks and ridiculed the idea of setting up such a huge apparatus so far away. Did those pygmy Romans, they asked, with their feeble hands and muscles, imagine that they could mount such a heavy tower on top of a wall? (All the Gauls are inclined to be contemptuous of our short stature, contrasting it with their own great height.)

31. But when they saw the tower in motion and approaching the fortress walls, the strange, unfamiliar spectacle frightened them into sending envoys to ask Caesar for peace. The envoys said they were forced to the conclusion that the Romans had divine aid in their warlike operations, since they could move up apparatus of such height at such a speed. 'We place ourselves and all we have at your disposal,' they continued, 'and make only one request: if in your clemency and kindness, of which we have often heard, you decide to spare us, do not deprive us of our arms. Almost all our

neighbours are hostile, being jealous of our bravery, and if we have to surrender our arms we cannot defend ourselves against them. We would rather suffer any fate at your hands, if it must be so, than be tortured to death by men whom we are used to ruling.'

32. To this appeal Caesar replied that he would spare the tribe – not because they deserved it, but because it was his habit to be merciful – provided they surrendered before the battering-ram touched the wall, but that he could not consider any terms of surrender unless they handed over their arms. He would do for them what he had done for the Nervii: he would forbid their neighbours to molest in any way a people who had submitted to Rome. After making a report to their countrymen, the envoys came again to say that they were ready to obey. A large quantity of arms was thrown from the wall into the moat that lay in front of the fortress, the piles reaching nearly to the top of the wall and of the siege terrace – although it appeared afterwards that they had about a third of their arms hidden inside. They opened the gates and were at peace for that day.

33. In the evening Caesar ordered the Roman soldiers in the fortress to leave it and had the gates closed, to prevent the men from doing any injury to the inhabitants during the night. But the enemy clearly had a preconcerted plan. Thinking that after their capitulation our pickets would either be withdrawn altogether or at any rate relax their vigilance, they equipped themselves with the arms that they had kept hidden, or with shields made of bark or wickerwork, hastily covered with skins to meet the emergency, and soon after midnight their whole force suddenly made a sortie at the point where our fortifications appeared easiest to scale. The alarm was quickly given by fire signals, in accordance with orders issued beforehand, and troops hastened up from the nearest redoubts. The Atuatuci struggled with the ferocity that was to be expected of brave men fighting a forlorn hope against an enemy who had the advantage of position and could hurl down missiles from an earthwork and towers, and knowing that courage was the one thing which could save them. About four thousand were killed and the rest driven back into the fortress. Next day the gates, now undefended, were smashed open and the soldiers let in; and Caesar sold all the inhabitants of the place by auction in one lot. The

purchasers reported that the number of persons included in the sale was fifty-three thousand.

34. About the same time Caesar was informed by Publius Crassus, whom he had sent with one legion against the Veneti and the other tribes on the Atlantic seaboard – the Venelli, Osismi, Coriosolites, Essuvii, Aulerci, and Redones – that all these had been subjected to Roman rule.

35. These various operations had brought about a state of peace throughout Gaul, and the natives were so much impressed by the accounts of the campaigns which reached them, that the tribes living beyond the Rhine sent envoys to Caesar promising to give hostages and obey his commmands. Being in a hurry to get away to northern Italy and Illyria, he told them to come again at the beginning of the following summer, and after quartering the legions for the winter, some in the territories of the Carnutes, Andes, and Turoni, the rest among tribes living near the scene of that year's fighting, he set out for Italy. On the receipt of his dispatches at Rome a public thanksgiving of fifteen days was decreed to celebrate his achievements – a greater honour than had previously been granted to anyone.[16]

BOOK III
THE FIRST REBELLION

1 Unsuccessful campaign in the Alps (57 B.C.)

1. When Caesar was starting for Italy, he sent Servius Galba with the 12th legion and a detachment of cavalry to the territories of the Nantuates, Veragri, and Seduni, which extend from the frontier of the Allobroges, the lake of Geneva, and the Rhône to the high Alps. His object was to open up the route over the Alps,[17] by which traders travelled only at great risk and on payment of heavy tolls. Galba was authorized to quarter his legion in the district for the winter, if he thought it necessary. After he had won several victories and taken a number of enemy fortresses, and all the tribes had sent envoys and given hostages, he made peace. He then decided to quarter two cohorts among the Nantuates, and to winter with the remainder in a village of the Veragri called Octodurus, situated in a rather narrow valley and completely surrounded by very high mountains. The village was divided by a river into two parts, one of which he let the natives keep, while the other, which he made them evacuate, was assigned to his cohorts and fortified with a rampart and trench.

2. Several days had been spent in this encampment, and Galba had ordered grain to be brought in, when suddenly he was informed by his patrols that during the night all the Gauls had quitted the part of the village allotted to them, and that the surrounding heights were occupied by an immense multitude of the Seduni and Veragri. Various reasons had led the Gauls to form the sudden resolution of renewing hostilities and overpowering the Romans. In the first place, they despised the numerical weakness of the legion, which was under strength owing to the detachment of the two cohorts and a number of individuals who had been sent out in search of supplies. Secondly, they had the advantage of position, being able to run down and hurl their javelins into the valley beneath, and thought they would carry all before them at their

very first charge. They also resented having their children torn
from them and kept as hostages, and were convinced that the
Romans were not merely seeking to open up communications, but
intended to occupy the alpine heights permanently and to annex
the district to the neighbouring province.

3. The work of entrenching the camp was not yet quite
completed, nor had a sufficient stock of grain and other supplies
been laid in, because after the enemy's submission and surrender
of hostages Galba did not think there was any reason to fear an
outbreak of hostilities. On receiving the news, therefore, he at once
called a council of war and invited opinions. The danger was as
serious as it was sudden and unexpected: nearly all the heights
were seen to be already swarming with armed men, and neither
relief nor supplies could be brought up, because the roads were
cut. Several members of the council were inclined to think the case
hopeless, and advised that they should abandon the baggage, force
their way out, and try to reach a place of safety by retracing their
steps. But the majority decided to reserve this plan as a last resort,
and in the meantime to defend the camp and await developments.

4. After a short interval, which barely gave time for posting the
troops and carrying out the measures decided on, the enemy ran
down from all sides at a given signal and began to hurl stones and
spears at the rampart. At first, while our soldiers were still fresh,
they resisted bravely, every missile they threw from their commanding position finding its mark, and ran to the relief of any part
of the camp that was stripped of defenders and seen to be in
danger. But what told against them was that the enemy, when
exhausted by prolonged fighting, could retire from the battle and
be relieved by fresh troops, which our men could not do on account
of their small numbers: not only had tired men to stay in the
fighting line, but even the wounded had to remain at their posts
without any chance of respite.

5. After more than six hours' continuous fighting the Romans
were at the end of their strength and had scarcely any weapons left
to throw, while the enemy was pressing them harder than ever and
took advantage of their exhausted state to break through the
palisade and fill up the trenches. The situation was as bad as it
could be; and Baculus – the chief centurion who, as already said,

was disabled by several wounds in the battle with the Nervii –
came running to Galba with Gaius Volusenus Quadratus, a military
tribune and a man of sound judgement and great courage, and told
him that their only hope of escape was to try their last resource –
a sortie through the enemy's lines. Accordingly Galba summoned
the centurions and immediately sent them to explain the new plan
to the troops. They were to cease offensive action for a time, merely
using their shields to intercept the enemy's missiles. When they
had had time to recover from their exertions, the signal would be
given to break out of the camp; then they would have to rely on
their courage to save their lives.

6. These orders were duly carried out. Suddenly they charged
out from all the gates, without giving the enemy a chance of
realizing what was happening or of preparing to meet their onset.
It was a complete reversal of fortune: the Gauls who had counted
on capturing the camp were surrounded and cut off. Of the forces
that had taken part in the attack – known to number over thirty
thousand – more than a third were killed; the rest fled in terror and
were not allowed to halt even on the mountain heights. Having
thus routed and disarmed the entire host, the Romans retired
within the shelter of their fortifications, and after this success Galba
did not want to take any more risks. The action which circumstances had compelled him to take was something that had never
been contemplated when he was sent there to winter, and there
was an alarming scarcity of corn and other supplies. Next day,
therefore, he burnt all the buildings in the village and started to
hasten back to the Province. No enemy barred his way or delayed
his march, and he conducted the legion safely through the territory
of the Nantuates into that of the Allobroges, where he spent the
winter.

2 The fight on the Atlantic coast (56 B.C.)

7. With the completion of these operations Caesar had every reason
to think that Gaul was pacified: the Belgae were overpowered, the
Germans driven out, and the Seduni defeated in the Alps. He had
therefore set out in the winter for Illyria, desiring to extend his

acquaintance with the countries under his command by visiting the tribes of that district, when war suddenly broke out again in Gaul.[18] The occasion of the outbreak was the action of young Publius Crassus, who with the 7th legion occupied the winter camp nearest the Atlantic, in the territory of the Andes. As food was scarce in that region, he sent a number of auxiliary officers and military tribunes to the neighbouring peoples to seek a supply of corn and other provisions. Among others, Titus Terrasidius was sent to the Essuvii, Marcus Trebius Gallus to the Coriosolites, Quintus Velanius and Titus Sillius to the Veneti.

8. The Veneti are much the most powerful tribe on this coast. They have the largest fleet of ships, in which they traffic with Britain; they excel the other tribes in knowledge and experience of navigation; and as the coast lies exposed to the violence of the open sea and has but few harbours, which the Veneti control, they compel nearly all who sail those waters to pay toll. They were the first to take action against the Romans by detaining Sillius and Velanius and any others they could catch, hoping by this to recover the hostages they had given to Crassus. Their neighbours followed their example with the impulsive haste that characterizes the actions of the Gauls and detained Trebius and Terrasidius with the same motive. Hurriedly dispatching envoys to one another, their leaders pledged the various tribes to take no separate action but to share alike whatever fortune might befall them. They urged the other tribes to preserve their inherited liberties and not submit to the Roman yoke, and quickly gained the adherence of all the maritime people, who sent a joint embassy calling upon Crassus to return their hostages if he wanted to recover his officers.

9. When Caesar was informed of these events by Crassus he was far away from Gaul, and therefore instructed his subordinates to use the time that must elapse before his arrival in building warships on the river Loire, which flows into the Atlantic, enlisting crews in the Province, and procuring seamen and captains. These orders were promptly attended to, and Caesar rejoined his troops as soon as the campaigning season started. On learning of his arrival and the Roman preparations, the Veneti and the other tribes, realizing the gravity of the crime they had committed in detaining and imprisoning envoys (an office that all nations had always held

sacred and inviolable), began to make ready for war on a scale commensurate with the seriousness of their peril, paying particular attention to the provision of equipment for their ships. Their hopes of success were increased by the confidence they placed in the natural strength of their country. They knew that the roads were intersected by tidal inlets, and that sailing would be difficult for us on account of our ignorance of the waterways and the scarcity of harbours; and they felt sure that our armies would be prevented by shortage of grain from staying there very long. And even if all their expectations were disappointed, they had a strong fleet, while we had no ships available and were unacquainted with the shoals, harbours, and islands of the coast on which we should have to fight; and sailing in a wide ocean was clearly a very different matter from sailing in a land-locked sea like the Mediterranean. Having resolved to fight, they fortified their strongholds, stocked them with corn from the fields, and assembled as many ships as possible on the coast of Venetia, where it was generally thought that Caesar would open hostilities. They secured the alliance of various tribes in the neighbourhood (the Osismi, Lexovii, Namnetes, Ambiliati, and Diablintes) and of the Morini and Menapii, and summoned reinforcements from Britain, which faces that part of Gaul.

10. In spite of the difficulties Caesar had several strong reasons for undertaking this campaign: the unlawful detention of Roman knights, the revolt and renewal of hostilities by enemies who had submitted and given hostages, the large number of tribes leagued against him, and above all the danger that if these were left unpunished others might think themselves entitled to follow their example. Knowing, too, that nearly all the Gauls were fond of political change and quickly and easily provoked to war, and that all men naturally love freedom and hate servitude, he thought it advisable to divide his forces and distribute them over a wider area before more tribes could join the coalition.

11. Accordingly he sent Labienus with some cavalry into the country of the Treveri, near the Rhine. His orders were to make contact with the Remi and the other Belgic tribes and see that they remained loyal; and if the Germans, whom some of the Gauls were said to have summoned to their assistance, should attempt to force a passage across the river in boats, to stop them. Publius Crassus

was instructed to march to Aquitania with twelve legionary cohorts and a strong force of cavalry, in order to prevent the dispatch of reinforcements to the Celtic Gauls and the formation of an alliance between such powerful peoples. Sabinus was sent with three legions against the Venelli, Coriosolites, and Lexovii, to keep that section of the rebels isolated. The young Decimus Brutus was placed in command of the fleet, including the Gallic ships that Caesar had ordered the Pictones, Santoni, and other tribes in the conquered areas to provide. Brutus' orders were to sail as soon as possible for Venetia. Caesar himself marched there with the land forces.

12. Most of the Veneti's strongholds were so situated on the ends of spits or headlands that it was impossible to approach them by land when the tide rushed in from the open sea, which happens regularly every twelve hours; and they were also difficult to reach by sea, because at low tide the ships would run aground on the shoals. For these reasons the strongholds were hard to attack. Sometimes the Romans made them untenable by building huge dykes, which both kept the sea away and enabled the besiegers to get on a level with the top of the walls; but as soon as the defenders saw that their position was hopeless, they would bring up numbers of ships, of which they had an unlimited supply, transfer all their property to them, and retire to neighbouring strongholds equally well situated for defence. They found it easy to pursue these tactics during most of the summer, because our ships were weather-bound and sailing was very hazardous in that vast, open sea, where the tides were high and harbours almost non-existent.

13. The Gauls' own ships were built and rigged in a different manner from ours. They were made with much flatter bottoms, to help them to ride shallow water caused by shoals or ebb-tides. Exceptionally high bows and sterns fitted them for use in heavy seas and violent gales, and the hulls were made entirely of oak, to enable them to stand any amount of shocks and rough usage. The cross-timbers, which consisted of beams a foot wide, were fastened with iron bolts as thick as a man's thumb. The anchors were secured with iron chains instead of ropes. They used sails made of raw hides or thin leather, either because they had no flax and were ignorant of its use, or more probably because they thought that

ordinary sails would not stand the violent storms and squalls of the
Atlantic and were not suitable for such heavy vessels. In meeting
them the only advantage our ships possessed was that they were
faster and could be propelled by oars; in other respects the enemy's
were much better adapted for sailing such treacherous and stormy
waters. We could not injure them by ramming because they were
so solidly built, and their height made it difficult to reach them
with missiles or board them with grappling-irons. Moreover, when
it began to blow hard and they were running before the wind, they
weathered the storm more easily; they could bring in to shallow
water with greater safety, and when left aground by the tide had
nothing to fear from reefs or pointed rocks – whereas to our ships
all these risks were formidable.

14. After taking several strongholds Caesar saw that all his
labour was being wasted: capturing their strongholds did not
prevent the enemy from escaping, and he was not in a position to
cripple them. He decided, therefore, that he must wait for his fleet
to be assembled and brought up. Directly it hove in sight, some
two hundred and twenty enemy ships, perfectly equipped and
ready for immediate action, sailed out of harbour and took up
stations facing it. Neither its commander Brutus nor the military
tribunes and centurions in charge of the individual ships could
decide what to do or what tactics to adopt. They knew that no
injury could be inflicted on the enemy by ramming, and when they
tried erecting turrets they found that they were still overtopped by
the foreigners' lofty sterns and were too low to make their missiles
carry properly, while the enemy's fell with great force. One device,
however, that our men had prepared proved very useful – pointed
hooks fixed into the ends of long poles, not unlike the grappling-
hooks used in sieges. With these the halyards were grasped and
pulled taut, and then snapped by rowing hard away. This of course
brought the yards down, and since the Gallic ships depended
wholly on their sails and rigging, when stripped of these they were
at once immobilized. After that it was a soldier's battle, in which
the Romans easily proved superior, especially as it was fought
under the eyes of Caesar and the whole army, so that any act of
special bravery was bound to be noticed; all the cliffs and hills that
commanded a near view of the sea were occupied by the troops.

15. When the yards of an enemy ship were torn down in the manner described, two or three of ours would get alongside and the soldiers would make vigorous efforts to board it. When the natives saw what was happening, and after the loss of several ships could still find no answer to these tactics, they tried to escape by flight. They had already put their ships before the wind when suddenly such a dead calm fell that they could not stir. Nothing could have been more fortunate for us. It enabled us to complete the victory by pursuing and capturing the vessels one after another, and only a very few managed to make land when night came on after a battle that lasted from about ten o'clock in the morning until sunset.

16. This victory ended the war with the Veneti and all the other maritime tribes, for besides assembling all their men of military age, and indeed all the older men of any standing or reputation for good judgement, they had also concentrated every one of their ships; and now that all these were lost, the survivors had no refuge left and no means of defending their strongholds, so they surrendered themselves and all their possessions to Caesar. He resolved to make an example of them in order to teach the natives to be more careful in future about respecting the rights of ambassadors; he had all their councillors executed and the rest of the population sold as slaves.[19]

17. While these events were taking place in the country of the Veneti, Sabinus arrived with the troops assigned to him in the territory of the Venelli. Their leader was Viridovix, the commander-in-chief of all the rebel tribes, from which he had raised a large army. Within a few days of Sabinus' arrival the Aulerci Eburovices and the Lexovii massacred their councillors because they would not sanction the policy of going to war, shut their gates and joined Viridovix; and there had also assembled from all over Gaul a host of desperadoes and bandits, to whom the prospect of fighting and plunder was more attractive than farming and regular work. Sabinus refused to leave his camp, which was ideally situated, while Viridovix, who had encamped opposite him at a distance of two miles, led his troops out daily and offered battle. The Gauls began to despise Sabinus, and even some of his own troops made insulting remarks; in the end he so convinced the enemy of his

timidity that they ventured close up to the rampart of the camp. The real reason for his inaction was his opinion that a subordinate ought not to engage such a large enemy force, especially in the absence of his commander-in-chief, without having either an advantage of position or some particularly favourable opportunity.

18. When everyone was fully persuaded that Sabinus was afraid, he selected from his auxiliaries a quick-witted Gaul, a man suitable for the purpose he had in mind, and induced him by liberal rewards and promises to go over to the enemy, explaining to him what he wanted done. The man came to them posing as a deserter, described the Romans' terror, and said that Caesar himself was hard pressed by the Veneti and that Sabinus planned to steal out of his camp the very next night and go to his aid. On hearing this they all cried that the chance of scoring a success should not be missed: they must march on the camp. In coming to this decision they were influenced by several things – the recent hesitation of Sabinus, the assurances of the deserter, their lack of supplies, for which they had not made proper provision, the hope of a victorious outcome of the Veneti's campaign, and the general tendency of mankind to wishful thinking. They were so possessed by these ideas that they would not let Viridovix and the other leaders leave the assembly until they consented to their arming and making a dash for the camp. When they got their way they were exultant, thinking that victory was within their grasp, and advanced to the camp with faggots and brushwood for filling up the trenches.

19. The camp stood at the top of a gentle slope about a mile long. The Gauls ran up it, so that the Romans might have no time to recover from their surprise and arm themselves, and they were out of breath when they arrived. After addressing his men Sabinus gave the signal which they were eagerly awaiting: while the enemy were hampered by the loads they carried, he ordered a sudden sortie from two of the gates. Thanks to the favourable position of the camp, the enemy's unskilfulness and exhausted condition, our soldiers' courage and the experience they had gained in previous battles, the very first charge made the Gauls turn tail. But they were in no condition to escape, and it was easy for our fresh troops to overtake them and to kill a large number; the remainder were rounded up by the cavalry, with the exception of a few who got

clean away. Sabinus heard of the naval battle at the same time as his own victory was reported to Caesar, and all the rebel states immediately submitted to him; for while the Gauls are quick and impetuous in taking up arms, they have not the strength of character to stand up against reverses.

3 Victorious campaign in Aquitania (56 B.C.)

20. About the same time Publius Crassus reached Aquitania.[20] This area, as already said, must be reckoned to be a third of Gaul, because of its extent and population. Knowing that he had to fight in a country where some years previously [78 B.C.] the general Lucius Valerius Praeconinus had been defeated and killed, and the proconsul Lucius Manlius compelled to retreat with the loss of all his heavy equipment, he realized that he must proceed with extreme caution. Accordingly he arranged for a supply of provisions, raised auxiliaries and cavalry, and called up individually many men of proved courage from Toulouse, Carcassonne, and Narbonne, towns in the Province not far distant from Aquitania. He then marched into the territory of the Sotiates, who on hearing of his approach assembled a large force and sent on ahead their cavalry, in which they were very strong. They attacked our column on the march, first of all with the cavalry; when this was repulsed and pursued by ours, they suddenly unmasked their infantry, which was ambushed in a valley. The infantry renewed the action by falling upon our troops while they were in disorder.

21. A prolonged and fierce struggle ensued; for the Sotiates were emboldened by their past victories and thought that the fate of all Aquitania depended on their bravery, while our men wanted to show what they could do without their commander-in-chief and the other legions, and under a youthful leader. At length, exhausted by wounds, the enemy turned and fled. After killing a large number Crassus advanced on their town and marched straight to the assault. As the garrison offered a stout resistance, he moved up mantlets and towers. Against these they first attempted a sortie, and then tunnelled in the direction of the siege terrace and the mantlets; the Aquitani excel in this work, as there are copper-mines and quarries

in many parts of their country. But when they found that the vigilance of our troops prevented their effecting anything by this means, they sent envoys to Crassus asking him to accept their surrender. He consented, and at his command they handed over their arms.

22. While everyone's attention was occupied by these events, the king of the tribe, Adiatuanus, attempted a sortie from another part of the town with six hundred followers who were bound to him by a vow of loyalty. The Sotiates call such persons *soldurii*. The friend to whom they attach themselves undertakes to share with them all the good things of life, on the understanding that, if he meets with a violent end, they shall either share his fate or make away with themselves; and within the memory of man none has yet been known to refuse to die when the friend to whom he had sworn allegiance was killed. Shouts arose from the nearest part of the fortifications, and the soldiers ran to arms. After a hard fight Adiatuanus was driven back into the town; but in spite of what had happened he prevailed on Crassus to let him surrender on the same terms as the rest.

23. After receiving the arms and hostages Crassus started for the country of the Vocates and Tarusates. The natives were now thoroughly alarmed, hearing that a town well protected both by its situation and by fortifications had fallen within a few days of our army's arrival. They therefore sent envoys to their neighbours on every side, made promises of mutual loyalty, exchanged hostages, and mobilized their troops. They even sent to the nearest tribes of northern Spain, and obtained from them reinforcements and generals, whose arrival enabled them to take the field with large forces under commanders of great prestige – men who had served throughout the Spanish War under Quintus Sertorius and were reputed military experts. Following Roman practice they occupied carefully chosen positions, entrenched a camp and took measures to intercept our convoys of supplies. Crassus' own forces were so small that they could not very well be divided, whereas the enemy could scour the countryside and block the roads, and at the same time leave an adequate guard in camp. Finding that this made it difficult to bring up grain and other supplies, and that the enemy's numbers were increasing daily, he thought he had better lose no

time in bringing them to a decisive action. On referring the question to a council of war he found that all the others were of the same opinion, and therefore determined to fight the next day.

24. At daybreak he brought out all his forces and deployed them in two lines, with the auxiliaries in the centre, and waited to see what plan of action the enemy would adopt. Although the Gauls, with their great numerical superiority and illustrious military record, had every confidence in the result of an engagement, they thought an even safer way would be to gain a bloodless victory by obstructing the roads and cutting off the army's supplies; and if a shortage of food compelled the Romans to retreat, their idea was to attack them on the march, when they would be hampered by the presence of the transport and dispirited by having to fight with their packs on their backs. Their leaders approved these plans, and when the Romans deployed their troops the Gauls remained in camp. Crassus took note of this; and as the enemy's reluctance to fight gave the impression that they were afraid, and increased the fighting spirit of his own men, who were all heard saying that the camp should be attacked without delay, he delivered the customary address and complied with their unanimous desire by advancing to the assault.

25. Some filled up the trenches, others drove the defenders from the rampart and entrenchments with a rain of missiles, while the auxiliaries, in whose fighting quality Crassus had little confidence, supplied the rest with stones and weapons and brought up sods for making a bank of earth, and so made a convincing show of fighting. The enemy, too, put up a determined and brave resistance, and the javelins that they hurled down from their elevated position did good execution. Meanwhile some cavalrymen who had ridden round the camp reported to Crassus that the back of it was not so carefully fortified, and offered easy access.

26. Crassus asked his cavalry officers to encourage their men by promises of liberal rewards to cooperate in a manoeuvre that he desired to execute. Under their guidance the cohorts that had been left to guard the Roman camp, which were still fresh, were quickly led out and conducted by a long detour, so that they could not be seen from the enemy's camp, to the section of the defences referred to, while everyone's attention was concentrated on the fighting.

Demolishing the fortifications, they gained a footing in the camp before the enemy could clearly see them or make out what was happening. On hearing the shouting at the back of the camp our soldiers felt their strength renewed, as generally happens when men have hopes of winning, and redoubled their efforts. The enemy, finding themselves completely surrounded, were overwhelmed with despair, and had no other thought than to throw themselves over the rampart and flee for their lives. Our cavalry pursued them over perfectly flat plains, and of the fifty thousand men known to have assembled from the Aquitani and Cantabri, barely a quarter escaped. It was late at night when the cavalry returned to camp.

27. On receiving news of this battle most of the Aquitanian tribes, including the Tarbelli, Bigerriones, Ptianii, Vocates, Tarusates, Elusates, Gates, Ausci, Garunni, Sibulates, and Cocosates, surrendered to Crassus and sent hostages of their own accord. Only a few of the most distant tribes, relying on the approach of winter to save them, neglected to follow their example.

4 Indecisive campaign against the Morini (56 B.C.)

28. About the same time, although the summer was nearly over, Caesar marched against the Morini and Menapii.[21] While peace was established throughout the rest of Gaul, they remained in arms and had never sent envoys to sue for peace; and he thought that a short campaign would suffice to conquer them. He found himself opposed by tactics quite different from those of the other Gauls. As they knew that the strongest tribes which had met Caesar in the field had been completely defeated, they took refuge with all their belongings in a region protected by a continuous belt of forests and marshes. On reaching the edge of the forests Caesar began to construct a camp. No enemy had yet been seen, and the men were working in scattered groups, when suddenly the Gauls rushed out to the attack from all parts of the forest. Our men hastily seized their arms and chased them back into it, but after inflicting heavy losses upon them pursued too far over rather difficult ground and themselves suffered a few casualties.

29. Some days were then spent in felling trees in the forest. To prevent his soldiers being surprised by flank attacks while they were unarmed, Caesar placed all the felled timber parallel with the enemy's line of retreat, piling it so as to form a rampart on both sides. In an incredibly short time a path was cleared for a considerable distance. But when the enemy's cattle and the tail-end of their transport were already in our hands, while they were making for the denser part of the forest, such bad weather came on that the work had to be stopped, and as the rain continued it became impossible to keep the soldiers under canvas any longer. Accordingly, after ravaging all the countryside and burning the villages and farms, Caesar withdrew his troops and quartered them in the countries of the Aulerci, the Lexovii, and the other tribes that had been recently in arms.

BOOK IV
INVASIONS OF GERMANY
AND BRITAIN

1 Massacre of the Usipetes and Tenctheri (55 B.C.)

1. In the following winter, in which the consulship of Pompey and Crassus began, the German tribes of the Usipetes and Tenctheri crossed the Rhine in large numbers not far from its mouth. They were forced to migrate because for several years they had been subjected to harassing attacks by the Suebi and prevented from tilling their land.

The Suebi are by far the largest and most warlike of the German nations. It is said that they have a hundred cantons, each of which provides annually a thousand armed men for service in foreign wars. Those who are left at home have to support the men in the army as well as themselves, and the next year take their turn of service, while the others stay at home. Thus both agriculture, and military instruction and training, continue without interruption. No land, however, is the property of private individuals, and no one is allowed to cultivate the same plot for more than one year. They do not eat much cereal food, but live chiefly on milk and meat, and spend much time in hunting. Their diet, daily exercise, and the freedom from restraint that they enjoy – for from childhood they do not know what compulsion or discipline is, and do nothing against their inclination – combine to make them strong and as tall as giants. They inure themselves, in spite of the very cold climate in which they live, to wear no clothing but skins – and these so scanty that a large part of the body is uncovered – and to bathe in the rivers.

2. Traders are admitted into their country more because they want to sell their booty than because they stand in any need of imports. Even horses, which the Gauls are inordinately fond of and purchase at big prices, are not imported by the Germans. They are content with their home-bred horses, which, although undersized

and ugly, are rendered capable of very hard work by daily exercise. In cavalry battles they often dismount and fight on foot, training the horses to stand perfectly still, so that they can quickly get back to them in case of need. In their eyes it is the height of effeminacy and shame to use a saddle, and they do not hesitate to engage the largest force of cavalry riding saddled horses, however small their own numbers may be. They absolutely forbid the importation of wine, because they think that it makes men soft and incapable of enduring hard toil.

3. They regard it as the proudest glory of a nation to keep the largest possible area round its frontiers uninhabited, because it shows that many other peoples are inferior to it in military might. It is said, for example, that on one side of the Suebic territory the country is uninhabited for a distance of more than five hundred and fifty miles. On the other side their nearest neighbours are the Ubii, who were once – by German standards – a considerable and prosperous nation. They are somewhat more civilized than the rest of the Germans; for living on the Rhine close to the frontier of Gaul, where traders visit them regularly, they have adopted Gallic customs. The Suebi, after repeated attempts to oust them from their home by force of arms, found them too numerous and strong to be dispossessed, but compelled them to pay tribute and greatly reduced their pride and power.

4. The Usipetes and Tenctheri were in the same case. For many years they withstood the Suebi's pressure, but eventually were driven from their country, and after wandering for three years in many parts of Germany reached the Rhine in the territory of the Menapii, who had lands, farmhouses, and villages on both banks of the river. Terrified by the arrival of such a multitude, the Menapii abandoned their dwellings on the German bank and placed outposts on the Gallic bank to prevent the emigrants from crossing. The Germans tried every expedient; but not having boats with which to force a passage and being unable to cross by stealth because of the Menapian pickets, they pretended to return to their home country, and marched in that direction for three days. Then they turned back again, and re-covering the whole distance in a single night, their cavalry made a surprise attack on the unsuspecting Menapii, who, on being informed by their patrols of their

enemy's departure, had fearlessly recrossed the Rhine and returned to their villages. The Germans slaughtered them, seized their boats, crossed the river before the Menapii on the Gallic side knew what was afoot, took possession of all their farmhouses, and lived on their provisions for the rest of the winter.

5. These events were reported to Caesar. The unstable character of the Gauls made him anxious – for they are easily induced to form new plans and generally welcome political change – and he thought it better to place no reliance on them. It is a custom of theirs to stop travellers, even against their will, and to question them about what they have heard by chance or by inquiry on this or that subject; and in the towns a crowd will gather round traders and demand to know what country they have come from and what they have learnt there. Such hearsay reports often induce them to make momentous decisions, which they are bound to repent immediately afterwards, since they credulously swallow unconfirmed rumours, and most of their informants invent such answers as they think will please them.

6. Caesar was aware of this habit and, not wishing to find himself faced with a dangerous war, set out to rejoin his army earlier in the season than usual. On his arrival he found that his suspicions were correct: a number of tribes had sent embassies to the Usipetes and Tenctheri, inviting them to go farther afield than the Rhineland and promising to supply all their requirements. This attractive prospect had induced the Germans to range over a wider area, and they had now reached the country of the Eburones and Condrusi, dependants of the Treveri. Caesar thought it advisable to say nothing to the Gauls about the information he had received. Summoning their leaders, therefore, he addressed them in soothing and reassuring terms, and told them to furnish cavalry for the campaign which he proposed to conduct against the Germans.

7. After arranging for his corn supply and making his selection of the cavalry, he marched towards the district where the invading Germans were said to be. He was a few days' march away, when envoys arrived from them with the following message: 'We Germans are not taking aggressive action against the Roman people, but we are ready to fight if provoked; for it is our custom to resist any attacker and to ask no quarter. We wish to say,

however, that we have come into Gaul not from choice but because we were expelled from our homes. If you Romans desire our friendship, we can be of service to you. Either grant us land to live in or let us keep what we have won by the sword. The only people whose superiority we acknowledge are the Suebi, with whom the gods themselves cannot compete. There is no one else on earth that we cannot conquer.'

8. Caesar made what he considered a suitable reply to this oration, but the upshot of his remarks was that there could be no friendship between him and the Germans if they remained in Gaul. He said that it was not reasonable for men who had been unable to protect their own territory to expect to occupy other people's. There was no land available in Gaul which he could justly assign to them, particularly in view of their large numbers; but they might settle if they chose in the country of the Ubii, whose ambassadors were then with him, complaining of the wrongs done them by the Suebi and asking for assistance. He would order the Ubii to admit them.

9. The German envoys said that they would refer Caesar's reply to their countrymen for consideration, and return in three days; in the meantime they asked him not to move his camp any nearer. But Caesar refused this request also. He knew that a large detachment of their cavalry had been sent across the Meuse some days before to the country of the Ambivariti, in search of corn and plunder; and he thought that they must be expecting these back, and that this was their reason for trying to gain time.

10. The Meuse rises in the Vosges mountains,[22] in the country of the Lingones. It is joined by a tributary from the Rhine, called the Waal, making the island of the Batavians, and flows into the Rhine some seventy-five miles from the sea. The Rhine rises in the country of the Lepontii in the Alps, and flows swiftly for a long distance through the lands of the Helvetii, Sequani, Triboci, Nemetes, Mediomatrici, and Treveri. As it nears the sea it divides into several channels, forming a number of very large islands (many of them inhabited by wild barbarian tribes, some of whom are supposed to live on fish and birds' eggs), and discharges itself by several mouths into the North Sea.

11. When Caesar was not more than twelve miles from the

Germans their envoys returned according to agreement, and meeting him on the march earnestly begged him to advance no farther. On Caesar's refusing to comply, they asked him to send word to the cavalry which had gone in advance of the column, forbidding them to engage in battle, and also requested leave to send an embassy to the Ubii. They said that if the Ubian chiefs and council would swear to keep faith with them, they would avail themselves of the offer that Caesar had made, and asked for three days to complete the necessary negotiations. Caesar believed that all these suggestions had the same object as their previous manoeuvre – to obtain a further three days' delay to give time for the return of the German cavalry from their foray. However, he said that he would restrict his advance that day to four miles – the distance that was necessary to get water. On the next day, if as many of them as possible would assemble at his halting-place, he would give their requests a formal hearing. In the meantime he sent orders to the officers who had gone on in front with the whole cavalry force that they were not to attack the enemy and, if attacked themselves, were to remain on the defensive until he approached with the main army.

12. But when the enemy caught sight of our cavalry, five thousand strong, although they themselves had not eight hundred horse – those who had crossed the Meuse to get corn having not yet returned – they immediately charged. Our men, who thought themselves safe from attack because the enemy's envoys had only just left Caesar and had asked for a truce for that day, were at first thrown into disorder. When they rallied, the German horsemen, following their usual practice, jumped down, unhorsed a number of our men by stabbing their horses in the belly, put the rest to flight, and kept them on the run in such a panic that they did not stop until they came in sight of the marching column of infantry. In this engagement seventy-four of our cavalrymen were killed, including Piso, a gallant Aquitanian of very good family, whose grandfather had been king of his tribe and had been granted the title of 'Friend' by the Roman Senate. He went to the assistance of his brother, who was cut off by some of the Germans, and succeeded in rescuing him; but his own horse was wounded and threw him. As long as he could, he resisted with the utmost

bravery, but eventually was surrounded and fell covered with wounds. When his brother, who by this time had got well away from the fight, saw what had happened, he galloped straight up to the enemy and let them kill him too.

13. After this treacherous and unprovoked attack by an enemy who had asked for peace, Caesar dismissed all further thought of giving audience to their envoys or accepting any overtures. At the same time he thought it would be sheer madness to wait till they were reinforced by the return of their cavalry. The Gauls were so scatter-brained that even this single German success had no doubt made a great impression upon them, and they must not be given time to concert plans. He told his generals and quaestor of his decision, and, not wanting to lose a single day in bringing the enemy to battle, marched forward. The next morning he had a great stroke of luck. Still pursuing their policy of treachery and deceit, a large deputation of Germans, comprising all their leaders and elder men of note, came to visit him in his camp. Their ostensible object was to apologize for attacking the day before in contravention of the agreement that they themselves asked for; but they also hoped to hoodwink Caesar into granting an extension of the truce. Caesar was delighted that they had put themselves in his power, and ordered them to be detained,[23] while he himself marched his whole army out of camp, with the cavalry bringing up the rear because he thought it had been demoralized by its recent defeat.

14. With the soldiers formed in three parallel columns, ready for wheeling into line of battle, he made a rapid march of eight miles and reached the enemy's camp before they realized his intention. The speed of his advance and the absence of their leaders combined to throw them into a sudden panic; they had no time to think what to do or to arm themselves, and were too distracted to decide whether it was best to march out against Caesar, to stay and defend the camp, or to flee for their lives. The Roman soldiers could tell that they were afraid by their cries and hurried movements, and, spurred on by the recollection of the previous day's treachery, burst into the camp. Those of the Germans who were quick enough in seizing their weapons resisted for a time, fighting under cover of their wagons and

baggage. But there was also a great crowd of women and children in the camp, for they had brought all their families with them when they left home and crossed the Rhine. These began to flee in all directions, and were hunted down by the cavalry which Caesar sent out for the purpose.

15. Hearing cries behind them and seeing that their people were being massacred, the Germans threw down their arms, deserted their standards, and rushed out of the camp. When they reached the confluence of the Moselle and the Rhine,[24] they realized that they could flee no farther. A large number were killed, and the rest plunged into the water and perished, overcome by the force of the current in their terror-stricken and exhausted state. The Romans returned to camp without a single fatal casualty, and with only a very few wounded, although a grim struggle had been anticipated against an enemy four hundred and thirty thousand strong. Caesar gave the prisoners detained in camp leave to depart, but as they were afraid of being killed or tortured by the Gauls whose lands they had ravaged, they said they wished to remain with him. They were allowed to retain their liberty.

2 *The first crossing of the Rhine* (55 B.C.)

16. On the conclusion of the German war Caesar thought it advisable for several reasons to cross the Rhine. His strongest motive was to make the Germans less inclined to come over into Gaul by giving them reason to be alarmed on their own account, and showing them that Roman armies could and would advance across the river. Another consideration was that the cavalry division which, as mentioned above, the Usipetes and Tenctheri sent across the Meuse in quest of plunder and corn, having taken no part in the battle and retired over the Rhine after the rout of their fellow countrymen, entered the territory of the Sugambri and joined forces with them; and when Caesar sent an embassy to the Sugambri to demand the surrender of men who had made war on him and on Gaul, they answered that the Rhine was the limit of Roman sovereignty: if Caesar held that the Germans had no right to cross into Gaul against his wishes, how could he claim any

dominion or authority beyond the Rhine? A third reason was that the Ubii – the only people in Germany who had sent envoys to Caesar, entered into alliance with him, and given hostages – were earnestly entreating him to come and defend them from the oppression of the Suebi or, if the public business with which he was occupied made that impossible, merely to bring his army across the river, which would suffice to deliver them from immediate danger and assure their security for the future. They said that by the defeat of Ariovistus, and by this latest victory, the Roman army had gained such renown and reputation, even among the most distant peoples of Germany, that the mere knowledge of their alliance with Rome would be enough to give them protection. They undertook to provide a large fleet of boats for the transportation of the army.

17. For these reasons Caesar had determined to cross the Rhine, but a crossing by means of boats seemed to him both too risky and beneath his dignity as a Roman commander. Therefore, although the construction of a bridge presented very great difficulties on account of the breadth, depth, and swiftness of the stream, he decided that he must either attempt it or give up the idea of crossing.[25] The method he adopted in building the bridge was as follows. He took a pair of piles a foot and a half thick, slightly pointed at the lower ends and of a length adapted to the varying depth of the river, and fastened them together two feet apart. These he lowered into the river with appropriate tackle, placed them in position at right angles to the bank, and drove them home with pile-drivers, not vertically, as piles are generally fixed, but obliquely, inclined in the direction of the current. Opposite these, forty feet lower down the river, another pair of piles was planted, similarly fixed together, and inclined in the opposite direction to the current. The two pairs were then joined by a beam two feet wide, whose ends fitted exactly into the spaces between the two piles forming each pair. The upper pair was kept at the right distance from the lower pair by means of iron braces, one of which was used to fasten each pile to the end of the beam. The pairs of piles being thus held apart, and each pair individually strengthened by a diagonal tie between the two piles, the whole structure was so rigid, that, in accordance with the laws of physics, the greater the

force of the current, the more tightly were the piles held in position. A series of these piles and transverse beams was carried right across the stream and connected by lengths of timber running in the direction of the bridge; on these were laid poles and bundles of sticks. In spite of the strength of the structure, additional piles were fixed obliquely to each pair of the original piles along the whole length of the downstream side of the bridge, holding them up like a buttress and opposing the force of the current. Others were fixed also a little above the bridge, so that if the natives tried to demolish it by floating down tree-trunks or beams, these buffers would break the force of the impact and preserve the bridge from injury.

18. Ten days after the collection of the timber had begun, the work was completed and the army crossed over. Leaving a strong guard at each end of the bridge, Caesar marched into the territory of the Sugambri. Meanwhile a number of tribes sent envoys with requests for peace and friendship, which Caesar graciously granted, bidding them bring hostages. But the Sugambri, who as soon as the construction of the bridge was begun had been advised by the fugitive Usipetes and Tenctheri to prepare for flight, had left their country with all their belongings and hidden themselves in forests and uninhabited districts.

19. Caesar remained for a few days in their territory, burning all the villages and farm buildings and cutting down the crops, and then returned to the Ubii, to whom he promised help if they were molested by the Suebi. They informed him that the Suebi, on learning from their scouts that a bridge was under construction, had convened a council – their usual procedure in such cases – and sent out word in all directions that the people should abandon their towns and hide their wives and children and property in the forests. All men capable of bearing arms had been ordered to assemble in one place, almost exactly in the middle of their territory. There they were awaiting the Romans, and had determined to fight a decisive battle on the spot. On receiving this news Caesar recrossed the bridge into Gaul and destroyed it behind him. He had achieved all the objects for which he had come – to overawe the Germans, punish the Sugambri, and relieve the Ubii from the harassing pressure of the Suebi – and after spending a total of eighteen days

across the Rhine he considered that he had done all that honour or interest required.[26]

3 The first invasion of Britain (55 B.C.)

20. It was now near the end of summer, and winter sets in early in those parts, because all that coast of Gaul faces north. Nevertheless, Caesar made active preparations for an expedition to Britain, because he knew that in almost all the Gallic campaigns the Gauls had received reinforcements from the Britons.[27] Even if there was not time for a campaign that season, he thought it would be of great advantage to him merely to visit the island, to see what its inhabitants were like, and to make himself acquainted with the lie of the land, the harbours, and the landing-places. Of all this the Gauls knew next to nothing; for in the ordinary way traders are the only people who visit Britain, and even they know only that part of the coast which faces Gaul. And so, although he interviewed traders from all parts, he could not ascertain anything about the size of the island, the character and strength of the tribes which inhabited it, their manner of fighting and customs, or the harbours capable of accommodating a large fleet of big ships.

21. In order to get this information before risking an expedition, he sent a warship in command of Volusenus, whom he considered a suitable man for the job. His orders were to make a general reconnaissance and return as soon as he could. Meanwhile Caesar marched the whole army into the country of the Morini, from which there was the shortest crossing to Britain, and ordered ships to assemble there from all the neighbouring districts, as well as the fleet that had been built the previous summer for the Venetian war. His design had become known in the meantime, and when the news was brought by traders to the Britons, envoys were sent by a number of tribes, offering to give hostages and submit to Rome. Caesar gave them audience, made them generous promises, and urged them to abide by their resolve. He then sent them home, accompanied by Commius, whom he had made king of the Atrebates after the conquest of that tribe – a man of whose courage, judgement, and loyalty he had a high opinion, and who was greatly

respected in Britain. He instructed Commius to visit as many tribes as possible, to urge them to entrust themselves to the protection of Rome, and to announce his impending arrival. Volusenus reconnoitred the coast as far as he could without disembarking and putting himself into the power of the natives, which he dared not do, and returned four days later with his report.

22. While Caesar was waiting in the country of the Morini for his fleet to be assembled, a large section of the tribe sent envoys to apologize for their previous hostile action, pleading that they were foreigners and ignorant of Roman ways, and promising to obey his commands in future. Caesar thought this very fortunate. He did not want to leave an enemy in his rear; yet it would have been too late in the season to start another campaign, and the expedition to Britain was much more important than the conquest of these petty tribes. He therefore demanded a large number of hostages, and on their arrival accepted the submission of the Morini.

In due course about eighty transports, which Caesar considered sufficient to convey two legions, were obtained and assembled, and also a number of warships, which were assigned to the quaestor, the generals, and the officers of the auxiliary troops. Besides these there were eighteen transports at a point eight miles along the coast, which were allotted to the cavalry.[28] The remainder of the army was entrusted to Sabinus and Cotta, with orders to march against the Menapii and those clans of the Morini which had not sent envoys. Another general, Publius Sulpicius Rufus, was ordered to hold the harbour and was given a force considered adequate for the purpose.

23. After the completion of these arrangements, Caesar took advantage of favourable weather and set sail about midnight, ordering the cavalry to proceed to the farther port, embark there, and follow him. As these conducted the operation too slowly, their transports were carried back to land by the tide. Caesar himself reached Britain with the first ships about nine o'clock in the morning, and saw the enemy's forces posted on all the hills. The lie of the land at this point was such that javelins could be hurled from the cliffs right on to the narrow beach enclosed between them and the sea. Caesar thought this a quite unsuitable place for landing, and therefore rode at anchor until three o'clock, in order to give

the rest of the ships time to come up. Meanwhile he assembled the generals and military tribunes and, telling them what he had learned from Volusenus, explained his plans. He warned them that the exigencies of warfare, and particularly of naval operations, in which things move rapidly and the situation is constantly changing, required the instant execution of every order. On dismissing the officers he found that both wind and tidal current were in his favour. He therefore gave the signal for weighing anchor, and after proceeding about seven miles ran his ships aground on an evenly sloping beach, free from obstacles.

24. The natives, on realizing his intention, had sent forward their cavalry and a number of the chariots which they are accustomed to use in warfare; the rest of their troops followed close behind and were ready to oppose the landing. The Romans were faced with very grave difficulties. The size of the ships made it impossible to run them aground except in fairly deep water; and soldiers, unfamiliar with the ground, with their hands full, and weighed down by the heavy burden of their arms, had at the same time to jump down from the ships, get a footing in the waves, and fight the enemy, who, standing on dry land or advancing only a short way into the water, fought with all their limbs unencumbered and on perfectly familiar ground, boldly hurling javelins and galloping their horses, which were trained to this kind of work. These perils frightened our soldiers, who were quite unaccustomed to battles of this kind, with the result that they did not show the same alacrity and enthusiasm as they usually did in battles on dry land.

25. Seeing this, Caesar ordered the warships – which were swifter and easier to handle than the transports, and likely to impress the natives more by their unfamiliar appearance – to be removed a short distance from the others and then to be rowed hard and run ashore on the enemy's right flank, from which position slings, bows, and artillery could be used by men on deck to drive them back. This manoeuvre was highly successful. Scared by the strange shape of the warships, the motion of the oars, and the unfamiliar machines, the natives halted and then retreated a little. But as the Romans still hesitated, chiefly on account of the depth of water, the man who carried the eagle of the 10th legion,

after praying to the gods that his action might bring good luck to the legion, cried in a loud voice: 'Jump down, comrades, unless you want to surrender our eagle[29] to the enemy; I, at any rate, mean to do my duty to my country and my general.' With these words he leapt out of the ship and advanced towards the enemy with the eagle in his hands. At this the soldiers, exhorting each other not to submit to such a disgrace, jumped with one accord from the ship, and the men from the next ships, when they saw them, followed them and advanced against the enemy.

26. Both sides fought hard. But as the Romans could not keep their ranks or get a firm foothold or follow their proper standards, and men from different ships fell in under the first standard they came across, great confusion resulted. The enemy knew all the shallows, and when they saw from the beach small parties of soldiers disembarking one by one, they galloped up and attacked them at a disadvantage, surrounding them with superior numbers, while others would throw javelins at the right flank of a whole group. Caesar therefore ordered the warships' boats and the scouting vessels to be loaded with troops, so that he could send help to any point where he saw the men in difficulties. As soon as the soldiers had got a footing on the beach and had waited for all their comrades to join them, they charged the enemy and put them to flight, but could not pursue very far, because the cavalry had not been able to hold their course and make the island. This was the one thing that prevented Caesar from achieving his usual success.

27. The defeated enemy, as soon as they rallied after their flight, hastened to send an embassy to ask for peace, promising to give hostages and carry out Caesar's commands. With these envoys came Commius the Atrebatian, whom Caesar had sent on ahead to Britain, as said above. When he had disembarked, and was delivering Caesar's message to them in the character of an ambassador, the natives had arrested and bound him. Now, after the battle, they sent him back, and in asking for peace threw the blame for this proceeding on the common people, begging Caesar to pardon an error due to ignorance. Caesar reproached them for making war on him without provocation, after sending envoys to the continent of their own accord to sue for peace, but said that he would pardon their ignorance, and demanded hostages. Some of

these they handed over at once; the rest they said would have to be fetched from a distance, and should be delivered in a few days' time. Meanwhile they bade their men return to the fields, and the chiefs began to come from all parts to solicit Caesar's favour for themselves and their tribes.

28. Peace was thus concluded. On the fourth day after Caesar's arrival in Britain the eighteen transports on which the cavalry had been embarked, as mentioned above, sailed from the northern port before a gentle breeze. When they were approaching Britain and were visible from the camp, such a violent storm suddenly arose that none of them could hold its course. Some were driven back to their starting-point; others, at great peril, were swept westwards to the south of the island. In spite of the danger they cast anchor, but as they were being filled with water by the waves, they were forced to stand out to sea into the darkness of the night and return to the continent.

29. It happened to be full moon that night, at which time the Atlantic tides are particularly high – a fact unknown to the Romans. The result was that the warships used in the crossing which had been beached, were waterlogged, and the transports, which were riding at anchor, were knocked about by the storm, without the soldiers having any chance of interfering to save them. A number of ships were shattered, and the rest, having lost their cables, anchors, and the remainder of their tackle, were unusable, which naturally threw the whole army into great consternation; for they had no other vessels in which they could return, nor any materials for repairing the fleet, and, since it had been generally understood that they were to return to Gaul for the winter, they had not provided themselves with a stock of grain for wintering in Britain.

30. On learning of this accident, the British chiefs who had assembled after the battle to execute Caesar's commands, put their heads together. Knowing that Caesar had no cavalry, ships, or corn, and inferring the weakness of his forces from the small size of the camp, which was all the smaller because he had come without most of the heavy luggage, they decided that their best course was to renew hostilities, to hinder the legions from obtaining corn and other supplies, and to prolong the war into the winter. If this army was conquered or prevented from returning, they felt

confident that no one would come across to invade Britain. Accordingly, after renewing their promises of mutual loyalty, they slipped away one by one from the camp and secretly called up once more the men who had returned to the fields.

31. Although Caesar had not yet heard of their intention, the disaster which had overtaken his fleet and the fact that they were no longer sending hostages led him to anticipate what was coming. He therefore prepared for anything that might happen. Corn was brought in daily from the fields, timber and bronze from the most severely damaged vessels were used to repair the others, and naval equipment was ordered to be sent from the continent. By the energetic efforts of the soldiers all but twelve ships were saved and rendered tolerably seaworthy.

32. While this work was proceeding, one legion, as usual, had been sent out to get corn – in this case the 7th. Nothing had yet occurred to raise any suspicion of a fresh attack, and some of the Britons were still working in the fields, while others were actually going backwards and forwards to the camp. Suddenly the guards on duty at the gates reported to Caesar that an unusually large cloud of dust was visible in the direction in which the legion had gone. Caesar guessed the truth – that the natives had hatched a new scheme – and ordered the cohorts on guard duty to set out with him in the direction indicated, two of the others to relieve them, and the rest to arm and follow immediately. After going some way he saw that the legion was hard pressed by enemy forces and holding its ground with difficulty, packed closely and pelted with missiles from all directions; for as the corn had already been cut everywhere except in one place, the enemy had expected that our men would go there and had hidden by night in the woods. Then, when the soldiers were scattered and busy cutting corn, with their arms laid down, they had made a sudden attack, killing a few and throwing the rest into confusion before they could form up, and also surrounding them with cavalry and chariots.

33. In chariot fighting the Britons begin by driving all over the field hurling javelins, and generally the terror inspired by the horses and the noise of the wheels are sufficient to throw their opponents' ranks into disorder. Then, after making their way between the squadrons of their own cavalry, they jump down from

the chariots and engage on foot. In the meantime their charioteers retire a short distance from the battle and place the chariots in such a position that their masters, if hard pressed by numbers, have an easy means of retreat to their own lines. Thus they combine the mobility of cavalry with the staying power of infantry; and by daily training and practice they attain such proficiency that even on a steep incline they are able to control the horses at full gallop, and to check and turn them in a moment. They can run along the chariot pole, stand on the yoke, and get back into the chariot as quick as lightning.[30]

34. The men of the 7th legion were unnerved by these tactics, and it was just at the right moment that Caesar came to their rescue. At his approach the enemy halted and the soldiers recovered from their alarm. But as he considered the situation too hazardous for attacking or engaging in battle, he stayed where he was, and after a short interval led the legions back to camp. While these events kept all our men occupied, the natives who were still in the fields made off.

There followed several days of continuous bad weather, which kept our men in camp and also prevented the enemy from attacking. During this time the natives sent messengers in all directions, who informed their people of the small numbers of our troops, and pointed out what a good opportunity they had of getting booty and liberating themselves for ever, if they could drive the Romans from their camp. By this means they quickly collected a large force of infantry and cavalry, which advanced towards the camp.

35. Caesar foresaw that what had happened before would happen again: even if the enemy were beaten, their speed would enable them to escape out of harm's way. Nevertheless, having luckily obtained about thirty horsemen whom Commius had brought across, he drew up the legions in battle formation in front of the camp. Before the engagement had lasted long the enemy were overpowered and took to flight. The Romans pursued as far as their strength enabled them to run, killing a number of the fugitives, and then set fire to all the buildings over a wide area and returned to camp.

36. The same day envoys came to Caesar to sue for peace. He

demanded twice as many hostages as before, and ordered these to be brought to the continent, as the equinox was close at hand and he thought it better not to expose his damaged ships to the dangers of a voyage in wintry weather. Taking advantage of a favourable wind he set sail shortly after midnight, and the whole fleet reached the continent safely.

Two transports, however, failed to make the same harbours as the rest and were carried a little farther south.

37. When about three hundred soldiers had disembarked from these two ships and were pushing towards the camp, the Morini, whom Caesar had compelled to make peace before setting out for Britain, thought they saw a chance of obtaining booty and surrounded them, at first with only a small force, bidding them lay down their arms if they did not want to be killed. The Romans formed a ring and defended themselves, but in a short time the shouts of their assailants brought some six thousand natives to the spot. On hearing what was happening Caesar sent all the cavalry to their aid. Meanwhile the soldiers held the enemy's attack, fighting with the utmost bravery for over four hours, and killed a number of them at the cost of only a few men wounded. As soon as the cavalry came in sight the Morini threw down their arms and fled, suffering very heavy casualties.

38. The next day Caesar sent Labienus against the rebellious Morini with the legions that had returned from Britain. As the marshes in which they had taken refuge the previous year were now dry, the natives had nowhere to retreat to, and nearly all fell into Labienus' hands. Sabinus and Cotta, however, who had led their legions into the territory of the Menapii, had to content themselves with destroying all the crops, cutting the corn, and burning the buildings, because all the inhabitants had concealed themselves in very dense forests. They then returned to Caesar, who arranged for all the legions to winter in Belgic territory. There he received the promised hostages from only two British tribes; the remainder neglected to send them.

On the conclusion of these campaigns and the receipt of Caesar's dispatches, the Senate decreed a public thanksgiving of twenty days.

BOOK V
THE SECOND REBELLION

1 The second invasion of Britain (54 B.C.)

1. In the consulship of Lucius Domitius and Appius Claudius, when Caesar was leaving his winter quarters as usual to go to Italy, he ordered the generals placed in command of the legions to have as many ships as possible built during the winter and the old ones repaired. He specified the dimensions and shape of the new ships. To enable them to be loaded quickly and beached easily he had them made slightly lower than those which we generally use in the Mediterranean – especially as he had found that owing to the frequent ebb and flow of the tides the waves in the Channel were comparatively small. To enable them, however, to carry a heavy cargo, including a large number of animals, they were made somewhat wider than the ships we use in other waters. They were all to be of a type suitable for both sailing and rowing – an arrangement which was greatly facilitated by their low freeboard. The materials required for fitting them out were to be imported from Spain.

On the completion of the assizes in northern Italy Caesar set out for Illyria, because he heard that the Pirustae were making damaging raids over the frontier of that province. On his arrival he ordered the tribes to levy troops and appointed a place for their assembly. When they heard this news the Pirustae sent representatives to say that their government was not responsible for what had happened, and that they were ready to make full reparation for the damage. He accepted their explanation and ordered them to deliver hostages by a certain day, failing which he would make war on them. The hostages were punctually delivered in obedience to his orders, and he then appointed arbitrators to assess the damage sustained by the various communities and fix the reparation.

2. After disposing of this matter and holding his assizes in

Illyria, Caesar returned to Italy and from there went to rejoin the army. On his arrival he made a tour of all the winter camps, and found that, in spite of a serious shortage of materials, the men had worked with such enthusiasm that they had built and equipped six hundred vessels of the type described and twenty-eight warships. These would all be ready for launching in a few days. Caesar congratulated the soldiers and the officers who had superintended the work, gave them further instructions and ordered all the ships to be assembled at Portus Itius, the starting-point for the easiest crossing to Britain – a run of about thirty miles. Leaving a sufficient number of troops to carry out this task, he took four legions, unencumbered by a baggage train, and eight hundred cavalry, and set out for the country of the Treveri, because they would not attend the annual councils of chieftains or submit to his authority, and were alleged to be making overtures to the Germans across the Rhine.

3. The Treveri have much the most powerful cavalry in Gaul, and also a considerable force of infantry. Their territory, it will be remembered, borders on the Rhine. Two rivals were struggling there for supremacy – Indutiomarus and Cingetorix. As soon as news came of Caesar's approach with the legions, Cingetorix presented himself, assured Caesar that he and all his followers would remain loyal to the Roman alliance, and explained the position of affairs among the Treveri. Indutiomarus, however, began to prepare for war, raising forces of cavalry and infantry, and hiding those too young or too old to fight in the huge forest of the Ardennes, which stretches from the Rhine through the middle of the Treveran country to the frontier of the Remi. Some of the other leaders of the tribe, who were friends of Cingetorix, were alarmed by the approach of the Roman army, and since it was not in their power, they said, to help their country, they came to Caesar and petitioned for their personal safety. Indutiomarus was now afraid of being completely isolated, and sent to Caesar to say that the reason why he had not wanted to leave his followers and wait upon him was that by remaining he had a better chance of keeping the tribe loyal. If all the men of rank left the country, the common people in their ignorance might fall into error. In this way he had kept control of his countrymen, and with Caesar's permission

would come to his camp and place himself and the tribe under his protection.

4. Caesar understood his motive in saying this, and knew what deterred him from prosecuting his original design. Nevertheless, to avoid having to waste the summer there after making all preparations for a campaign in Britain, he told Indutiomarus to present himself with two hundred hostages, including his son and all his relations, who were mentioned by name. When these were brought, Caesar reassured him and urged him to remain loyal. But he also summoned the other leaders of the tribe and called on them individually to support Cingetorix. He thought that Cingetorix deserved this help, and that it was important to do all he could to increase the power of a man who had proved himself so devoted a friend. This abatement of his influence provoked Indutiomarus to bitter resentment, which greatly inflamed the hostility that he already felt towards the Romans.

5. After settling this matter Caesar proceeded with the legions to Portus Itius. He found that sixty ships which were built in the country of the Meldi had been driven out of their course by a storm and had returned to their starting-point.[31] All the rest were completely equipped and ready for sea. Four thousand cavalry from all parts of Gaul assembled at the port, and the leaders of all the tribes. Caesar had decided to leave behind only a few of these who had proved their loyalty, and to take all the rest with him as hostages, because he was afraid of a rising in Gaul during his absence.

6. Among the Gallic leaders was Dumnorix the Aeduan, spoken of above. He was one whom Caesar was particularly determined to keep with him, because he knew him to be a political intriguer, ambitious, bold, and very influential with the Gauls. Moreover, Dumnorix had said in the Aeduan council that Caesar had offered to make him king of the tribe – a statement that was much resented by the Aedui, although they dared not protest to Caesar or ask him to give up the idea. Caesar learnt these facts from some Gauls in whose house he had lodged. Dumnorix began by begging hard to be allowed to stay at home, saying that he was unused to sailing and afraid of the sea, and also that he was debarred from leaving the country by religious duties. When he found that there was no

hope of altering Caesar's determination not to leave him behind, he began to intrigue with the other chiefs, taking them aside one by one, urging them to remain on the continent, and working on their fears. He said that Caesar had an ulterior object in thus stripping Gaul of all her leading citizens: he shrank from killing them under the eyes of their countrymen, but his purpose was to put them all to death when he had got them across to Britain. He pledged his word to work with the others for what they saw to be the interest of Gaul, and called on them to take an oath to the same effect.

7. When these facts were reported to Caesar by a number of informants, he decided that in view of the high regard which he had for the Aedui he ought to do everything possible to restrain Dumnorix and deter him from pursuing his design; and as the man's obsession was clearly increasing, it must be put beyond his power to do any injury to Caesar or to Roman interests. For between three and four weeks the army was delayed at the port because the north-west wind – the prevailing wind at all seasons on that coast – made it impossible to sail; and in the meantime Caesar took measures to make Dumnorix behave himself, but at the same time to obtain information about any plans he might form. At length, taking advantage of favourable weather, Caesar ordered the infantry and cavalry to embark. But while everyone's attention was occupied with this operation, Dumnorix took some Aeduan horsemen out of the camp without Caesar's knowledge and started for home. On hearing of this Caesar postponed the sailing. Letting everything else wait, he sent a strong detachment of cavalry to pursue him and bring him back; if he showed fight and refused to obey, their orders were to kill him, since Caesar thought that a man who flouted his authority under his very eyes could not be expected to behave rationally behind his back. On being summoned to return Dumnorix began to resist, sword in hand, begging his followers to protect him, and shouting over and over again that he was a free man and a citizen of a free state. In obedience to Caesar's orders he was surrounded and killed, and all the Aeduan horsemen returned to the Roman camp.

8. Caesar then set sail, leaving Labienus on the continent with three legions and two thousand cavalry, with orders to guard the ports, provide for a supply of corn, watch events in Gaul, and act

as circumstances from time to time might require. Caesar took with him five legions and the remaining two thousand cavalry,[32] and putting out about sunset was at first carried on his way by a light south-westerly breeze. But about midnight the wind dropped, with the result that he was driven far out of his course by the tidal current and at daybreak saw Britain left behind on the port side. When the set of the current changed he went with it, and rowed hard to make the part of the island where he had found the best landing-places the year before. The soldiers worked splendidly, and by continuous rowing enabled the heavily laden transports to keep up with the warships. When the whole fleet reached Britain about midday, no enemy was to be seen. Caesar discovered afterwards from prisoners that, although large numbers had assembled at the spot, they were frightened by the sight of so many ships and had quitted the shore to conceal themselves on higher ground. Including those retained from the previous year and the privately owned vessels built by individuals for their own use, over eight hundred ships were visible simultaneously.

9. Caesar disembarked his army and chose a suitable spot for a camp. On learning from prisoners where the enemy were posted, he left ten cohorts and three hundred cavalry on the coast to guard the fleet and marched against the Britons shortly after midnight, feeling little anxiety about the ships because he was leaving them anchored on an open shore of soft sand. The fleet and its guard were put under the command of Quintus Atrius. A night march of about twelve miles brought Caesar in sight of the enemy, who advanced to a river with their cavalry and chariots, and tried to bar his way by attacking from a position on higher ground. Repulsed by his cavalry they hid in the woods, where they occupied a well-fortified post of great natural strength, previously prepared, no doubt, for some war among themselves, since all the entrances were blocked by felled trees laid close together. Scattered parties made skirmishing attacks out of the woods, trying to prevent the Romans from penetrating the defences. But the soldiers of the 7th legion, locking their shields together over their heads and piling up the earth against the fortifications, captured the place and drove them out of the woods at the cost of only a few men wounded. Caesar forbade them to pursue far, however, because he did not

know the ground and because he wanted to devote the few remaining hours of the day to the fortification of his camp.

10. The next morning he sent out a force of infantry and cavalry in three columns to pursue the fleeing enemy. They had advanced some way and were in sight of the nearest fugitives, when dispatch riders brought news from Atrius of a great storm in the night, by which nearly all the ships had been damaged or cast ashore: the anchors and cables had not held, and the sailors and their captains could not cope with such a violent gale, so that many vessels were disabled by running foul of one another.

11. Caesar at once ordered the legions and cavalry to be halted and recalled. He himself went back to the beach, where with his own eyes he saw pretty much what the messengers and the dispatch described. About forty ships were a total loss; the rest looked as if they could be repaired at the cost of much trouble. Accordingly he called out all the skilled workmen from the legions, sent to the continent for more, and wrote to tell Labienus to build as many ships as possible with the troops under his command. Further, although it was a task involving enormous labour, he decided that it would be best to have all the ships beached and enclosed together with the camp by one fortification. This work, although it was continued day and night, took some ten days to complete. As soon as the ships were hauled up and the camp strongly fortified, Caesar left the same units as before to guard them, and returned to the place from which he had come. On arriving there he found that larger British forces had now been assembled from all sides by Cassivellaunus, to whom the chief command and direction of the campaign had been entrusted by common consent. Cassivellaunus' territory is separated from the maritime tribes by a river called the Thames, and lies about seventy-five miles from the sea. Previously he had been continually at war with the other tribes, but the arrival of our army frightened them into appointing him their supreme commander.

12. The interior of Britain is inhabited by people who claim, on the strength of an oral tradition, to be aboriginal; the coast, by Belgic immigrants who came to plunder and make war – nearly all of them retaining the names of the tribes from which they originated – and later settled down to till the soil. The population

is exceedingly large, the ground thickly studded with homesteads, closely resembling those of the Gauls, and the cattle very numerous. For money they use either bronze, or gold coins, or iron ingots of fixed weights. Tin is found inland, and small quantities of iron near the coast; the copper that they use is imported. There is timber of every kind, as in Gaul, except beech and fir. Hares, fowl, and geese they think it unlawful to eat, but rear them for pleasure and amusement. The climate is more temperate than in Gaul, the cold being less severe.[33]

13. The island is triangular, with one side facing Gaul. One corner of this side, on the coast of Kent, is the landing-place for nearly all the ships from Gaul, and points east; the lower corner points south. The length of this side is about 475 miles. Another side faces west, towards Spain. In this direction is Ireland, which is supposed to be half the size of Britain, and lies at the same distance from it as Gaul. Midway across is the Isle of Man, and it is believed that there are also a number of smaller islands, in which according to some writers there is a month of perpetual darkness at the winter solstice. Our inquiries on this subject were always fruitless, but we found by accurate measurements with a water-clock that the nights are shorter than on the continent. This side of Britain, according to the natives' estimate, is 665 miles long. The third side faces north; no land lies opposite it, but its eastern corner points roughly in the direction of Germany. Its length is estimated at 760 miles. Thus the whole island is 1,900 miles in circumference.[34]

14. By far the most civilized inhabitants are those living in Kent (a purely maritime district), whose way of life differs little from that of the Gauls. Most of the tribes in the interior do not grow corn but live on milk and meat, and wear skins. All the Britons dye their bodies with woad, which produces a blue colour, and shave the whole of their bodies except the head and the upper lip. Wives are shared between groups of ten or twelve men, especially between brothers and between fathers and sons; but the offspring of these unions are counted as the children of the man with whom a particular woman cohabited first.

15. The British cavalry and charioteers had a fierce encounter with our cavalry on the march, but our men had the best of it

everywhere and drove them into the woods and hills, killing a good many, but also incurring some casualties themselves by a too eager pursuit. The enemy waited for a time, and then, while our soldiers were off their guard and busy fortifying the camp, suddenly dashed out of the woods, swooped upon the outpost on duty in front of the camp, and started a violent battle. Caesar sent two cohorts – the first of their respective legions – to the rescue, and these took up a position close together; but the men were unnerved by the unfamiliar tactics, and the enemy very daringly broke through between them and got away unhurt. That day Quintus Laberius Durus, a military tribune, was killed. The attack was eventually repulsed by throwing in some more cohorts.

16. Throughout this peculiar combat, which was fought in front of the camp in full view of everyone, it was seen that our troops were too heavily weighted by their armour to deal with such an enemy: they could not pursue them when they retreated and dared not get separated from their standards. The cavalry, too, found it very dangerous work fighting the charioteers; for the Britons would generally give ground on purpose and after drawing them some distance from the legions would jump down from their chariots and fight on foot, with the odds in their favour. In engaging their cavalry our men were not much better off: their tactics were such that the danger was exactly the same for both pursuers and pursued. A further difficulty was that they never fought in very close order, but in very open formation, and had reserves posted here and there; in this way the various groups covered one another's retreat and fresh troops replaced those who were tired.

17. Next day the enemy took up a position on the hills at a distance from the camp. They showed themselves now only in small parties and harassed our cavalry with less vigour than the day before. But at midday, when Caesar had sent three legions and all the cavalry on a foraging expedition under his general Gaius Trebonius, they suddenly swooped down on them from all sides, pressing their attack right up to the standards of the legions. The legionaries drove them off by a strong counter-attack and continued to pursue until the cavalry, emboldened by the support of the legions which they saw close behind them, made a charge that sent

the natives flying headlong. A great many were killed and the rest were given no chance of rallying or making a stand or jumping from their chariots. This rout caused the immediate dispersal of the forces that had assembled from various tribes to Cassivellaunus' aid, and the Britons never again joined battle with their whole strength.

18. On learning the enemy's plan of campaign, Caesar led his army to the Thames in order to enter Cassivellaunus' territory. The river is fordable at one point only, and even there with difficulty. At this place he found large enemy forces drawn up on the opposite bank. The bank was also fenced by sharp stakes fixed along the edge, and he was told by prisoners and deserters that similar ones were concealed in the river-bed. He sent the cavalry across first and then at once ordered the infantry to follow. But the infantry went with such speed and impetuosity, although they had only their heads above water, that they attacked at the same moment as the cavalry. The enemy was overpowered and fled from the river-bank.

19. Cassivellaunus had now given up all hope of fighting a pitched battle. Disbanding the greater part of his troops, he retained only some four thousand charioteers, with whom he watched our line of march. He would retire a short way from the route and hide in dense thickets, driving the inhabitants and cattle from the open country into the woods wherever he knew we intended to pass. If ever our cavalry incautiously ventured too far away in plundering and devastating the country, he would send all his charioteers out of the woods by well-known lanes and pathways and deliver very formidable attacks, hoping by this means to make them afraid to go far afield. Caesar was thus compelled to keep the cavalry in touch with the column of infantry and to let the enemy off with such devastation and burning as could be done under the protection of the legionaries – tired as they often were with marching.

20. During this march envoys arrived from the Trinovantes, about the strongest tribe in south-eastern Britain. Mandubracius, a young prince of this tribe, had gone over to the continent to put himself under Caesar's protection, having fled for his life when his father the king of the Trinovantes was killed by Cassivellaunus.

The envoys promised to surrender and obey Caesar's commands, and asked him to protect Mandubracius from Cassivellaunus and send him home to rule this people as king. Caesar demanded forty hostages and grain for his troops, and then allowed Mandubracius to go. The Trinovantes promptly sent the required number of hostages and the grain.

21. When they saw that the Trinovantes had been protected against Cassivellaunus and spared any injury on the part of the Roman troops, several other tribes, the Cenimagni, Segontiaci, Ancalites, Bibroci, and Cassi, sent embassies and surrendered. From them Caesar learnt that he was not far from Cassivellaunus' stronghold, which was protected by forests and marshes and had been filled with a large number of men and cattle. (The Britons apply the term 'strongholds' to densely wooded spots fortified with a rampart and trench, to which they retire in order to escape the attacks of invaders.) He marched to the place with his legions, and found that it was of great natural strength and excellently fortified. Nevertheless, he proceeded to assault it on two sides. After a short time the enemy proved unable to resist the violent attack of the legions and rushed out of the fortress on another side. A quantity of cattle was found there, and many of the fugitives were captured or killed.

22. While these operations were proceeding in his territory, Cassivellaunus sent envoys to Kent ordering the four kings of that region, Cingetorix, Carvilius, Taximagulus, and Segovax, to collect all their troops and make a surprise attack on the naval camp. When these forces appeared the Romans made a sortie, in which without suffering any loss they killed a great many of them and captured Lugotorix, a leader of noble birth. On receiving news of this action, Cassivellaunus, alarmed by so many reverses, by the devastation of his country, and above all by the defection of his allies, sent envoys to Caesar to obtain terms of surrender, employing Commius as an intermediary. Caesar had decided to return to the continent for the winter, for fear any sudden rising should break out in Gaul. The summer, too, was nearly over, and he knew that the Britons could easily hold out for the short time that remained. Accordingly he granted Cassivellaunus' request for terms, demanding hostages, fixing an annual tribute to be paid by the Britons to

the Roman government, and strictly forbidding Cassivellaunus to molest Mandubracius or the Trinovantes.[35]

23. As soon as the hostages were delivered he led the army back to the coast, where he found the ships repaired. He had them launched, and as he had a large number of prisoners, and some of the ships had been destroyed by the storm, decided to make the return voyage in two trips. It happened that of all these large fleets, which made so many voyages in this and the preceding year, not a single ship with troops on board was lost, while very few of the vessels coming over empty from the continent (i.e., those which had returned to Gaul after landing troops in Britain and sixty that Labienus had built after the start of the expedition) reached their destination, nearly all the rest being forced back to land. After waiting a long time for them in vain, Caesar was afraid of being prevented from sailing by the approaching season of the equinox, and so had to pack the men more tightly than usual on the ships he had. The sea becoming very calm, he set sail late in the evening and brought all the fleet safely to land at dawn.

2 Destruction of Sabinus' army by the Eburones (54 B.C.)

24. The harvest that year in Gaul was a poor one on account of drought. Accordingly, after beaching the ships and holding a council of Gallic leaders at Samarobriva, Caesar was compelled to change his previous method of quartering the army for the winter, and distribute the legions among a larger number of tribes. One was sent to the Morini under the general Gaius Fabius, another to the Nervii under Quintus Tullius Cicero, a third to the Essuvii under Lucius Roscius. A fourth, under Labienus, was ordered to winter in the country of the Remi near the frontier of the Treveri, and three more were placed in Belgic territory under the quaestor Marcus Crassus and the generals Lucius Munatius Plancus and Gaius Trebonius. One of the legions recently raised in the country north of the Po, and a further detachment of five cohorts, were sent under the command of Sabinus and Cotta[36] to the Eburones, who live principally between the Meuse and the Rhine, and were

at that time ruled by Ambiorix and Catuvolcus. This wide distribution Caesar thought would be the easiest way of meeting the shortage of corn. In fact, however, the quarters of all the legions except that under Roscius, which had been sent to a perfectly quiet and peaceful district, were within a hundred miles of one another. Caesar determined to stay in Gaul himself until he knew that all the troops had reached their destinations and fortified their camps.

25. In the land of the Carnutes was a man of noble birth called Tasgetius, whose ancestors had been kings of the tribe. In recognition of his merit and devotion – for in all the campaigns his services had been exceptionally valuable – Caesar had placed him upon the throne of his ancestors. In the third year of his reign he was assassinated by enemies with the avowed approval of many members of the tribe. The crime was reported to Caesar and, as the number of persons implicated was large, he feared lest they might instigate the tribes to revolt. Accordingly he at once transferred Plancus to the country of the Carnutes from his quarters among the Belgae, with orders to stay there for the rest of the winter, and to arrest and send to him those whom he found to be responsible for Tasgetius' death. Meanwhile Caesar heard from all the generals and quaestors in command of the legions that they had reached their quarters and completed the fortification of their camps.

26. About a fortnight later an open revolt was suddenly started by the Eburonians Ambiorix and Catuvolcus. They had waited on Sabinus and Cotta at the frontier of their kingdom and brought a supply of grain to the Roman camp, but were then induced by a message from Indutiomarus the Treveran to call their subjects to arms. Making a sudden attack on a party collecting wood, they came with a large force to assault the camp. The legionaries quickly armed and mounted the rampart, and some Spanish horsemen who were sent out by one of the gates were victorious in a cavalry engagement. The Eburones realized that they had no hope of success, and retired from the attack; then they shouted aloud, after the manner of their nation, for someone from our side to go out and parley with them, declaring that they had something to say which concerned us as well as themselves, and which they hoped might bring the conflict to an end.

27. Gaius Arpineius, a Roman knight and a friend of Sabinus, was sent to confer with them, accompanied by a Spaniard named Quintus Junius, who had already been employed by Caesar on many missions to Ambiorix. They were addressed by Ambiorix in the following terms: 'I admit,' he said, 'that I am greatly indebted to Caesar for the services which he has rendered me. It was he who relieved me of the tribute that I used to pay to my neighbours the Atuatuci, and restored to me my son and my brother's son, who, when sent to them as hostages, had been enslaved and kept in chains. In attacking your camp I acted against my better judgement and my own wishes. I was constrained by my subjects – for I am not an absolute ruler: the people have as much power over me as I have over them. And the reason why the tribe took up arms was because it could not oppose the movement in which all the Gauls suddenly leagued themselves together. The insignificance of my power clearly proves the truth of what I say: I am not so ignorant as to imagine that my army by itself is strong enough to defeat the Romans. The whole of Gaul is united in this attempt, and they have arranged to attack all the camps today simultaneously, so that the legions shall not be able to help one another. It would have been difficult for us to refuse help to our fellow countrymen, especially as we knew that their object was the recovery of our national liberty. But having now discharged the duty which patriotism required of me, I remember what I owe to Caesar for his favours, and I urge and implore Sabinus, as my friend and host, to consider his own and his soldiers' safety. A large force of German mercenaries has crossed the Rhine and will be here in a couple of days. It is for you to decide whether you will withdraw your troops from the camp before the neighbouring tribes can find out what you are doing, and take them either to Cicero, who is less than fifty miles away, or to Labienus – a somewhat greater distance. I swear to grant them safe conduct through my territory. In so doing I am acting in the interest of my people, who will be relieved from the burden of the camp in their midst, and at the same time repaying Caesar for his kindnesses.' After making this speech Ambiorix retired.

28. These remarks were reported by Arpineius and Junius to the generals, who heard them with surprise and alarm; and

although the suggestion came from an enemy, they did not think it ought to be disregarded. The most disquieting thing was that it really did seem scarcely credible that an obscure and insignificant tribe like the Eburones could have dared of its own initiative to make war on Rome. Accordingly the matter was referred to a council of war, where it was hotly debated. Cotta and many of the military tribunes and first-grade centurions thought that they ought not to take any hasty step or leave the camp without Caesar's authority. 'We can resist any number of Gauls,' they said, 'and a large force of Germans into the bargain, in this fortified camp. We have proof of that; for the men put up a very brave resistance against the enemy's first attack, and indeed took the offensive and inflicted heavy loss upon them. We are not short of grain, and before we run short help will come from the nearest camps and from Caesar. In any case, what could be more irresponsible or unsoldierly than to follow the advice of an enemy in a matter of prime importance?'

29. In reply to this Sabinus insisted that it would be too late to do anything when the Gauls had assembled in greater numbers, reinforced by the Germans, or when some disaster had occurred in the other camps that were within reach. 'We have only a short time to decide,' he said, 'and as for Caesar, I think he must have started for Italy. Otherwise, the Carnutes would not have resolved on the murder of Tasgetius, nor would the Eburones, if Caesar had been in Gaul, have held us in such contempt as to attack the camp. It is irrelevant to say that the suggestion comes from the enemy. It is the facts of the case that I am looking at. The Rhine is close by, and the Germans are bitterly resentful of Ariovistus' death and of our victories in earlier campaigns. Gaul is blazing with indignation at all the humiliations she has suffered by being brought under Roman dominion, and at the eclipse of her former military prestige. And it is inconceivable that Ambiorix would have taken such action without being sure of his ground. My policy is safe either way. If nothing serious is afoot, we shall make our way to the nearest legion without any risk; if the Gauls are united and in league with the Germans, our only chance of escape is to act quickly. As to the plan recommended by Cotta and the others who differ from me, what would be the result of adopting it? It may or may not involve

immediate danger; it certainly means a long blockade and the threat of starvation.'

30. After these divergent views had been put forward, Cotta and the centurions continued to oppose Sabinus vigorously. 'Have your own way, then, if you will,' cried Sabinus, raising his voice so that many of the soldiers could hear. 'I am not more afraid of death than the rest of you. The men will understand: if disaster follows, it is you, Cotta, that they will hold responsible. If you would give your consent, by the day after tomorrow they would have reached the nearest camp, and would have their comrades by their side to share the fortune of war with them, instead of remaining isolated like outcasts and exiles, to be massacred or to die of starvation.'[37]

31. The officers rose from their places, laid hold of the two generals, and implored them not to persist in a dispute which must gravely imperil the army. 'Whether we go or stay,' they said, 'there is no real difficulty, if only we all agree on one course of action; but if we go on quarrelling, there is no chance of escape.' The debate dragged on till midnight, but at last Cotta, greatly distressed, gave in. Sabinus' plan was adopted, and it was announced that they would march at dawn. The soldiers stayed up for the rest of the night, each man going through his kit to see what he could take with him, and how much of his winter equipment must be abandoned. They thought of every possible argument to persuade themselves that there was no danger in going, and considerable danger in remaining, and tired themselves so much with loss of sleep that the actual peril was increased. At daybreak they started out, apparently quite convinced that the enemy who had suggested the plan was the best of friends – for they went in a long, straggling column, encumbered with a very heavy load of baggage.

32. Hearing the sound of voices in the night, the Gauls knew that the soldiers were awake, and concluded that they were leaving the camp. They therefore placed two ambushes at a likely place some two miles away in the woods, where they were screened from observation, and there awaited the Roman column. When the greater part of it had descended into a large defile, they suddenly appeared at either end, harassed the rearguard, prevented the head of the column from climbing the hill which led out of the defile, and forced the soldiers to fight on very unfavourable ground.

33. Sabinus, having failed to foresee what might happen, now got excited and ran to and fro arranging the cohorts; but even this he did nervously and in a way which showed that he was at his wits' end – as generally happens to those who are compelled to make decisions when a battle has actually begun. Cotta, however, who had foreseen the possibility of a surprise attack on the march, and for that reason had opposed the idea of leaving the camp, did everything possible to save the army – calling upon the men and encouraging them as their commander-in-chief might have done, and fighting in the ranks like any soldier. As the length of the column made it difficult for the generals to attend to everything personally and to see what was required in every part of the field, they passed word along to abandon the baggage and form a circle. Although this measure cannot be condemned in such circumstances, it had unfortunate results: it discouraged the soldiers and increased the enemy's ardour for the fight, because it clearly indicated an extremity of fear and desperation. It inevitably meant, too, that men were everywhere leaving their units and running to the baggage to look for their most cherished possessions and pull them out, amid a hubbub of shouting and cries.

34. The enemy, for their part, showed no lack of resources. Their leaders passed word along the whole line that no one was to leave his post; all the plunder that the Romans left would be theirs, and should be kept for them alone, so they must realize that everything depended on victory. The Gauls were equal to our troops in fighting quality, and superior in numbers. Yet our men, although their general had failed them and fortune deserted them, relied on their courage to save them, and every time a cohort charged, a large number of the enemy fell. Seeing this, Ambiorix ordered his men to throw their javelins without going too close, and to give ground before the Roman charges; being lightly armed and trained by daily practice to execute such manoeuvres, they would still be able to inflict heavy casualties. As soon as the Romans began to retire to their main body, they were to give chase.

35. These instructions were carefully obeyed. Whenever a cohort made a charge out of the circle, the enemy retreated at full speed. A temporary gap was bound to be left in the circle, so that the unit which stood next was exposed to missiles on its right flank;

and when the cohort began to return to its original place, it was surrounded by the Gauls who had fallen back and by the nearest of those who had remained in position. If the Romans tried simply holding their ground in the circle, there was no scope for any courageous effort, and they were huddled together too closely to avoid the javelins that the huge Gallic host rained upon them. Yet, notwithstanding all the disadvantages that they had to contend with, and in spite of heavy losses, they still held out, and throughout a fight that lasted for a considerable part of the day – from dawn till two o'clock – did nothing to be ashamed of. In this battle Titus Balventius, who the previous year had been chief centurion of his legion, a brave and highly respected man, had both his thighs pierced by a javelin; another centurion of the same rank, Quintus Lucanius, was killed in a very courageous attempt to rescue his son, who had been surrounded; and Cotta himself, while engaged in cheering on each cohort and company, was wounded by a slingstone which struck him full in the face.

36. Sabinus was so much alarmed by these events that on catching sight of Ambiorix, who was addressing his troops at some distance, he sent his interpreter Gnaeius Pompeius to ask for quarter for himself and his soldiers. In response to this appeal Ambiorix said that Sabinus might speak to him if he wanted. He hoped that his men could be induced to spare the Roman soldiers' lives; in any case Sabinus himself should come to no harm – that much he would personally guarantee. Sabinus proposed to the wounded Cotta that they should withdraw from the fight and together confer with Ambiorix, who he hoped could be induced to spare them and the troops. But Cotta refused to go to an enemy who had not laid down his arms, and would not budge from his resolve.

37. Sabinus ordered the military tribunes who were with him at the moment, and the first-grade centurions, to follow him. On approaching Ambiorix he was told to lay down his arms. He obeyed, and commanded the others to do the same. While he was discussing terms with Ambiorix, who purposely prolonged the conversation, he was gradually surrounded, and then killed. At this the Gauls raised their customary shout of triumph, and with a loud yell charged and broke our ranks. Cotta fell fighting where

he stood, and most of the soldiers with him. The survivors retreated into the camp from which they had come. Lucius Petrosidius, the standard-bearer of the legion, seeing himself beset by a large crowd of Gauls, threw his eagle inside the rampart and died fighting heroically outside the camp. The rest had hard work to withstand the enemy's onslaught till nightfall; in the night, seeing that all hope was gone, every single man committed suicide. A few who had escaped from the battle made their way by scarcely distinguishable woodland tracks to Labienus' camp and told him what had happened.[38]

3 Attack by the Nervii on Cicero's winter camp (54 B.C.)

38. Elated by his victory, Ambiorix at once started with his cavalry for the country of the Atuatuci, which bordered on his kingdom, marching day and night without a halt. His infantry had orders to follow. Explaining to the Atuatuci what had occurred, he roused them to arms. The next day he reached the Nervii, and urged them not to lose the chance of freeing themselves for ever and avenging the wrongs they had suffered at the hands of the Romans. Two generals, he told them, were killed, and a large part of the Roman army annihilated; it would be easy to surprise and destroy Cicero's legion in its winter quarters.[39] He promised to aid them in this enterprise, and easily persuaded them to undertake it.

39. Accordingly the Nervii hastened to send messengers to the tribes under their rule, the Ceutrones, Grudii, Levaci, Pleumoxii, and Geidumni, and, raising as large a force as they could, swooped down on Cicero's camp before he had received news of Sabinus' death. Like him, Cicero could not help being taken by surprise: some soldiers who had gone into the woods to get firewood and timber for building fortifications were cut off by the unexpected arrival of the enemy's cavalry. Then a large-scale attack on the legion was begun by the Eburones, Nervii, and Atuatuci, accompanied by their allies and satellites. The soldiers rushed to arms and mounted the rampart. A very hard day's fighting ensued, because the enemy staked all their hopes on swift action, and were

confident that success in that engagement would assure them final victory.

40. Cicero immediately wrote to Caesar, and offered large rewards to the couriers if they succeeded in delivering his letter; but all the roads were guarded, and they were intercepted. During the night, the timber that had been collected for the defence works was used to build towers, as many as a hundred and twenty of these being run up with incredible speed, and all defects in the fortifications were made good. Next day the enemy, considerably reinforced, renewed their attack on the camp and filled up the trench, while the Romans resisted with the same determination. Similar attacks followed day after day, and work had to be continued throughout the night, so that even the sick and the wounded could get no sleep. Everything necessary for repelling the next day's assault was got ready by night, including large numbers of siege spears and stakes charred at the point. The towers were provided with additional storeys, and with wicker breastworks surmounted by a crenellated top. Cicero himself, though in very poor health, would not rest even at night, until a crowd of soldiers actually went to him and by their remonstrances made him take care of himself.

41. At length a number of the Nervian leaders and chieftains, who had some claim to consider themselves friends of Cicero, and therefore entitled to speak to him, asked for an interview. Their request was granted, and they told him the same as Ambiorix had told Sabinus – that the whole of Gaul was in arms, the Germans had crossed the Rhine, and the camps of Caesar and the other generals were being attacked. They also described the death of Sabinus, and, to prove the truth of their account, pointed to the presence of Ambiorix with their army.

'You are mistaken,' they continued, 'if you expect any help whatever from troops who know that they are in extreme peril themselves. However, we have no quarrel with Cicero or the Roman people, except that we object to the establishment of winter camps in our country, and do not want it to become a regular practice. As far as we are concerned, you can leave the camp without being molested, and go where you please without fear.'

By way of reply, Cicero contented himself with saying that it was not the habit of the Roman people to accept any terms from an armed enemy. If they would lay down their arms, and send an embassy to Caesar to ask for terms, he would support their request, and hoped that Caesar in his justice would grant it.

42. After this disappointment, the Nervii surrounded the camp with a rampart ten feet high and a trench fifteen feet wide. They had learnt something of the art of entrenchment by observing our methods in previous years, and also got hints from prisoners belonging to our army whom they had taken. But as they lacked the proper tools for the work, they had to cut the sods with their swords, and remove the earth in their hands and in their cloaks. From this one could get some idea of their great number: in less than three hours they completed a fortified line three miles in circumference and during the next few days set to work, under the prisoners' instruction, to erect towers high enough to overtop the rampart of the camp, and to make grappling-hooks and sappers' huts.

43. On the seventh day of the siege a great gale sprang up, and the enemy began slinging moulded bullets of red-hot clay and hurling incendiary darts at the huts in the camp, which, as usual in Gaul, were thatched. The huts quickly caught fire, and the strong wind spread the flames throughout the camp. The enemy raised a loud cheer, as if victory were now a certainty, and began to move up their towers and sappers' huts and to scale the rampart with ladders. The defenders showed the greatest courage and coolness. They were surrounded by scorching heat and pelted with a hail of missiles, and knew that all their baggage, containing everything they possessed, was being burnt. Yet not a single man deserted his post on the rampart, and hardly anyone even turned his head to look at what was happening; every man fought in this great crisis with the utmost energy and heroism. This was by far the worst day's fighting for them; nevertheless, it ended in their killing and wounding more of the enemy than on any other day, because the Gauls were crowded in a tightly packed mass at the very foot of the rampart and those at the back prevented the front ranks from retreating. When the fire had died down a little, one of the enemy's towers was pushed right up to the rampart at one point. The centurions of the 3rd cohort retired from the spot where

they were stationed, withdrew all their men, and then made signs and called to the Gauls to come inside if they liked; but not one of them dared to move. They were then driven from their position on the tower by a volley of stones from every direction, and the tower was itself set on fire.

44. In the legion were two very brave centurions named Titus Pullo and Lucius Vorenus, both of them nearly qualified for the first grade. They were always disputing which was the better soldier, and every year the competition for promotion set them quarrelling. When the fighting at the entrenchment was as its height, Pullo cried: 'Why hesitate, Vorenus? What better opportunity do you want to prove your courage? Today shall decide between us.' With these words he advanced outside the fortification and rushed into the thickest place he could see in the enemy's line. This brought Vorenus too over the rampart, hastening after his rival for fear of what everyone would think if he lagged behind.

Pullo stopped a short way from the Gauls, hurled his spear and transfixed one of them who was running forward from the ranks. The man fainted from the wound, and his comrades covered him with their shields, at the same time showering missiles upon Pullo and preventing him from advancing further. His shield was pierced by a javelin, which stuck in his sword-belt; and as the blow knocked his scabbard out of place, he could not get his hand quickly to his sword when he tried to draw it, and was surrounded by the enemy while unable to defend himself.

His rival Vorenus ran up to rescue him in his distress, and all the Gauls immediately left Pullo, who they thought had been mortally wounded by the javelin, and turned upon Vorenus. Vorenus drew his sword and fighting hand to hand killed one of his assailants and drove the rest back a little; but pressing on too eagerly he stumbled down a steep slope and fell. It was now his turn to be surrounded, but Pullo came to his aid; both of them escaped unhurt and after killing a number of the enemy returned to camp covered with glory. Thus Fortune played with them in their struggle for pre-eminence: bitter rivals though they were, each helped and saved the other, so that it could not be decided which was the more deserving of the prize of valour.

45. Day by day the peril and hardship of the siege increased,

especially as so many of the men were incapacitated by wounds that few were now available for the defence. As the situation became worse, Cicero made still more frequent attempts to get a letter through to Caesar. Some of the messengers were detected at once and tortured to death under the eyes of the soldiers. There was one Nervian in the camp, a man of good birth named Vertico, who had deserted to Cicero at the start of the siege and served him very faithfully. The man induced his slave, by the promise of freedom and a large reward, to carry a dispatch to Caesar. He took it tied round a javelin, passed through his fellow countrymen's lines without exciting any suspicion, and reached Caesar, who learned from him the perils that surrounded Cicero and his legion.

46. On receiving the dispatch in the late afternoon, Caesar at once sent a messenger to his quaestor Marcus Crassus, whose camp was twenty-four miles away in the country of the Bellovaci, ordering him to march at midnight with his legion and join him with all speed. Accordingly, Crassus left his camp with the messenger.

Another message was sent to Fabius, bidding him march his legion into the country of the Atrebates, through which Caesar would have to pass on his way to Cicero's camp. He also directed Labienus to bring his legion to the frontier of the Nervii, if he could do so without risk. As the remaining legions were a long way off, Caesar did not think it advisable to wait until they could be assembled; but he collected about four hundred cavalry from the nearest camps.

47. The next morning, on learning from Crassus' scouts that he was approaching, Caesar set out about nine o'clock and marched twenty miles.[40] He directed that Crassus, with the legion which he was bringing with him, should take charge of everything left behind at Samarobriva – the heavy baggage, the hostages furnished by various tribes, the state papers, and the whole of the grain that had been collected to last through the winter. Fabius and his legion, in accordance with their orders, joined Caesar on the march without much delay. As for Labienus, he had heard the bad news about the destruction of Sabinus and the fifteen cohorts; all the forces of the Treveri were close upon him, and he feared the consequences of a departure from his camp which must look like

a flight: the enemy would be sure to attack, and he doubted his ability to resist, especially as he knew that they were elated by the recent Gallic victory. Accordingly he wrote back to Caesar saying that it would be very dangerous for him to move his legion from its quarters; he described in detail what had happened in the country of the Eburones, and told him that the whole army of the Treveri, infantry and cavalry, had taken up a position three miles from his camp.

48. Caesar approved of Labienus' decision. Although this meant that he had only two legions instead of the three he had expected, he thought that the only possible way to save the situation was to act quickly. He proceeded by forced marches to the territory of the Nervii, and there learnt from prisoners what was happening in Cicero's camp, and how critical the position was. He then induced one of his Gallic horsemen, by the promise of a large reward, to convey a letter to Cicero, which he wrote in Greek characters, for fear it might be intercepted and his plans become known to the enemy. If he was unable to get into the camp, the man was to tie the letter to the thong of a javelin and throw it in over the rampart. The letter informed Cicero that Caesar was on the way with some legions and would be there shortly, and told him to keep up a bold front. The Gaul was afraid to enter the camp and therefore threw the javelin in, according to his instructions. It happened to stick in one of the towers, where it remained unnoticed for two days. Then a soldier saw it, pulled it out, and took it to Cicero, who after reading it paraded the troops and read it aloud, to their great joy. By this time the smoke of burning buildings was visible in the distance, which dispelled all doubt about the approach of the legions.

49. On hearing the news from their patrols, the Gauls raised the siege and marched out to meet Caesar with all their forces, about sixty thousand men. With the help of Vertico – the man already mentioned – Cicero again found a Gaul to carry a dispatch to Caesar, in which he advised him to march warily and carefully, because the enemy had left the camp and diverted all their forces to oppose him. When the dispatch reached him, about midnight, Caesar informed his troops of its contents and told them to summon up their courage for a battle. At daybreak he broke up the camp,

and had advanced about four miles, when he saw the Gallic host on
the other side of a wide valley with a stream running through it. It
would have been very risky to fight on unfavourable ground with
such a small force; and knowing that Cicero was now released from
blockade, he felt that he had no cause for anxiety, and had better
take his time. He therefore halted and made a fortified camp on the
most advantageous site he could find. The camp would have been
small in any case, since he had barely seven thousand men and no
heavy baggage; but he reduced its size still further by making the
camp roads narrower than usual, so that his forces would seem
contemptibly small. At the same time he sent out scouts in all
directions to find the most convenient place for crossing the valley.

50. Some cavalry skirmishes took place that day near the stream,
but the two armies maintained their positions. The Gauls were
awaiting the arrival of larger forces. Caesar hoped, by feigning
fear, to entice them on to his own ground, and so to be able to fight
in front of his camp on his own side of the valley; or, failing that,
to cross the valley and the stream with less risk by reconnoitring
the available routes beforehand. At dawn the enemy's cavalry came
up to the camp and engaged the Roman horse. Caesar ordered
them to give ground voluntarily and fall back into the camp, and
told the legionaries to increase the height of the rampart all round
and block up the gateways; in doing so they were to run about as
much as possible and pretend to be afraid.

51. By these feints the enemy were induced to cross the valley
and form up in a disadvantageous position. After Caesar had
enticed them still nearer by withdrawing his men from the rampart,
they threw javelins from all directions over the fortifications, and
sent heralds round with orders to announce that anyone, Gaul or
Roman, who liked to come over and join them might safely do so
before nine o'clock; after that, no one would be admitted. They
were so contemptuous of the Roman army, that when they found
the gateways blocked and thought they could not break in that way
– though actually the barricades were shams, consisting of a single
thickness of sods – they began to fill up the trenches and make
openings in the palisade with their bare hands. Suddenly, while
the infantry made sorties from all the gates, Caesar sent out the
cavalry. The Gauls fled so precipitately that not a single one stayed

to strike a blow; many were killed, and all the rest threw away their arms.

52. Caesar was afraid to pursue too far, because there were woods and marshes in the way, and because he saw that he would incur serious losses by abandoning his position. As it was, he joined Cicero the same day without having suffered any casualties. He saw with astonishment the towers, sappers' huts, and earthworks constructed by the Gauls, and, when Cicero's legion was paraded, found that not one man in ten remained unwounded. He was thus able to realize how grave the peril had been, and with what resolution the defence had been conducted. He gave Cicero the high praise he deserved, congratulated the whole legion, and spoke individually to the centurions and military tribunes who were mentioned by Cicero as having specially distinguished themselves. Obtaining from prisoners more precise information about the fate of Sabinus and Cotta, he paraded the legion next day, described the disaster that had taken place, and reassured the men. The defeat, he said, was due to the blundering rashness of the general, and they had no reason to be upset about it, since with the help of Providence their valour had avenged it; the enemy's triumph had been short, and there was no need for them to be depressed any longer.

4 Widespread revolts in northern and central Gaul (54–53 B.C.)

53. The news of Caesar's success was brought to Labienus by the Remi with extraordinary speed. He was more than fifty-five miles from Cicero's camp, and it was after two o'clock in the afternoon when Caesar reached it; yet before midnight some of the Remi were shouting at the camp gates, announcing the victory and offering their congratulations. When the news reached the Treveri, Indutiomarus, who had intended to attack Labienus' camp on the following day, fled home in the night with all his forces. Caesar sent Fabius back to his camp with his legion, and decided to winter himself with three legions in separate camps near Samarobriva, and in view of the serious disturbances that had occurred to remain

with the army throughout the winter.[41] Since the disaster in which
Sabinus met his death became generally known, nearly all the
tribes had been discussing warlike projects, sending messengers
and embassies in all directions, trying to find out one another's
plans and see who would take the initiative, and holding meetings
at night in deserted spots.

All through the winter Caesar had scarcely a moment's respite
from anxiety: he was continually receiving some report about plans
for revolt. The quaestor Roscius, for example, whom he had placed
in command of the 13th legion, reported that large forces belonging
to the tribes called Aremorican had assembled to attack him and
had been within eight miles of his camp, but on hearing of Caesar's
victory had made off with a haste that suggested an army in flight.

54. Caesar summoned the leading men of each tribe and partly
by intimidation, letting them know that he was aware of what was
going on, partly by persuasion, succeeded in keeping a large part
of the country obedient. The government of the Senones, however,
a very powerful tribe with great influence over the others, tried to
kill their king Cavarinus, whom Caesar had set on his ancestral
throne in succession to his brother Moritasgus, who occupied it at
the time of Caesar's arrival in Gaul. When Cavarinus got wind of
their intention and fled, they pursued him as far as the frontier,
dethroned him, and banished him. On receiving a deputation sent
to justify their action, Caesar ordered the whole of the tribal council
to appear before him; but they disregarded his command. The fact
that someone had been bold enough to take the initiative in hostile
action made a deep impression on the ignorant natives, and
produced such a profound change in their attitude that nearly every
tribe was suspected by Caesar of disloyalty. Almost the only
exceptions were the Aedui, whom he always held in special esteem
for their long-standing record of unbroken loyalty, and the Remi,
who had earned similar regard by their recent services in the Gallic
campaigns. Perhaps there is nothing very surprising in their
readiness to revolt; among many other reasons, tribes which were
considered the bravest and most warlike in the world naturally felt
bitter resentment at the complete loss of this reputation which
submission to Rome rule entailed.

55. Indutiomarus and the Treveri were particularly active. All

through the winter they never ceased sending embassies across the Rhine, intriguing with the German tribes, promising them money, and assuring them that the great losses which the Roman army had sustained had left only a small part of it in existence. Not a single German tribe, however, could be induced to cross the river; they said that they had twice had experience of the Roman arms – in the campaign of Ariovistus, and at the time of the migration of the Tenctheri – and did not intend to tempt fortune again. In spite of this disappointment Indutiomarus proceeded to raise and drill troops, to procure horses from the neighbouring states, and by large rewards to entice exiles and condemned criminals from all over Gaul to join him. Indeed, he soon acquired such prestige in the country by these measures that embassies poured in from all quarters, requesting his favour and alliance either for tribal governments or for individuals.

56. From these unsolicited overtures he inferred that he would have no lack of volunteers when he began to advance beyond his own frontier. In one direction were the Senones and Carnutes, incited to revolt by their consciousness of guilt, while on another side the Nervii and Atuatuci were preparing to attack the Romans. So he gave notice of a muster in arms. This is the customary method of opening hostilities in Gaul. A law, common to all the tribes alike, requires all adult males to arm and attend the muster, and the last to arrive is cruelly tortured and put to death in the presence of the assembled host. At this meeting Indutiomarus declared his son-in-law Cingetorix a public enemy and confiscated his property. Cingetorix was the leader of the rival party and had remained faithful to Caesar since putting himself under his protection, as described above. Indutiomarus next announced to the assembly that his aid had been invoked by the Senones, the Carnutes, and several other tribes: he intended in due course to march to their country, ravaging the territory of the Remi on his way, but would first attack Labienus' camp. He then gave the necessary orders.

57. Labienus was safe in a camp well protected both by its situation and by fortifications, and felt no anxiety for himself or his legion; his only concern was not to lose any opportunity of scoring a success against the enemy. Accordingly, when Cingetorix and his

relatives told him what Indutiomarus had said in the assembly, he sent messages to all the neighbouring tribes, calling upon them to supply contingents of cavalry by a certain date. Meanwhile Indutiomarus came prowling round the camp nearly every day with all his cavalry, either to reconnoitre its position or to get into conversation with the soldiers; and usually all the horsemen tried to frighten them by throwing javelins over the rampart. Labienus kept his men within the entrenchment and did all he could to confirm the enemy's belief that they were afraid.

58. Each day as he moved up to the Roman lines Indutiomarus showed greater contempt for his adversary. Eventually Labienus brought into the camp, in a single night, the cavalry which he had summoned from all the neighbouring tribes, and by setting a guard succeeded so well in keeping all his men inside, that there was no means by which the news could get abroad or be carried to the Treveri. Indutiomarus came up to the camp as usual and spent the greater part of the day there, his cavalrymen throwing javelins and shouting insults to provoke the soldiers to fight. They got no reply, and towards evening, when they felt like it, went off in scattered groups. Suddenly Labienus sent out all his cavalry through two of the gates. He gave strict orders that as soon as the enemy were scared off and put to flight – as he foresaw they would be – every man was to look for Indutiomarus, and not strike a blow at anyone else until they saw him killed; for he was anxious that they should not give him time to escape by going in pursuit of the others. He set a big price on his head, and to make doubly sure sent some cohorts to support the cavalry. Fortune aided the plan that human foresight had devised. With every man after him, and him alone, Indutiomarus was caught and killed in the very act of fording a river, and his head brought back to camp. On their way back the cavalry pursued and killed as many as they could, and all the forces which had assembled from the Eburones and the Nervii departed when they heard the news. This success made Gaul a little quieter for the time being.

BOOK VI
OPERATIONS NEAR THE RHINE

1 The Treveri routed (53 B.C.)

1. Caesar had many reasons, however, for expecting still more serious disturbances before long. He therefore charged three of his generals, Marcus Silanus, Gaius Antistius Reginus, and Titus Sextius, with the duty of raising fresh troops. He also sent a message to Pompey – who, though vested as proconsul with military command, was remaining for political reasons in the neighbourhood of Rome – requesting him to mobilize the recruits from northern Italy whom he had sworn in during his consulship and to send them out to him. Caesar considered it very important, with a view to making a permanent impression upon the tribesmen, to let it be seen that the manpower of Italy was sufficient not only to repair speedily any loss sustained in the field, but actually to increase the size of the expeditionary force. Pompey acceded to this request from motives of patriotism as well as of friendship, and Caesar's officers promptly enlisted further recruits, so that before the end of the winter three legions were formed and brought to Gaul, making double the number of the cohorts lost under Sabinus. This large reinforcement, and the speed with which it was effected, showed what Roman organization and resources were capable of.[42]

2. After the death of Indutiomarus, related above, his command was transferred by the Treveri to members of his family, who persisted in trying to obtain the support of the nearest German tribes by promises of money. Failing in this, they made overtures to more distant tribes, a number of which consented. The alliance was confirmed by an exchange of oaths, and hostages were given as security for the payment of the money. Ambiorix also was admitted as a partner to the league. Caesar was informed of these intrigues, and saw warlike preparations going on all around. The Nervii,

Atuatuci, and Menapii, together with all the tribes of German origin on the west bank of the Rhine, were in arms; the Senones refused to attend at his bidding, and were concerting plans with the Carnutes and others of their neighbours; and the Treveri were sending embassy after embassy to obtain German aid. He therefore decided that he must take the field in advance of the usual season.

3. Accordingly, before the winter was over, he assembled the four nearest legions and made an unexpected attack on the country of the Nervii. Before they could either concentrate their forces or flee, a large number of cattle and prisoners were captured and handed over as booty to the soldiers; the country was ravaged, and the Nervii forced to surrender and give hostages. After this quick success Caesar took the legions back into winter quarters. In the early spring he convoked the usual Gallic council, which was attended by all those summoned except the Senones, Carnutes, and Treveri. He regarded their non-appearance as the first step towards an armed revolt, and in order to make it clear that he considered its suppression of paramount importance, he decided to transfer the meeting to Lutetia, a town of the Parisii. They inhabited a territory adjoining that of the Senones, and a generation before had united with them to form one state; but they appeared to have had no hand in the present policy of the Senones. After announcing his decision from the platform in his camp, Caesar started with his legions the same day and made his way by forced marches to the country of the Senones.

4. On learning of his approach, Acco, the ringleader of the conspiracy, ordered the population to gather in their strongholds. Before they had time to complete this operation they heard that the Romans were at hand. The Senones had no choice but to abandon their project and send envoys to ask Caesar's pardon. These were introduced by the Aedui, under whose protection their tribe had been from ancient times. Caesar willingly pardoned them at the request of the Aedui and accepted their excuses; for he thought that the summer should be devoted to the impending war, and not wasted in holding an inquest. He ordered them, however, to provide a hundred hostages, whom he entrusted to the custody of the Aedui. The Carnutes, too, sent envoys and hostages while Caesar was in the district, pleading their cause with the support of

the Remi, whose dependants they were, and received the same reply. Caesar then completed the business of the council and requisitioned cavalry from the various tribes.

5. Now that this part of Gaul was tranquillized, Caesar devoted all his energies to the war against the Treveri and Ambiorix. He bade Cavarinus accompany him with the cavalry of the Senones, lest his hasty temper or the hatred that he had earned should cause trouble in the tribe. Then, since he felt certain that Ambiorix did not intend to fight a battle, he cast about to discover what other plans he might have.

Close to the Eburones and protected by a continuous line of marshes and forests dwelt the Menapii, the only Gallic people who had never sent envoys to Caesar to sue for peace. He knew that Ambiorix was united to them by ties of hospitality and also that, through the agency of the Treveri, he had formed an alliance with the Germans. He thought it advisable to deprive Ambiorix of these allies before attacking him directly, for fear desperation should make him hide among the Menapii or join the tribes beyond the Rhine. Therefore, after sending the baggage of the entire army to Labienus' camp in the country of the Treveri and ordering two legions to proceed there too, he started himself for the territory of the Menapii with five legions in light marching order. The Menapii did not collect any troops, but relying on the protection of the terrain took refuge with all their belongings in the forests and marshes.

6. Caesar put Fabius and the quaestor Marcus Crassus in command of detachments, and the three columns advanced with the aid of hastily constructed causeways, burning farms and villages, and taking a large number of cattle and prisoners. By this means the Menapii were compelled to send envoys to sue for peace. Caesar took the hostages they offered and told them that he would treat them as enemies if they admitted Ambiorix or his agents into their territory. With this warning, he left Commius the Atrebatian with a force of cavalry to keep the Menapii under surveillance, while he marched against the Treveri.

7. Meanwhile the Treveri had collected large forces of infantry and cavalry and were preparing to attack Labienus and the single legion which was wintering in their territory. They were within

two days' march of his camp, when they heard of the arrival of the
two legions dispatched to him by Caesar and, encamping at a
distance of fifteen miles, they decided to wait for reinforcements
from the Germans. Apprised of their intention, Labienus hoped
that their imprudence would give him some opportunity of bringing
them to action. He left five cohorts to guard the baggage, marched
against the enemy with the other twenty-five and a strong force of
cavalry, and entrenched a camp a mile away from them.

Between the two camps was a river with steep banks, difficult to
cross; Labienus had no intention of crossing it himself and did not
think the enemy would. The Gauls' hope of being reinforced was
increasing daily, and Labienus purposely let the soldiers hear him
say that, since the Germans were said to be approaching, he would
not jeopardize their safety and his own by remaining, but would
break up the camp next morning at dawn. This remark was soon
reported to the enemy, since among the large number of Gallic
horsemen it was only natural that there should be some who
sympathized with their fellow countrymen's cause. At night
Labienus summoned the military tribunes and first-grade centurions and explained his plans; then, to help in making the enemy
think they were afraid, he ordered the camp to be broken up with
more noise and disturbance than is customary with Roman armies,
and so made his departure resemble a flight. This also was reported
to the Gauls by their patrols before daybreak, for the camps were
very close together.

8. They urged one another not to let the hoped-for prize slip
from their grasp: to wait for German aid when the Romans were
panic-stricken would mean unnecessary delay and with such a large
army it would be disgraceful to shrink from attacking a mere
handful of men, especially men who were running away and
hampered by baggage. Accordingly, when the rearguard of the
Roman column had barely got outside the entrenchment, they
boldly began to cross the river and join battle in an unfavourable
position. Labienus had expected this, and enticed them all across
by continuing to advance slowly, keeping up the pretence that he
was marching away. Then, sending the baggage a short distance
ahead and parking it on a piece of rising ground, he said to the
soldiers: 'Here is your chance. You have got the enemy where you

wanted them – in a bad position, where they are not free to manoeuvre. Fight as bravely under me as you often have under the commander-in-chief; imagine that he is here, watching the battle in person.' With these words he bade the units turn to face the enemy and form a line of battle, sent a few squadrons of cavalry to protect the baggage, and posted the rest on the flanks. The men at once raised a shout and launched their spears.

The enemy were amazed to see the enemy that they thought to be in flight advancing to the attack. They had not the courage to face its charge; directly the lines met, they turned tail and made for the nearest woods. Labienus hunted them down with his cavalry, killing many of them and taking a number of prisoners, and a few days later had recovered his hold over the tribe; for the Germans who were coming to aid them returned home when they found the Treveri routed. The relatives of Indutiomarus who had instigated the revolt fled the country and went along with the Germans. Cingetorix, who had remained loyal right from the outset, was invested with civil and military control of the tribe.

2 The second crossing of the Rhine (53 B.C.)

9. After marching from the country of the Menapii to that of the Treveri, Caesar determined to cross the Rhine for two reasons: first, because the Germans had sent the Treveri reinforcements to use against him; secondly, to prevent Ambiorix's finding an asylum in Germany. He therefore proceeded to build a bridge a little above the place where he had crossed before. As the method of construction was familiar to the soldiers from the previous occasion, they were able by energetic efforts to complete the task in a few days. Leaving a strong guard on the Gallic side of the bridge to prevent any sudden rising on the part of the Treveri, he led across the remainder of his forces, including the cavalry. The Ubii, who had previously given hostages and submitted, sent envoys to clear themselves by explaining that they had not broken their word: the aid sent to the Treveri did not come from their state. They begged him to spare them, and not to let an indiscriminate animosity against the Germans make the innocent suffer for the guilty; if he

wanted more hostages they should be given. On investigating the matter he found that the reinforcements had been sent by the Suebi. He therefore accepted the Ubii's explanation and made careful inquiry about the routes leading to the territory of the Suebi.

10. A few days later Caesar was told by the Ubii that the Suebi were concentrating all their forces and calling upon their subject tribes to furnish contingents of infantry and cavalry. Thereupon he arranged for a supply of grain, selected a suitable site for a camp, and directed the Ubii to remove their cattle and transfer all their possessions from the fields into their strongholds, hoping that the ignorant and uncivilized Germans might be induced by shortage of food to fight a battle on unequal terms. He also told the Ubii to keep sending scouts into Suebic territory and find out what the enemy were about. The Ubii carried out these instructions, and a few days later reported that on the receipt of reliable information about the Roman army all the Suebi had retired, with the whole of their forces and those which they had raised from their allies, to the farthest extremity of their country, where there was an immense forest called Bacenis, stretching far into the interior and forming a natural barrier between the Suebi and the Cherusci, which prevented them from raiding and damaging each other's territory. On the edge of this forest, they said, the Suebi had resolved to await the arrival of the Romans.

3 Customs and institutions of the Gauls

11. At this point, it seems not inappropriate to give an account of the customs of the Gauls and the Germans and the differences between these peoples.

In Gaul, not only every tribe, canton, and subdivision of a canton, but almost every family, is divided into rival factions.[43] At the head of these factions are men who are regarded by their followers as having particularly great prestige, and these have the final say on all questions that come up for judgement and in all discussions of policy. The object of this ancient custom seems to have been to ensure that all the common people should have protection against the strong; for each leader sees that no one gets the better of his supporters by force or by cunning – or, if he fails to do so, is utterly discredited.

The same principle holds good in intertribal politics: all the tribes are grouped in two factions.

12. At the time of Caesar's arrival, these were headed respectively by the Aedui and the Sequani. As the Aedui had long enjoyed very great prestige and had many satellite tribes, the Sequani were the weaker of the two, depending on their own resources. They therefore secured the alliance of Ariovistus and his Germans, at the cost of heavy sacrifices and the promise of still further concessions [70–65 B.C.]. Then, as a result of several victories in which all the Aeduans of rank were killed, the Sequani became so much stronger than their rivals that they were able to bring over to their side a considerable part of the Aeduan dependencies, and to make the Aeduans surrender the sons of their chiefs as hostages and swear to form no hostile designs against the Sequani. They had also seized and retained a part of the Aeduan territory that lay near their own frontier and had in fact established a hegemony over the whole of Gaul. Reduced to this extremity, Diviciacus the Aeduan went to Rome to solicit aid from the Senate, but returned without success [61 B.C.].

Caesar's arrival changed the situation: the Aedui had their hostages restored to them, and not only regained their former dependencies but acquired new ones with Caesar's help, because those who became their allies found that they were better off and more equitably governed than before. In other respects, too, their influence and standing were enhanced, and the Sequani lost their supremacy. Their place was taken by the Remi; and as it was known that they stood as high in Caesar's favour as the Aedui, tribes which on account of old feuds could not be induced to join the Aedui were placing themselves under the protection of the Remi, who by taking good care of them were able to maintain the unaccustomed power that they had suddenly acquired. At this time, therefore, the position was that, while the Aedui were acknowledged to be easily ahead of all the other tribes, the Remi came next in importance.

13. Everywhere in Gaul there are only two classes of men who

are of any account or consideration. The common people are
treated almost as slaves, never venture to act on their own initiative,
and are not consulted on any subject. Most of them, crushed by
debt or heavy taxation or the oppression of more powerful persons,
bind themselves to serve men of rank, who exercise over them all
the rights that masters have over slaves. The two privileged classes
are the Druids[44] and the knights. The Druids officiate at the
worship of the gods, regulate public and private sacrifices, and give
rulings on all religious questions. Large numbers of young men
flock to them for instruction, and they are held in great honour by
the people. They act as judges in practically all disputes, whether
between tribes or between individuals; when any crime is committed, or a murder takes place, or a dispute arises about an inheritance
or a boundary, it is they who adjudicate the matter and appoint the
compensation to be paid and received by the parties concerned.
Any individual or tribe failing to accept their award is banned from
taking part in sacrifice – the heaviest punishment that can be
inflicted upon a Gaul. Those who are laid under such a ban are
regarded as impious criminals. Everyone shuns them and avoids
going near or speaking to them, for fear of taking some harm by
contact with what is unclean; if they appear as plaintiffs, justice is
denied them, and they are excluded from a share in any honour.
All the Druids are under one head, whom they hold in the highest
respect. On his death, if any one of the rest is of outstanding merit,
he succeeds to the vacant place; if several have equal claims, the
Druids usually decide the election by voting, though sometimes
they actually fight it out. On a fixed date in each year they hold a
session in a consecrated spot in the country of the Carnutes, which
is supposed to be the centre of Gaul. Those who are involved in
disputes assemble here from all parts, and accept the Druids'
judgements and awards. The Druidic doctrine is believed to have
been found existing in Britain and thence imported into Gaul; even
today those who want to make a profound study of it generally go
to Britain for the purpose.

14. The Druids are exempt from military service and do not pay
taxes like other citizens. These important privileges are naturally
attractive: many present themselves of their own accord to become
students of Druidism, and others are sent by their parents or

relatives. It is said that these pupils have to memorize a great number of verses – so many, that some of them spend twenty years at their studies. The Druids believe that their religion forbids them to commit their teachings to writing, although for most other purposes, such as public and private accounts, the Gauls use the Greek alphabet. But I imagine that this rule was originally established for other reasons – because they did not want their doctrine to become public property, and in order to prevent their pupils from relying on the written word and neglecting to train their memories; for it is usually found that when people have the help of texts, they are less diligent in learning by heart, and let their memories rust. A lesson which they take particular pains to inculcate is that the soul does not perish, but after death passes from one body to another; they think that this is the best incentive to bravery, because it teaches men to disregard the terrors of death. They also hold long discussions about the heavenly bodies and their movements, the size of the universe and of the earth, the physical constitution of the world, and the power and properties of the gods; and they instruct the young men in all these subjects.

15. The second class is that of the knights.[45] When their services are required in some war that has broken out – and before Caesar's arrival in the country the Gallic states used to fight offensive or defensive wars almost every year – these all take the field, surrounded by their servants and retainers, of whom each knight has a greater or smaller number according to his birth and fortune. The possession of such a following is the only criterion of position and power that they recognize.

16. As a nation the Gauls are extremely superstitious; and so persons suffering from serious diseases, as well as those who are exposed to the perils of battle, offer, or vow to offer, human sacrifices, for the performance of which they employ Druids. They believe that the only way of saving a man's life is to propitiate the god's wrath by rendering another life in its place, and they have regular state sacrifices of the same kind. Some tribes have colossal images made of wickerwork, the limbs of which they fill with living men; they are then set on fire, and the victims burnt to death. They think that the gods prefer the execution of men taken in the act of theft or brigandage, or guilty of some offence; but when they

run short of criminals, they do not hesitate to make up with innocent men.

17. The god they reverence most is Mercury. They have very many images of him, and regard him as the inventor of all arts, the god who directs men upon their journeys, and their most powerful helper in trading and getting money. Next to him they reverence Apollo, Mars, Jupiter, and Minerva, about whom they have much the same ideas as other nations – that Apollo averts illness, and Minerva teaches the principles of industries and handicrafts; that Jupiter is king of the gods, and Mars the lord of war. When they have decided to fight a battle they generally vow to Mars the booty that they hope to take, and after a victory they sacrifice the captured animals and collect the rest of the spoil in one spot. Among many of the tribes, high piles of it can be seen on consecrated ground; and it is an almost unknown thing for anyone to dare, in defiance of religious law, to conceal his booty at home or to remove anything placed on the piles. Such a crime is punishable by a terrible death under torture.

18. The Gauls claim all to be descended from Father Dis,[46] declaring that this is the tradition preserved by the Druids. For this reason they measure periods of time not by days but by nights; and in celebrating birthdays, the first of the month, and new year's day, they go on the principle that the day begins at night. As regards the other usages of daily life, the chief difference between them and other peoples is that their children are not allowed to go up to their fathers in public until they are old enough for military service; they regard it as unbecoming for a son who is still a boy to stand in his father's sight in a public place.

19. When a Gaul marries he adds to the dowry that his wife brings with her a portion of his own property estimated to be of equal value. A joint account is kept of the whole amount, and the profits which it earns are put aside; and when either dies, the survivor receives both shares together with the accumulated profits. Husbands have power of life and death over their wives as well as their children. When a high-born head of a family dies, his relatives assemble, and if the circumstances of his death are suspicious, they examine his widow under torture, as we examine slaves; if her guilt is established, she is consigned to the flames and put to death with

the most cruel torments. Gallic funerals are splendid and costly, for a comparatively poor country. Everything that the dead man is supposed to have been fond of, including even animals, is placed upon his pyre; and not long ago there were people still alive who could remember the time when slaves and retainers known to have been beloved by their masters were burnt with them at the conclusion of the funeral rites.

20. The tribes which are considered to manage their affairs best have a law that if anyone hears from a neighbouring country any rumour or news that concerns the State, he is to communicate it to a magistrate without speaking of it to anyone else; for experience has shown that impulsive and ignorant persons are often frightened by false reports into subversive action, and meddle with important affairs of state. The magistrates suppress what they think it advisable to keep secret, and publish only what they deem it expedient for the people to know. The discussion of politics is forbidden except in a public assembly.

4 Customs and institutions of the Germans

21. The customs of the Germans are entirely different. They have no Druids to control religious observances and are not much given to sacrifices. The only beings they recognize as gods are things that they can see, and by which they are obviously benefited, such as Sun, Moon, and Fire; the other gods they have never even heard of. They spend all their lives in hunting and warlike pursuits, and inure themselves from childhood to toil and hardship. Those who preserve their chastity longest are most highly commended by their friends; for they think that continence makes young men taller, stronger, and more muscular. To have had intercourse with a woman before the age of twenty is considered perfectly scandalous. They attempt no concealment, however, of the facts of sex: men and women bathe together in the rivers, and they wear nothing but hides or short garments of hairy skin, which leave most of the body bare.

22. The Germans are not agriculturalists, and live principally on milk, cheese, and meat. No one possesses any definite amount

of land as private property; the magistrates and tribal chiefs annually assign a holding to clans and groups of kinsmen or others living together, fixing its size and position at their discretion, and the following year make them move on somewhere else. They give many reasons for this custom: for example, that their men may not get accustomed to living in one place, lose their warlike enthusiasm, and take up agriculture instead; that they may not be anxious to acquire large estates, and the strong be tempted to dispossess the weak; to prevent their paying too much attention to building houses that will protect them from cold and heat, or becoming too fond of money – a frequent cause of division and strife; and to keep the common people contented and quiet by letting every man see that even the most powerful are no better off than himself.

23. The various tribes regard it as their greatest glory to lay waste as much as possible of the land around them and to keep it uninhabited. They hold it a proof of a people's valour to drive their neighbours from their homes, so that no one dare settle near them, and also think it gives them greater security by removing any fear of sudden invasion. When a tribe is attacked or intends to attack another, officers are chosen to conduct the campaign and invested with powers of life and death. In peacetime there is no central magistracy; the chiefs of the various districts and cantons administer justice and settle disputes among their own people. No discredit attaches to plundering raids outside the tribal frontiers; the Germans say that they serve to keep the young men in training and prevent them from getting lazy. When a chief announces in an assembly his intention of leading a raid and calls for volunteers, those who like the proposal, and approve of the man who makes it, stand up and promise their assistance amid the applause of the whole gathering; anyone who backs out afterwards is looked on as a deserter and a traitor and no one will ever trust him again. To wrong a guest is impious in their eyes. They shield from injury all who come to their houses for any purpose whatever, and treat their persons as sacred; guests are welcomed to every man's home and table.

24. There was a time when the Gauls were more warlike than the Germans, when they actually invaded German territory, and sent colonists across the Rhine because their own country was too

small to support its large population. It was in this way that the most fertile district of Germany, in the neighbourhood of the Hercynian forest (which I see was known to Eratosthenes and other Greeks, who call it Orcynia) was seized and occupied by the Volcae Tectosages, who remain there to this day and have a high reputation for fair dealing and gallantry. Nowadays, while the Germans still endure the same life of poverty and privation as before, without any change in their diet or clothing, the Gauls, through living near the Roman Province and becoming acquainted with sea-borne products, are abundantly supplied with various commodities. Gradually accustomed to inferiority and defeated in many battles, they do not even pretend to compete with the Germans in bravery.

25. This Hercynian forest is so wide that it takes a lightly equipped traveller nine days to cross it; this is the only way the Germans have of estimating its size, as they know nothing of measures of length. Starting from the frontiers of the Helvetii, Nemetes, and Rauraci, it runs straight along the Danube to the country of the Dacians and the Anartes. At this point it turns north-east away from the river, and in its huge length extends through the territories of many different peoples. No western German claims to have reached its eastern extremity, even after travelling for two months, or to have heard where it ends. The forest is known to contain many kinds of animals not seen elsewhere, some of which seem worthy of mention because they differ greatly from those found in other countries.

26. There is an ox shaped like a deer, with a single horn in the middle of its forehead between the ears, which sticks up higher and straighter than those of the animals we know, and at the top branches out widely like a man's hand or a tree. The male and female are alike, and their horns are of the same shape and size.

27. There are also animals called elks, which resemble goats in shape and in their piebald colouring, but are somewhat larger, and have stunted horns and legs without joints or knuckles. They do not lie down to rest, and if they fall by accident, cannot get up or raise themselves from the ground. Trees serve them as resting-places: they support themselves against the trunks and rest in that way, leaning over only slightly. When the hunters have found out their usual retreats by following their tracks, they either sever the

roots of all the surrounding trees or cut nearly through the trunks, so that they only *look* as if they are still standing firm. When the elks lean against them as usual, they push over the insecure trunks with their weight, and fall down with them.[47]

28. A third species is the aurochs, an animal somewhat smaller than the elephant, with the appearance, colour, and shape of a bull. They are very strong and agile, and attack every man and beast they catch sight of. The natives take great pains to trap them in pits, and then kill them. This arduous sport toughens the young men and keeps them in training; and those who kill the largest number exhibit the horns in public to show what they have done, and earn high praise. It is impossible to domesticate or tame the aurochs, even if it is caught young. The horns are much larger than those of our oxen, and of quite different shape and appearance. The Germans prize them greatly: they mount the rims with silver and use them as drinking-cups at their grandest banquets.

5 Devastation of the country of the Eburones (53 B.C.)

29. Learning from the scouts of the Ubii that the Suebi had retired into the forests, Caesar was afraid that if he followed them he might run short of corn, since, as already said, none of the Germans pay much attention to agriculture. He therefore decided to advance no farther.[48] However, so as not to let the natives think they had seen the last of him, he left the greater part of the bridge standing. In order to hold up any reinforcements which they might try to send to Gaul, after withdrawing his army he broke down the end that touched the Ubian bank for a distance of two hundred feet, and at the Gallic end erected a four-storeyed tower, posted a detachment of twelve cohorts to protect the bridge and fortified the position with strong defence works. A young officer named Gaius Volcacius Tullus was placed in command of it.

When the crops were beginning to ripen Caesar set out through the Ardennes to fight Ambiorix. He sent Lucius Minucius Basilus in advance with all the cavalry, to see if he could gain any advantage by travelling quickly and striking at a favourable opportunity.

Caesar told him to forbid fires to be lighted in his camps, so as not to give the enemy warning of his approach from a distance, and promised to follow him immediately.

30. Basilus duly carried out his instructions. Completing the journey more quickly than anyone had thought possible, he surprised a number of Eburones working in the fields, and following their directions hurried on to a place where Ambiorix, guarded only by a few horsemen, was said to be. Much depends on fortune, in war, as in all other things. It was a lucky chance that enabled Basilus to catch Ambiorix unprepared and off his guard and to appear on the scene before his approach was reported or even rumoured. But by an equally great stroke of luck Ambiorix escaped alive, although he lost all the military equipment that he had with him, his carriages, and his horses. His house was in a wood, like most Gallic houses – for they generally choose sites near woods and rivers, to avoid the heat. So, fighting in a confined space, his attendants and friends were able to resist the attack of Basilus' cavalry for a time. Meanwhile, one of them mounted him on a horse, and his flight was covered by the wood. In this way he was first brought into danger, and then delivered from it, by the all-prevailing power of fortune.

31. Ambiorix did not assemble his troops – either on purpose, because he thought it better not to give battle, or through lack of time, because his plans were upset by the sudden arrival of the Roman cavalry, which he assumed would be followed up by the rest of the army. At all events he sent out messengers through the countryside, bidding every man shift for himself. Some fled into the Ardennes, others into a continuous belt of marshes, while those who lived nearest the sea hid in places cut off from the mainland at high tide. Many left their own country and entrusted their lives and all their possessions to complete strangers. Catuvolcus, who as king of one half of the Eburones had joined in Ambiorix's enterprise, was now a weak old man, unable to face the hardships of war or flight; solemnly cursing Ambiorix for having suggested the plan, he poisoned himself with yew, a tree which is very common in Gaul and Germany.

32. The Segni and Condrusi, peoples of Germanic origin and generally counted as Germans, living between the Eburones and

the Treveri, sent ambassadors to ask Caesar not to regard them as enemies and not to assume that all the Germans in Gaul were leagued together against him. They said that they had never thought of making war upon him, and had not sent any help to Ambiorix. After confirming their statements by interrogating prisoners, Caesar ordered them to bring to him any Eburonian fugitives who had come to their country; if they obeyed, he would respect their territory.

He then separated his forces into three divisions and took all the heavy baggage to Atuatuca, a fortress situated about in the middle of the country of the Eburones, where Sabinus and Cotta had had their winter quarters. He had several reasons for selecting this place: the principal one was that the fortifications constructed in the previous year were still intact, which would save the soldiers the labour of building new ones. He left the baggage under the protection of the 14th legion, one of the three which he had recently brought from Italy, where they had been levied. He placed this legion and the camp in charge of Cicero, assigning him also two hundred cavalry.

33. After dividing the army, Caesar ordered Labienus to advance with three legions towards the coast, into the region bordering on the country of the Menapii, and sent Trebonius with three more to ravage the district lying on the frontiers of the Atuatuci. He took the remaining three himself, and decided to march to the river Scheldt, which flows into the Meuse,[49] and to the western end of the Ardennes, where he heard Ambiorix had gone with a small number of cavalry. Before setting out he promised to return in a week, when a distribution of rations to the legion left at the fortress would be due. He asked Labienus and Trebonius to return by the same date if the military situation allowed, so that after holding a further discussion they might be able to restart the campaign on new lines, in the light of what they would have learnt by that time of the enemy's plans.

34. It has been explained that the Eburones had no regular force assembled, no stronghold, and no garrison capable of armed resistance: their population was scattered in all directions. Each man had installed himself in any remote glen, any wooded spot, or impenetrable morass, that offered a chance of protection or escape.

These hiding-places were known to the natives living in the neighbourhood, and great care was needed to ensure the safety of the Roman troops. So long as they kept together, they were in no danger from a panic-stricken and scattered enemy; but losses severe enough to weaken the army might easily be sustained by the waylaying of individual soldiers, who were tempted far afield by the hope of plunder, or got separated from the rest because the ill-defined and half-concealed paths through the woods were not practicable for columns in close formation. The only way to make an end of the business, and exterminate this race of criminals, would have been to break up the army into a large number of detachments which could be sent out separately. But it was safer to keep the companies in their regular formation, according to the established practice of the Roman army, although this meant that they could not injure the Gauls in such country. Even so, any men who strayed apart from the main body were liable to be ambushed and surrounded by some of the bolder spirits among them. In these difficult circumstances the most careful precautions were taken; Caesar thought it better to let the enemy off comparatively lightly, in spite of the men's burning desire for revenge, than to punish them severely at the cost of serious loss to his own troops. He preferred to expose Gauls, instead of Roman legionaries, to the dangers of fighting in the forests, and also wanted to envelop the Eburones with a great multitude of men, in order to punish their heinous crime with total annihilation. Large numbers soon assembled from every side.

35. While the whole of the Eburonian territory was being plundered, it was getting near the day on which Caesar had intended to return to the legion left in charge of the baggage. At this moment an instance occurred of the important part played in war by accident, which can have far-reaching consequences. After the panic-stricken flight of the enemy, already described, there was no hostile force in the field to give the slightest occasion for alarm. But the Germans across the Rhine heard that the Eburones were being plundered, and that all comers were invited to share the spoil. Immediately a force of two thousand cavalry was raised by the Sugambri, who live close to the Rhine – the people who, as said above, sheltered the fugitive Tenctheri and Usipetes. They crossed

149

the river on boats and rafts, some thirty miles below the place where Caesar's bridge had been built and the garrison left, entered the territory of the Eburones, caught a number of the scattered fugitives and seized a quantity of cattle – a prize much sought after by the barbarians. Lured on by the hope of more plunder, they advanced farther; for these born fighters and bandits were not to be stopped by marshes or forests. On asking their prisoners where Caesar was, they were told that he had started on a campaign some distance away, and that all the army had left the district. One of the prisoners added: 'Why go after this paltry miserable loot, when you have the chance of making your fortunes right away? In three hours you can reach Atuatuca, where the Romans have stored all their property. The garrison is so small that they can't even man the wall, and not a man dare set foot outside the entrenchments.' The offer of such a chance decided the Germans. They hid the booty they had got, and guided by their informant made straight for Atuatuca.

36. Throughout the previous week Cicero had been most careful to keep the soldiers in camp according to Caesar's instructions, not allowing even a single servant to go outside the entrenchment. But on the seventh day he began to fear that Caesar would not keep his appointment; it was said that he had advanced a long way, and there was no news of his return. The soldiers, too, were grumbling at Cicero's patient acceptance of the situation: to be cooped up like this in camp, they said, was almost as bad as a blockade. With nine legions and a strong cavalry force in the field, and the enemy scattered and very nearly destroyed, he had no reason to expect a serious accident within three miles of his camp. Accordingly he sent five cohorts to get corn from the nearest fields, which were separated from the camp by only a single hill. A number of sick men had been left behind by the legions; from these there went with the cohorts, as a separate detachment, some three hundred men who had recovered from illness during the week, and permission to accompany them was granted also to a large number of servants, who took out a great many of the animals that were being kept in the camp.

37. It happened that just at this moment the German cavalry appeared and, riding right on without slackening speed, tried to

break in by the back gate. As the view was obstructed by woods on that side, they were not seen until they were quite close to the camp – so close that the traders who had their tents at the foot of the rampart had no time to get away. The suddenness of the attack upset the soldiers, and the cohort on guard had difficulty in withstanding the first rush. The enemy spread out all round, trying to find a way in. The soldiers had hard work to defend the gates; elsewhere the lie of the land and the entrenchments gave protection. The whole camp was in a state of alarm; the men were asking one another the cause of the disturbance, and could not tell where to assemble or in which direction to advance. Some said the camp was already taken; others maintained that the Germans had come in triumph after destroying the Roman army and its commander-in-chief. Most of them were filled with strange superstitious fancies suggested by the spot on which they stood, and saw in imagination the disaster that had befallen Cotta and Sabinus, who perished not far from that same fort. Everyone was so paralysed by fear that the Germans believed the prisoner had spoken the truth when he told them that there was no garrison in the camp. They strove hard to force their way in, calling on one another not to let such a piece of luck slip through their fingers.

38. Among the sick men left with the garrison was Baculus, who had served under Caesar as chief centurion of his legion, and has been mentioned in connection with earlier engagements. For five days he had been too ill to eat. Feeling anxious for his own and his comrades' safety, he walked unarmed out of his tent, and, on seeing the enemy close at hand and the situation extremely critical, borrowed arms from the nearest soldiers and posted himself in the gateway. He was joined by the centurions of the cohort on guard, and for a time they fought together to hold the enemy's attack. Baculus was severely wounded and fainted, and the others just managed to save him by passing him back from hand to hand. This respite gave the rest of the troops time to recover courage enough to man the fortifications and make a show of defence.

39. Meanwhile the reaping party, which had finished its work, heard the shouting at the camp. The horsemen hurried on, and discovered how serious the peril was. Out there in the open there was no fortification to shelter the frightened men – raw recruits

without any experience – and they turned to the military tribune and centurions, waiting to be told what to do; even the bravest were unnerved by the emergency. The Germans caught sight of the standards in the distance, and desisted from their attack on the camp. At first they thought it was the legions, returned from the distant expedition on which the prisoners said they had gone; but when they saw how small the force was, they regarded it with contempt and attacked from all sides.[50]

40. The servants ran forward to the nearest rising ground, from which they were quickly dislodged and, by rushing to the standards round which the companies were formed up, increased the nervous soldiers' alarm. Since the camp was so near, some were for adopting a wedge formation and making a quick dash through, feeling confident that, though a few might be surrounded and killed, the rest could escape. Others preferred to make a stand on the hill, and all take their chance together. The latter plan was rejected by the detachment of veterans which had gone out with the cohorts. The veterans, therefore, with words of mutual encouragement, advanced under their commander Gaius Trebonius, a Roman knight, broke right through the enemy, and reached the camp without a single casualty. Close behind them, in the gap made by their courageous charge, the servants and the cavalry got safely through. But those who had taken their stand on the hill showed that they had still learnt nothing of the art of war: they failed either to stick to the plan they had chosen of defending themselves on the high ground, or to imitate the swift and vigorous action which they could see had saved their comrades. Instead, in an attempt to regain the camp, they let themselves be caught in a bad position on low-lying ground. The centurions, some of whom had been promoted for gallantry from lower grades in other legions to the higher grades in this one, were determined not to forfeit the reputation they had won in previous actions, and fell fighting with the utmost courage. Some of the soldiers were saved by the centurions' brave stand, which made the enemy fall back, and – to their surprise – reached the camp in safety. The rest were surrounded by the enemy and killed.

41. As the Germans saw that the Roman troops had now manned the fortifications, they gave up hope of taking the camp by storm,

and retired across the Rhine with the booty that they had hidden in the woods. Even after their departure, the defenders were still so frightened that Volusenus, who was sent ahead by Caesar with the cavalry and arrived that night in the camp, could not make them believe that Caesar was close at hand, with his army safe and sound. Fear had so completely possessed them all that they nearly took leave of their senses, and would have it that the whole army had been cut to pieces, and that the cavalry had managed to escape by flight: if the army were not destroyed, they maintained, the Germans would never have attacked the camp. The panic was eventually stopped by Caesar's arrival.

42. He was well aware of the way things happen in war, and on his return made only one criticism – that the cohorts had been allowed to leave their post in the garrison: Cicero should have avoided running even the slightest risk.[51] For the rest, he recognized that what had happened was largely the result of accident: it was a strange chance that had brought the enemy to the camp so suddenly, and a still stranger chance that had sent them away when they were almost masters of the rampart and gates. And the strangest thing of all was that although their object in crossing the Rhine was to plunder Ambiorix's country, circumstances had led them to attack the Roman camp instead, and thus render Ambiorix the greatest service he could have desired.

43. Setting out once more to harass the Eburones, Caesar sent out in all directions a large force of cavalry that he had collected from the neighbouring tribes. Every village and every building they saw was set on fire; all over the country the cattle were either slaughtered or driven off as booty; and the crops, a part of which had already been laid flat by the autumnal rains, were consumed by the great numbers of horses and men. It seemed certain, therefore, that even if some of the inhabitants had escaped for the moment by hiding, they must die of starvation after the retirement of the troops. With such a large number of horsemen scouring the country in separate parties, it happened time and again that prisoners were taken who had just seen Ambiorix in flight; they would actually look round to see where he was, insisting that he was barely out of sight. This raised his pursuers' hopes of running him down, and so standing high in Caesar's favour. They took

endless pains and made almost superhuman efforts. But they always seemed just to have missed what they so ardently desired; Ambiorix would escape by hiding in a wood or ravine, and under cover of night would make off in some new direction, escorted only by four horsemen – for to no one else did he dare entrust his life.

44. After ravaging the country in this way, Caesar withdrew his army – minus the two cohorts of Cicero's legion which had been lost – to Durocortorum, a town of the Remi, where he convened a Gallic council and held an inquiry into the conspiracy of the Senones and Carnutes. Acco, the instigator of the plot, was condemned to death and executed in the ancient Roman manner.[52] Some others, who fled in fear of being brought to trial, were outlawed. Caesar then distributed the legions in winter quarters – two on the frontier of the Treveri, two among the Lingones, and the other six at Agedincum in the country of the Senones – and after provisioning them, since Gaul was quiet, set out for northern Italy as usual to hold his assizes.

BOOK VII
THE REBELLION OF
VERCINGETORIX

1 *The opening stage* (*52* B.C.)

1. On his arrival in Italy Caesar was told of the assassination of Publius Clodius, and of a senatorial decree ordering all Italians of military age to be sworn in. He proceeded to enrol recruits in all parts of the Cisalpine Province. The news of these events soon reached Gaul; and the Gauls, drawing what they thought was the natural inference, invented a story that Caesar was detained by the disturbances in Rome, where political strife was so acute, they said, that he could not rejoin his army. The prospect of such a chance spurred them into action. They were already smarting under their subjection to Rome, and now began to plan war with greater confidence and boldness. The leading men arranged meetings at secluded spots in the woods, where they spoke bitterly of the execution of Acco and pointed out that the same fate might befall them next. They complained of the miserable condition of the whole country and offered tempting rewards to induce some of their hearers to open hostilities and risk their lives for the liberty of Gaul. The first step, they said, was to contrive means of cutting Caesar off from his army before their plot was divulged. This could easily be done, because the legions would not dare to leave their winter quarters in the absence of their commander-in-chief, and he would not be able to reach them without an escort. In any case it was better to die in battle than to resign themselves to the loss of their ancient military glory and the liberty inherited from their ancestors.

2. These discussions ended with a declaration by the Carnutes that they were prepared to face any danger for the common cause, and would undertake to strike the first blow. As it was not possible at the moment to give mutual guarantee by exchange of hostages, for fear their design should be betrayed, the Carnutes called upon

the others to stack their military standards together – a most solemn rite, according to Gallic custom – and to bind themselves by an oath not to desert them when once hostilities were begun. The Carnutes were warmly congratulated by the assembly; all present took the oath and before separating fixed a date for the rising.

3. When the appointed day arrived, the Carnutes, led by two desperadoes named Gutuater and Conconnetodumnus, swooped down at a given signal on Cenabum, killed the Romans who had settled there for purposes of commerce – including Gaius Fufius Cita, a Roman knight of high standing, whom Caesar had put in charge of the commissariat – and plundered their property. Tidings of these events sped swiftly to all the tribes of Gaul; for when anything specially important or remarkable occurs, the people shout the news to one another through the countryside and villages, and others in turn take up the cry and pass it on to their neighbours. Thus, on the present occasion, what happened at Cenabum at dawn was known before eight o'clock at night in the country of the Arverni, about a hundred and fifty miles away.

4. There, the lead given by the Carnutes was followed by Vercingetorix, a very powerful young Arvernian, whose father Celtillus had held suzerainty over all Gaul, and had been put to death by his compatriots for seeking to make himself king. Assembling his retainers, Vercingetorix had no difficulty in exciting their passions, and the news of what was afoot soon brought others out in arms. An effort to restrain him was made by his uncle Gobannitio and other chiefs, who thought the enterprise too risky, and he was expelled from the town of Gergovia. Undeterred, however, he went round the countryside raising a band of vagabonds and beggars. With these at his back he was able to win over all the Arvernians whom he approached. Calling upon them to take up arms for the freedom of Gaul, he assembled a large force and succeeded in expelling the opponents by whom, not long before, he had been driven out himself. He was proclaimed king by his adherents, and sent embassies in every direction adjuring the tribes to keep faith. In a short time he had secured the support of the Senones, Parisii, Cadurci, Turoni, Aulerci, Lemovices, Andes, Pictones, and all the other

tribes of the west coast, who unanimously elected him comman-der-in-chief. Armed with this power, he ordered each tribe to give hostages, to bring a specified quota of troops at once, and to manufacture a specified quantity of arms by a certain date – paying particular attention to the cavalry arm. Himself a man of boundless energy, he terrorized waverers with the rigours of an iron discipline. Serious cases of disaffection were punished by torture and death at the stake, and even for a minor fault he would cut off a man's ears or gouge out one of his eyes and send him home to serve as a warning to others of the severe chastisement meted out to offenders.

5. By this terrorism he quickly raised an army, part of which he sent into the territory of the Ruteni under a Cadurcan of great daring named Lucterius. Vercingetorix himself marched against the Bituriges, who at his approach sent envoys to their overlords the Aedui, asking for help to enable them to offer a more effective resistance. On the advice of the generals whom Caesar had left with the army, the Aedui sent cavalry and infantry to aid the Bituriges. When these reached the Loire, however, the boundary between the Bituriges and the Aedui, they halted and after a few days turned back without venturing to cross it. The explanation they gave to the generals was that they were afraid of treachery on the part of the Bituriges, who, according to information they had received, had concerted a plan with the Arverni to cut them off on both sides if once they crossed the river. Whether they really acted for the reason they alleged, or from motives of treachery, I do not know for certain, and therefore do not feel justified in making a positive statement. On the departure of the Aedui, the Bituriges immediately joined forces with the Arverni.

6. By the time news of these events reached Caesar in Italy, the situation in Rome had improved, thanks to the resolute action of Pompey; and accordingly he set out for Gaul. On arriving he was faced with a difficult problem: how was he to rejoin his army? If he summoned the legions to the Transalpine Province, they would clearly have to fight a pitched battle on the march without him; and to travel across Gaul without an escort would mean risking his own life, since in the circumstances even the tribes that were apparently quiet could not be relied upon.

7. In the meantime Lucterius, the Cadurcan who had been sent to the Ruteni, induced them to join the Arverni. Advancing into the territories of the Nitiobroges and Gabali, he took hostages from both, and after assembling a strong force attempted to make a raid into the Province in the direction of Narbonne. Caesar decided that he must let everything else wait. Marching at once to the town, he reassured the frightened inhabitants and posted detachments of the garrison troops in the districts that lay near the point of attack, i.e. the part of the Province inhabited by the Ruteni, Volcae Arecomici, and Tolosates and the neighbourhood of Narbonne itself. He also ordered a part of the Provincial garrison and a fresh draft that he had brought from Italy to concentrate in the territory of the Helvii, which adjoins that of the Arverni.

8. These measures checked Lucterius and made him keep his distance, because he was afraid to venture into the area encircled by the Roman detachments. Accordingly Caesar joined the forces assembled in the country of the Helvii. The Cevennes mountains, which form a barrier between the Helvii and the Arverni, were at this season – the severest part of the winter – covered with very deep snow, and the passes blocked. But the soldiers cleared stretches of the path by shovelling away drifts up to six feet deep, and by prodigious exertions enabled Caesar to get across into the land of the Arverni. Taking them completely by surprise – for they thought that the Cevennes gave them as secure protection as a solid wall, since the passes had never been considered practicable even for single travellers at that time of year[53] – Caesar ordered his cavalry to scour the widest possible area and frighten the Gauls as much as they could. Rumours and dispatches soon brought the news to Vercingetorix, and in the greatest alarm all his Arvernian supporters came running to him, begging him to save them from ruin and not to let their country be pillaged by the enemy; they had a right to claim protection, they said, since it was obvious that they were now bearing the brunt of the attack. In response to their entreaties he moved his camp from the country of the Bituriges and marched towards that of the Arverni.

9. But Caesar stayed there only two days, because he had anticipated Vercingetorix's move. Then, on the pretext of collecting reinforcements and cavalry, he went away, leaving the troops

under the command of the young Brutus. He instructed him to send out the cavalry as far as possible in every direction, and announced that he would try not to be away from the camp longer than three days. After making these arrangements, to the great surprise of his escort he made his way post-haste to Vienne. There he picked up some fresh cavalry which he had sent on some time before, and without stopping night or day pushed on through the country of the Aedui into that of the Lingones, where two legions were wintering – for he thought it possible that the Aedui might go so far as to make an attempt on his life, and wished to forestall this by making all the speed he could. Directly he arrived at the winter camp, he sent word to the other legions, and had them all concentrated before the news of his coming could reach the Arverni. When he did get to know of it Vercingetorix led his army back into the country of the Bituriges, and from there marched to attack Gorgobina, a stronghold of the Boii, whom Caesar, after defeating them in the battle with the Helvetii, had established there under the suzerainty of the Aedui.

10. This move greatly embarrassed Caesar. If he kept the legions all together until the end of the winter and allowed a people subject to the Aedui to be overpowered without interference, it was only too likely that the whole of Gaul would desert his cause, since it would be evident that his friends could not look to him for protection. On the other hand, if he withdrew the troops from their quarters so early in the year, he might be hard put to it to supply them with food, owing to the difficulties of transport. He thought it better, however, to face any risk, rather than alienate all his supporters by submitting to such a loss of prestige. Accordingly he asked the Aedui to send up supplies, and sent forward a message to the Boii saying that he was on his way to their relief, and urging them to remain loyal and resist the enemy's attack courageously. Then, leaving two legions at Agedincum with the heavy baggage of the entire army, he set out for the country of the Boii.

11. The next day he reached Vellaunodunum, a stronghold of the Senones, and in order to facilitate the movement of supplies by ensuring that he left no enemy in his rear, laid siege to it. In two days he had encircled it with entrenchments, and on the third day the garrison sent out envoys to surrender. Caesar ordered them to

deposit all their arms in one place, bring out their horses, and give six hundred hostages. As he wanted to complete his journey to Gorgobina as soon as possible, he left Trebonius to see to the execution of these orders and himself set out for Cenabum, in the territory of the Carnutes. The Carnutes, who had only just heard of the siege of Vellaunodunum and expected that it would last some time, were engaged in collecting troops to send to the defence of Cenabum. Caesar reached this town in two days, but by the time he had encamped in front of it, it was too late to attack that day. He therefore directed the necessary preparations to be made for an assault on the next day, and as there was a bridge over the Loire right under the town walls, and he was afraid that the inhabitants might escape under cover of night, he ordered two legions to remain under arms all night.

Shortly before midnight the people of Cenabum moved silently out of the town and began to cross the river. Apprised of this by the patrols, Caesar set the gates on fire and sent inside the legions he had kept ready for action. The town was captured, and all but a very few of the enemy taken prisoner – for the narrow streets and bridge were blocked by the crowd of fugitives. After plundering and burning Cenabum, and distributing among his soldiers the booty it contained and the prisoners, Caesar marched across the Loire and made his way into the territory of the Bituriges.

12. At his approach Vercingetorix raised the siege of Gorgobina and marched to meet him. Caesar had laid siege to a stronghold of the Bituriges called Noviodunum, which lay upon his line of march, when envoys came to him from the garrison, begging him to pardon them and spare their lives. As he wanted to complete the campaign with the same speed that had already brought him so many successes, he granted their petition, ordering them to collect all their arms in one place, bring out their horses, and furnish hostages.

A part of the hostages had already been delivered up, and some centurions had been sent into the town with a small party of soldiers to collect the arms and horses, when the cavalry preceding Vercingetorix's main body was seen in the distance. Directly the besieged townsmen caught sight of it and thought there was a chance of being relieved, they raised a cheer and began to snatch up their arms, shut the gates, and man the wall. The centurions inside the town, realizing from the cheering that some fresh scheme was afoot, seized the gates sword in hand and got their men away without a single casualty.

13. Caesar ordered his Gallic cavalry out of camp and engaged Vercingetorix's horse; when the cavalry got into difficulties, he reinforced it with four hundred German horsemen whom he had kept with his army from the start of this campaign. Their charge overpowered the enemy, who were put to flight and fell back with heavy loss on their main body. Their defeat made the defenders of Noviodunum change their minds once more. Terror-stricken, they laid hands on those they thought responsible for instigating the people against the Romans, hauled them off to Caesar, and surrendered. Noviodunum being thus disposed of, Caesar advanced on Avaricum, a very large and strongly defended town situated in a particularly fertile part of the Biturigan country, as he felt sure that its capture would secure the submission of the whole tribe.

2 Siege and capture of Avaricum (52 B.C.)

14. After this series of reverses at Vellaunodunum, Cenabum, and Noviodunum, Vercingetorix summoned his followers to a council of war and told them that their plan of campaign must be completely changed.

'We must strive by every means,' he said, 'to prevent the Romans from obtaining forage and supplies. This will be easy, since we are strong in cavalry and the season is in our favour. There is no grass to cut; so the enemy will be forced to send out parties to get hay from the barns, and our cavalry can go out every day and see that not a single one of them returns alive. What is more, when our lives are at stake we must be prepared to sacrifice our private possessions. Along the enemy's line of march we must burn all the villages and farms within the radius that their foragers can cover. We ourselves have plenty of supplies, because we can rely upon the resources of the people in whose territory the campaign is conducted; but the Romans will either succumb to starvation or have to expose themselves to serious risk by going far from their camp in search of food. We can either kill them or strip them of their baggage – which will be equally effective, since without it they cannot keep the field. We should also burn all the towns except those which are rendered impregnable by natural and artificial defences; otherwise they may serve as refuges for shirkers among our own numbers, and give the enemy the chance of looting the stores of provisions and other property that they contain. You may think these measures harsh and cruel, but you must admit that it would be a still harsher fate to have your wives and children carried off into slavery and be killed yourselves – which is what will inevitably befall you if you are conquered.'

15. This proposal was unanimously approved and in a single day more than twenty of the Bituriges' towns were fired. The same was done in the territory of the neighbouring tribes, until fires were visible in every direction; and although this was a grievous sorrow to all Gauls, they found consolation in the thought that victory was practically assured and that they would soon repair the loss. In a second joint council of war the question was debated whether Avaricum was to be burnt or defended. The Bituriges went down on their knees and implored the representatives of the other tribes not to compel them to set fire with their own hands to a town that was almost the finest in Gaul, the chief defence and pride of their state. It could easily be held, they said, in view of its natural strength; for it was almost completely surrounded by river and marsh, in which there was only one narrow opening. Their petition was granted – Vercingetorix, though he opposed it at first, was at length prevailed upon by their entreaties and by the general sympathy felt for them – and a careful choice was made of officers to defend the town.⁵⁴

16. Following Caesar's march by easy stages, Vercingetorix selected for his encampment a spot sixteen miles from Avaricum protected by marshes and forests. By an organized liaison service he was informed hourly of events at Avaricum and transmitted his orders accordingly. He was constantly on the watch for parties going out for forage or corn, and by attacking them when they were isolated – for they were obliged to go far afield – he inflicted heavy losses, although they tried everything they could think of to baffle him, setting out at irregular intervals and by different routes.

17. Caesar encamped on the side of the town where there was a narrow gap in the marshes and watercourses surrounding it, and began to build a siege terrace, form lines of mantlets, and erect two towers upon the terrace; for the lie of the land made it impossible to invest the place. To maintain a supply of corn he kept importuning the Boii and the Aedui; but the Aedui were lukewarm and gave little help, while the Boii, a small and feeble tribe, had only slender resources, which were quickly exhausted. The troops were brought to such straits by the inability of the Boii to relieve them and the indifference of the Aedui, as well as by the burning of the granaries, that for several days they had no grain and saved themselves from starvation only by bringing in cattle from distant villages. Yet not a word were they heard to utter that was unworthy of Roman soldiers with successful campaigns to their credit. Indeed, when Caesar addressed the men of each legion at their work, and told them that if they found their privations unbearable he would abandon the siege, with one voice they begged him not to do so, saying that they had served under him for many years without suffering any humiliation or ever being forced to relinquish a task that they had set their hands to. They would feel it a humiliation to abandon the siege now, and would rather suffer any hardship than fail in avenging the Romans who had fallen victims to Gallic treachery at Cenabum. They said the same to their centurions and military tribunes, asking them to pass it on to Caesar.

18. The siege towers had already been moved close to the wall, when Caesar learnt from prisoners that Vercingetorix, having run out of forage, had moved nearer Avaricum, and had taken command in person of the cavalry and the light-armed infantry who regularly fought among the cavalry, in order to ambush the place where he expected our men would go the next day to forage. Accordingly Caesar set out silently at midnight and reached the enemy's camp in the morning. But they received speedy warning of his approach from their patrols, hid their wagons and baggage in the densest parts of the woods, and drew up all their forces on open rising ground. On hearing of this Caesar at once ordered his men to pile their packs and get their arms ready.

19. The hill that the enemy occupied had a gentle gradient at

the bottom, and was almost surrounded by a marsh which was extremely difficult to negotiate, although only fifty feet wide. The Gauls had broken down the causeways leading over the marsh, and relying on the strength of their position refused to budge from the hill. Formed up in tribal groups, they held all the fords and the thickets that bordered the marsh, determined, if the Romans tried to force a passage, to overpower them by running down to the attack while they were stuck fast in the mud. Awaiting us at such a short distance, they looked as if they were prepared to fight a battle on more or less equal terms; but their position was so much stronger than ours that this show of courage was clearly a mere pretence. The legionaries were indignant at the enemy's daring to face them at such close range, and clamoured for the signal to attack. But Caesar pointed out how costly a victory would be in these conditions, how many brave men's lives must be sacrificed; when they showed such steadfast loyalty and were willing to face any danger for his honour, he would be guilty of the grossest injustice if he did not consider their lives before his own interests. After addressing them in this way to alleviate their disappointment, he led them back to camp the same day and proceeded to complete his preparations for the siege of the town.

20. On returning to his main body Vercingetorix was accused of treachery for having moved his camp nearer the Romans, for going off with all the cavalry, and for leaving such a large army without anyone in supreme command, with the result that the Romans had taken advantage of his departure to make a swift move against it. All this could not have happened by chance, they said, but must have been deliberately planned; evidently he would rather become king of Gaul by Caesar's favour than by the gift of his fellow countrymen. To these charges Vercingetorix replied that he moved camp because he was short of forage, and they themselves had pressed him to do so; he went nearer the Romans because he had found a very favourable position, so well protected by nature that no defence works were required.

'I knew,' he continued, 'that the cavalry would not be missed on this marshy ground, whereas it was very useful in the place to which I took it. I purposely did not delegate the command to anyone when I went away, for fear the person I chose might be induced by the enthusiasm of the rank and file to give battle; for I could see that that was what they all desired, because they were soft and incapable of prolonged exertion. If the arrival of the Romans during my absence was an accident, it was a stroke of luck for us; if it was the result of information conveyed by a traitor, you ought to be grateful to him for enabling you to see from your commanding position how weak are their forces and how contemptible is their cowardice, since they slunk back ignominiously to their camp without daring to fight. I have no need to obtain from Caesar by treachery the power that I can secure by victory – a victory already in my grasp, and to be shared by the whole Gallic people. You may take back the command you entrusted me with, if you imagine that you are conferring a favour on men when in reality you owe your lives to me. To satisfy yourselves that what I say is true, hear what these Roman soldiers have to say.'

With these words he brought forward some camp servants whom he had captured on a foraging expedition some days previously and had subjected to the tortures of chains and starvation. These he had carefully primed beforehand with the answers they were to make when questioned. They said that they were legionaries, and that the hunger and want they had suffered made them steal out of camp to see if they could find any corn or cattle in the fields. The whole army, they added, was in the same plight; every man was at the end of his strength and unfit for work, and their commander had decided to raise the siege in three days' time unless some progress was made.

'That,' cried Vercingetorix, 'is what you owe to me, whom you charge with treachery. Thanks to me, without shedding a drop of your own blood, you see a great and victorious army almost destroyed by starvation; and when it is routed and retreats in disgrace, I have taken good care that no people shall admit it into their territory.'

21. The whole concourse cheered and clashed their weapons, as the Gauls are accustomed to do when they approve of what a speaker says. Vercingetorix was a great leader, they declared, his loyalty above suspicion, and no one could conduct the campaign with greater skill. They determined to send into Avaricum ten thousand men picked from all the contingents, not wishing to

entrust the national cause to the Bituriges alone, because they realized that if the Bituriges saved the town the victory would be entirely theirs.

22. To baffle the extraordinary bravery of our troops the Gauls resorted to all kinds of devices; for they are a most ingenious people and very clever at borrowing and applying ideas suggested to them. They pulled aside our wall hooks with lassoes, for example, and when they had made them fast hauled them inside with windlasses. They made our terraces fall in by undermining, at which they were expert because they have extensive iron mines in their country and are thoroughly familiar with every kind of underground working. They had also equipped the whole circuit of the wall with towers, furnished with platforms and protected by hides. They made frequent sorties by day and night, either to set fire to the terrace or to attack our soldiers at work. As our towers were raised higher by the material added each day to the terrace, they increased the height of theirs correspondingly by inserting floors between the upright posts forming the framework. They countermined the subterranean galleries that we were digging towards the walls, and prevented their continuation by throwing into them stakes sharpened and hardened in a fire, boiling pitch, and very heavy stones.

23. Gallic walls are always built more or less on the following plan. Balks of timber are laid on the ground at regular intervals of two feet along the whole line on which the wall is to be built, at right angles to it. These are made fast to one another by long beams running across them at their centre points, and are covered with a quantity of rubble; and the two-foot intervals between them are faced with large stones fitted tightly in. When this first course has been placed in position and fastened together, another course is laid on top. The same interval of two feet is kept between the balks of the second course, but they are not in contact with those of the first course, being separated from them by a course of stones two feet high; thus every balk is separated from each of its neighbours by one large stone, and so held firmly in position. By the addition of further courses the fabric is raised to the required height. This style of building presents a diversified appearance that is not unsightly, with its alternation of balks and stones each preserving

their own straight lines. It is also very serviceable and well adapted
for defending a town: the masonry protects it from fire, the timber
from destruction by the battering-ram, which cannot either pierce
or knock to pieces a structure braced internally by beams running
generally to a length of forty feet in one piece.

24. The besiegers were continually hampered, not only by these
various devices, but also by incessant rain following a thaw. By
unremitting toil, however, they overcame all these hindrances and
in twenty-five days raised a terrace three hundred and thirty feet
wide and eight feet high. It was now almost touching the wall; and
one night when Caesar was staying up as usual with the working
parties, urging them not to lose an instant, smoke was noticed
rising from the terrace shortly before midnight. The enemy had
dug a tunnel under it and set it on fire. At the same moment the
Gauls raised a cheer all along the wall and came pouring out of two
gates on either side of our towers. Others flung torches and dry
wood on to the terrace from their position on the wall and dropped
pitch and other inflammable material, so that it was hard to decide
which points to defend or which attack to counter first. It was
Caesar's practice, however, to have two legions on duty all night in
front of the camp, while a larger number laboured at the works by
shifts. So the defence was quickly organized: some checked the
sorties while others pulled back the towers and made a gap in the
terrace, and all the rest of the troops ran from the camp to
extinguish the flames.

25. The fight went on everywhere throughout the remainder of
the night, and the enemy's hope of victory was continually
renewed, especially as they saw that the sheds used to protect the
men who moved the towers were burnt and that it was not easy for
our soldiers to advance without cover to help their comrades, while
in their own ranks fresh men kept relieving those who were worn
out. They felt that the fate of Gaul depended entirely on what
happened at that moment, and performed before our eyes an
exploit so memorable that I felt I must not leave it unrecorded.

There was a Gaul standing before one of the gates and throwing
into the flames, opposite one of our towers, lumps of tallow and
pitch that were passed along to him. An arrow from a catapult
pierced his right side and he fell dead. Another near him stepped

over his prostrate body and took over his job. When he likewise was killed by the catapult, a third took his place, and so they went on. The post was not abandoned by the defenders until the fire on the terrace was extinguished, the Gauls repulsed all along the line, and the battle at an end.

26. The enemy had now tried everything without success, and the next day determined to abandon the town, a course to which Vercingetorix was urgently pressing them. By making the attempt when all was quiet at night they hoped to bring it off without serious loss; Vercingetorix's camp was not far away, and the continuous stretch of marshland that lay between the town and the Romans would hinder pursuit. They were already preparing to execute this plan the following night, when suddenly their wives came running out into the streets and in tears threw themselves at the men's feet.

'Do not abandon us,' they begged, 'and the children who are yours as much as ours, to a cruel enemy. We cannot fly with you because we have not the strength.'

When they saw that their minds were made up – for men who stand in extreme peril are generally too scared to feel pity – they started shrieking and gesticulating to the Romans to warn them of the men's intention. This frightened the Gauls into giving up the idea; for they were afraid that the Roman cavalry would have seized the roads before they could get away.

27. The next day Caesar completed the siege works which he had under construction and moved forward one of the towers. It began to rain heavily and he thought this a good opportunity to attempt an assault, especially as he saw that the guards on the wall had been carelessly posted. He told the men to go about their work in a half-hearted fashion and explained his plan to them. The legions were got ready for action, as far as possible under cover of mantlets, and Caesar, calling upon them to seize the chance of victory and reap at long last the fruit of all their toil, promised rewards to those who were first to mount the wall. He then gave the signal for the assault. The soldiers suddenly darted out everywhere and quickly lined the wall.

28. Taken by surprise and panic-stricken, the enemy were dislodged from the wall and towers, but re-formed in the market

place and other open spaces in wedge-shaped masses, determined to fight a pitched battle against attackers from any direction. But when they saw the Romans occupying the entire circuit of the wall around them, and not a man coming down to meet them on level ground, they were afraid of being cut off from all chance of escape, and throwing down their arms ran without stopping to the farthest corners of the town. There, some were cut down by our infantry as they jammed the narrow gateways and others by the cavalry after making their way out. None of our soldiers thought about making money by taking prisoners. They were exasperated by the massacre of Romans at Cenabum and the labour of the siege and spared neither old men nor women nor children. Of the whole population – about forty thousand – a bare eight hundred who rushed out of the town at the first alarm got safely through to Vercingetorix. He took them in silently, late at night. Afraid that if numbers of them entered the camp together the compassion they would arouse among the rank and file of his army might cause a riot, he stationed his trusted friends and the tribal leaders some distance along the road, with orders to sort them out and convey them to the various parts of the camp allotted to each tribe at the start of the campaign.

29. The next day Vercingetorix called a council of war and encouraged his followers, telling them not to be unduly disheartened or upset by this reverse.

'The Romans have not won by superior courage or in fair fight,' he said, 'but by their expert knowledge of siegecraft, a special technique that we were unacquainted with. It is idle to expect invariable success in war. I personally was never in favour of defending Avaricum, as you yourselves can testify. It was the imprudence of the Bituriges and the too ready acquiescence of the rest that caused this setback. However, the successes that I shall soon gain will more than make up for it. I am working hard to bring over the tribes which are standing aloof from us. The whole of Gaul will then be united, and when we are all of one mind the entire world cannot stand against us. I have already nearly succeeded in this. Meanwhile it is only fair that you should do what I ask for the safety of us all – fortify the camp, so that we can more easily resist any sudden attack.'

30. This speech was well received by the Gauls, who were especially pleased to find that Vercingetorix had not lost heart after such a serious defeat, and faced them instead of hiding himself. They credited him with extraordinary foresight and prudence because, while there was still time, he had twice given them good advice about Avaricum – in the first place to burn it, later to evacuate it. And so, unlike most commanders, whose position is weakened by failure, Vercingetorix gained reputation with every day that followed the reverse. Their hopes were raised by his assurances that other tribes could be induced to join them. They even built a fortified camp – an unheard-of thing in Gaul. The shock had been so severe that, unused to hard work though they were, they felt they must submit to anything that was demanded of them.

31. Vercingetorix kept his promise and used every means he could think of to gain the adherence of the tribes outside the alliance. He tried to entice their chiefs by presents and offers of reward, employing the agents whom he thought best qualified for the purpose; some were personal friends of the chiefs, other were chosen for their powers of subtle speech. The refugees who came in after the fall of Avaricum were provided with arms and clothes, and to bring his army up to its former strength Vercingetorix called for reinforcements from the various tribes, fixing the precise number of each quota and the date by which it was to arrive at the camp. He also ordered all the archers who could be found (there were a very large number of them in Gaul) to be sent to him. By these measures he quickly repaired the losses at Avaricum, and Teutomatus, king of the Nitiobroges (son of Ollovico, who was granted the title of 'Friend' by the Roman Senate), now joined him with a strong force of cavalry from his own tribe and some mercenaries whom he had raised in Aquitania.

3 Roman reverse at Gergovia (52 B.C.)

32. Caesar stayed several days at Avaricum, where he found abundance of grain and other provisions, so that the troops were able to recover from their fatigue and undernourishment. It was

now near the end of the winter and the start of the campaigning season; and Caesar had just decided to march against the enemy, in the hope of either manoeuvring them out of the marshes and forests or blockading them where they were, when some of the leading men of the Aedui came to ask for his help in a serious emergency. The situation, they said, was critical. Their old-established practice was to elect a single magistrate to hold sovereign power for a year. Now, however, there were two magistrates in office, each of whom claimed to have been legally appointed. One was Convictolitavis, a young man of wealth and distinction; the other was Cotus, a descendant of a very old house and a man with great personal influence and numerous family connections whose brother Valetiacus had held the same office the year before. The country had become an armed camp; both council and people were divided in their loyalty and each claimant was supported by his retainers. If the quarrel was kept up much longer it would mean civil war. The only way of preventing this was for Caesar to intervene and exert his authority.

33. It was most unfortunate for Caesar to have to leave the fighting front, but he knew what serious harm such disputes often cause. The Aedui were a powerful tribe, bound by the closest ties to Rome. He himself had done all in his power to strengthen them and had shown them every mark of favour; and now that there was a prospect of their coming to blows with each other, and a risk that the side which felt itself the weaker might call in help from Vercingetorix, he thought it was his first duty to prevent such a catastrophe. As Aeduan law forbade the chief magistrate to leave the country and Caesar wished to avoid the appearance of violating this rule of its constitution, he decided to go there in person, and summoned the whole council and the two disputants to meet him at Decetia. Almost all the councillors assembled there, and informed Caesar that the announcement of Cotus' election had been made by his brother, the magistrate of the previous year, in the presence of a mere handful of people called together in secret, neither in the proper place nor at the proper time. It was further pointed out that Aeduan law forbade the election, not merely to the magistracy but even to a seat on the council, of a near relation of a person previously elected and still living. Caesar therefore

made Cotus resign his claims and told Convictolitavis, who had been appointed constitutionally, under the presidency of the priests and at a time when the magistracy was vacant, to continue in office.

34. After deciding the matter in this way, Caesar advised the Aedui to forget their disputes and quarrels and allow nothing to distract them from the war they had on hand. They might look forward to receiving from him the rewards they deserved when the conquest of Gaul was completed. In the meantime they must send him without delay all their cavalry, and ten thousand infantry to be distributed at various places for the protection of his convoys. He then divided his army into two parts. Four legions and a part of the cavalry were assigned to Labienus to lead against the Senones and Parisii. Caesar himself took the other six legions and the rest of the cavalry, and marched into the country of the Arverni towards Gergovia, following the course of the Allier. On learning this, Vercingetorix broke down all the bridges over that river and began to march along the opposite bank.

35. The two armies were within sight of one another and Vercingetorix was generally encamped opposite Caesar, placing patrols to prevent the Romans from making a bridge anywhere and getting across. Thus Caesar found himself in a very difficult position: it looked as if his progress might be barred by the river for most of the summer, since it is not usually fordable until autumn. To get out of this impasse he encamped in a wooded spot opposite one of the bridges destroyed by the enemy and next day stayed there in concealment with two legions, sending on the rest as usual with all the baggage, and breaking up some of the cohorts into companies so as to make it appear that the number of legions was unchanged. He ordered them to march on as far as they could, and when he had allowed enough time for them to reach their next encampment, he began to rebuild the bridge on the original piles, the lower parts of which were still intact. The work was quickly completed and the legions were taken across. Then, choosing a suitable site for a camp, Caesar recalled the other legions. When Vercingetorix heard of it, he was afraid of being compelled to fight a pitched battle, and therefore pushed on ahead by forced marches.

36. Five days' march brought Caesar to Gergovia, where on the day of his arrival he fought a cavalry skirmish and reconnoitred the

position of the town. As it was situated on a high mountain and difficult of access on every side, he decided that it was hopeless to attempt an assault and that it would be better not to start a siege until he had secured his food supply. Vercingetorix, who had encamped near the town, placed the various tribal contingents at short distances round his headquarters; they occupied all the mountain heights within view and presented a terrifying appearance. The chieftains whom he had chosen to form his council of war were summoned every morning at daybreak to exchange intelligence or make arrangements, and almost daily the cavalry were sent into action with archers dispersed among their ranks, to test each man's courage and fighting spirit. Opposite the town, there projected from the foot of the mountain a very steep hill of great natural strength. Once in possession of this, we should clearly be able to deprive the enemy of a considerable part of his water supply and restrict the movements of his foragers; but it was held by a fairly strong garrison. By starting out of camp at dead of night, however, Caesar dislodged the garrison before relief could come from the town, and making himself master of the position installed two legions there in a camp connected with his larger camp by a double trench twelve feet wide,[55] so that men could pass to and fro even singly, without fear of being surprised by the Gauls.

37. While these events were taking place at Gergovia, Convictolitavis, the Aeduan in whose favour, as told above, Caesar had decided the dispute about the magistracy, was bribed by the Arverni and entered into negotiation with certain young men of his tribe, chief among whom were Litaviccus and his brothers, members of a very illustrious family. He shared the money with them and bade them remember that they were free men and born to rule. It was the Aedui alone, he said, who hindered the Gallic victory which, but for them, would be certain. Their influence kept the other tribes loyal to Rome; and if they changed sides, the Romans would be unable to maintain their position in Gaul.

'It is true,' he went on, 'that I am under some obligation to Caesar – though the justice of my case was so apparent that he could hardly help deciding in my favour. But the cause of national liberty outweighs any such consideration. Why should we call Caesar in to adjudicate questions involving our rights and the interpretation of our laws? We do not expect him to submit questions of Roman law to our arbitration.'

The young men soon yielded to the combined persuasions of Convictolitavis' eloquence and gold, and professed themselves ready to take the lead in the enterprise; but how to put it into execution required some thought, since they knew that it would be no easy task to induce the Aeduan people to take up arms against Rome. It was decided that Litaviccus should march at the head of the ten thousand men who were to be sent to Caesar as reinforcements, while his brothers hurried on ahead to Caesar; and the remainder of their programme was agreed upon.

38. On taking command of the army Litaviccus marched to a point within thirty miles of Gergovia, and then suddenly halted and paraded his troops.

'Soldiers,' he said with tears in his eyes, 'where are we going? All our cavalry and all our men of high rank have perished. Two of our leading citizens, Eporedorix and Viridomarus, have been accused of treason and put to death by the Romans without trial. Learn the facts from these men who have escaped from the actual scene of the massacre. I cannot bear to describe what has happened myself; for my brothers and all my other relations have been killed.'

He then produced some men whom he had carefully coached and they repeated to the troops the tale that he had already told. All the Aeduan cavalry, they said, had been butchered because it was alleged that they had entered into negotiation with the Arverni; they themselves had hidden among the crowd of soldiers and escaped while the slaughter was still going on. With shouts of indignation all the Aedui begged Litaviccus to consider what they were to do.

'It needs no consideration,' he replied. 'Obviously we must march straight to Gergovia and join the Arverni. After such a crime, can we doubt that the Romans are even now hastening here to kill us too? So if we have a spark of courage in us, let us avenge this foul murder by wiping out these ruffians.' With these words he indicated some Romans who had been travelling with him in reliance on his protection. The Gauls cruelly tortured and killed them and plundered a large quantity of grain and other supplies that they had with them. Litaviccus then sent messengers into

every part of the Aeduan country and inflamed the people by the
same propaganda about the massacre of cavalrymen and chiefs,
calling on them to avenge their wrongs by doing the same as he had
done.

39. The two Aeduans who were alleged to have been killed were
serving in the contingent of Gallic cavalry, having been called up
by a special summons from Caesar. Eporedorix was a young man
of the noblest birth and very powerful in his own country;
Viridomarus, a man of the same age and equally influential, though
not of good birth, had been raised by Caesar, on Diviciacus'
recommendation, from a humble position to the highest honour.
They were rivals for power; and in the recent struggle for the
magistracy Eporedorix had been a strong supporter of Convictolitavis, and Viridomarus of Cotus. On hearing of Litaviccus' project,
Eporedorix came about midnight to inform Caesar of it, and begged
him not to allow the misguided counsels of raw youths to detach
the tribe from its friendship with Rome – which must happen if
Litaviccus' army joined Vercingetorix, since neither their relations
nor the tribal authorities could be indifferent to the safety of so
many thousand men.

40. Caesar was much perturbed by the news that the Aedui were
turning disloyal in spite of the special favour that he had always
shown them. Without a moment's hesitation he started out with
four legions in light marching order and all his cavalry.[56] There
was no time to reduce the size of the camp, since in such an
emergency everything depended on prompt action, but he left
Fabius to guard it with two legions. He ordered Litaviccus'
brothers to be arrested, but found that he was just too late; they
had already deserted to the enemy. Urged by Caesar to submit
without complaint to the laborious march that the crisis necessitated, all ranks followed him with enthusiasm, and an advance of
twenty-four miles brought him within sight of the Aeduan army.
By sending forward the cavalry he forced them to halt and
prevented them from resuming their march. Orders were given
that no one was to kill any of them, and Eporedorix and
Viridomarus, who were believed by the Aedui to have been put to
death, were told to go to and fro among the cavalrymen and speak
to their fellow countrymen. As soon as the Aedui recognized them

and realized that Litaviccus had imposed upon them, they stretched out their hands in token of surrender and throwing down their arms begged for quarter. Litaviccus escaped to Gergovia, accompanied by his retainers; for Gallic custom regards it as a crime, even in a desperate situation, for retainers to desert their lord.

41. Caesar sent a message to the Aeduan authorities informing them that by an act of grace he had spared men whom the laws of war entitled him to put to the sword; and after giving his army three hours' rest he started for Gergovia. When he had covered about half the distance he met a party of horse sent by Fabius, who told him that a dangerous situation had arisen. The enemy, they said, had assaulted the camp in full force, and, by continually sending in fresh troops to relieve their tired comrades, had exhausted our men, who on account of the size of the camp had to remain hard at work on the rampart without relief. Showers of arrows and every other kind of missile had wounded many of the defenders, but the artillery was of great use in helping them to hold out. The enemy had at length retired, and Fabius was now blocking up all but two of the camp gates, strengthening the rampart with breastworks, and preparing to meet a similar attack the next day. At this Caesar accelerated his march and the soldiers made such exertions that they reached the camp before sunrise.

42. In the meantime Litaviccus' first messages reached the country of the Aedui. Without waiting for confirmation they accepted an idle rumour as an established fact, some excited by greed, others carried away by anger and impetuosity – the most striking characteristic of the Gallic race. All the Romans in their power were killed or enslaved and their property was plundered. Convictolitavis added fuel to the fire and goaded the people to frenzy, in the hope that if once they committed a serious crime they would be ashamed to return to reason. Marcus Aristius, a military tribune on his way to rejoin his legion, was ejected from the town of Chalon-sur-Saône with the promise of safe conduct, and the Roman merchants living there were also compelled to leave. Directly they started the Gauls set on them and stripped them of all their baggage. As the Romans resisted, they continued harassing them all that day and the following night, and when

many had been killed on both sides, called a larger number of their countrymen to arms.

43. Meanwhile news arrived that the whole Aeduan army was in Caesar's power. At this the tribal leaders came running to Aristius, saying that the government had no hand in what had occurred. They ordered an inquiry into the robberies, confiscated the property of Litaviccus and his brothers, and sent a deputation to make their excuses to Caesar. The object of these moves was to secure the release of their army. But the number of people involved in the outrages was large. Fascinated by the profits of the plunder, yet at the same time dreading retribution for their crimes, they began to make secret preparation for war and sent envoys to obtain the support of other tribes. Caesar understood this perfectly well, but answered the deputation in the most conciliatory terms: in spite of the ignorance and irresponsibility of the populace, he still felt the same goodwill towards the Aedui and would not judge them too harshly. Anticipating a widespread rising, however, and afraid of being surrounded by rebellious tribes, he began to consider how he could draw off from Gergovia and reunite the whole army without making his departure look like a flight occasioned by the fear of revolt.

44. He was still occupied with this problem when he thought he saw a chance of striking an effective blow. On going to inspect the defence works at the smaller of his two camps, he noticed that a hill within the enemy's lines was completely deserted, although previously they had been so thick upon it that the ground was scarcely visible. He inquired the reason for this surprising circumstance from the deserters who daily flocked to him. They all confirmed what he had already discovered from his patrols – that the heights adjoining this hill formed a ridge that was almost level, but narrow and wooded where it gave access to the farther side of the town. The Gauls, they said, were very anxious for the safety of this ridge, feeling sure that if they lost a second height in addition to the one already occupied by the Romans, it would be obvious to everyone that they were all but imprisoned and unable to get away or to send out foraging parties; so every man who could be spared had been summoned by Vercingetorix to fortify the ridge.

45. About midnight, therefore, Caesar sent several squadrons

THE CONQUEST OF GAUL

of cavalry in that direction with orders to scour the whole district and make as much disturbance as possible. At daybreak he had a large number of packhorses and mules brought out of camp, unsaddled them, and ordered the drivers to put on helmets and ride round over the high ground masquerading as cavalry. A few cavalrymen who were sent with them were told to range over a wide area with the object of letting themselves be seen. All were to make a long circuit and converge upon the same place. These movements could be seen from the town, which commanded a view of the camp, but at such a distance it was impossible to make out with certainty what was going on. Next, a single legion was sent along the same line of heights by which the horsemen had gone, and after advancing a short way was stationed on lower ground, concealed in a wood. The Gauls now became even more alarmed and the whole of their forces were transferred to the threatened ridge to aid in the work of fortification. When he saw their camps empty, Caesar told his soldiers to cover the crests of their helmets, hide their standards, and move across in small parties – so as not to attract the defenders' attention – from the larger to the smaller camp. He explained his plan to the generals in command of the various legions, warning them above all to keep their men well in hand and not let them be tempted to advance too far by over-eagerness for battle or hope of plunder. He pointed out that their inferior position placed them at a disadvantage which could be remedied only by quick action: it was a case for a surprise attack, not a regular battle. He then gave the signal to advance, at the same time sending the Aedui up the hill by another route on the right.

46. The distance, as the crow flies, between the town ramparts and the point on the plain from which the ascent began was a little over a mile; but the turns that had to be made in order to ease the ascent increased its length. About half way up the Gauls had built a six-foot wall of large stones, which followed the contour of the mountain and was intended to impede any attack. All the lower part of the slope was left unoccupied, while the higher part, between this wall and the town ramparts, was covered with their camps, placed close together. Advancing at the signal, the Romans soon reached the wall, climbed over, and captured three of the

camps – so quickly that Teutomatus, king of the Nitiobroges, was surprised in his tent, where he was taking his siesta, and only just managed to escape, naked to the waist and riding a wounded horse, from the soldiers who entered in search of plunder.

47. As his purpose had now been achieved, Caesar ordered the recall to be sounded[57] and the 10th legion, which was with him, immediately halted. The other legions did not hear the trumpet, because a fairly wide hollow intervened; but the military tribunes and the generals did their best, in accordance with Caesar's orders, to hold them back. The soldiers, however, elated by the hope of a quick victory, by the enemy's flight, and by the recollection of their past triumphs, thought that nothing was too hard for their valour to achieve, and continued their pursuit until they got close to the ramparts and gates of the town. Then shouts came from every part of the fortress, and those of the defenders who were farthest away, alarmed by the sudden uproar, thought that the attackers were inside the gates and rushed out. The married women threw clothes and money down from the ramparts and leaning over with bared breasts and outstretched hands besought the Romans to spare them, and not to kill the women and children as they had done at Avaricum. Some were lowered from the rampart by their companions and gave themselves up to the soldiers. Lucius Fabius, a centurion of the 8th legion, who had said that day in the hearing of his men that he meant to win a reward such as Caesar had offered at Avaricum, by mounting the rampart before any other man, got three men of his company to hoist him up, and after clambering to the top himself, pulled up each of the others after him.

48. Meanwhile the Gauls who had assembled, as related above, on the other side of the town to construct defence works had heard the shouting and were recalled by a succession of messengers telling them that the town was in the Romans' hands. Their cavalry loped up first, with the whole horde of infantrymen racing after them. Every man as he arrived took his stand under the ramparts and swelled the ranks of fighters. When a great crowd of them had gathered, the women who a moment before had been holding out their hands in supplication to the Romans began to appeal to their own folk, leaning over the wall with their hair flung loose in Gallic

fashion, and bringing out their children for the men to see. It was an unequal struggle for the Romans, with both position and numbers against them; tired out with hurrying uphill and fighting a long engagement, they found it difficult to hold their own against troops just come fresh into action.

49. Seeing his men harassed on such unfavourable ground by continually increasing numbers, Caesar became anxious for their safety, and sent orders to Titus Sextius, the general left in charge of the small camp, to lead his cohorts out immediately and station them at the foot of the hill, facing the enemy's right flank, where he could cover the legions' retreat, if he saw them driven from their position, by frightening off their pursuers. Caesar also moved his own legion to a slightly more forward position and there awaited the issue of the battle.

50. Fierce hand-to-hand fighting was in progress, the Gauls relying on their superior numbers and position, while our men trusted in their courage to see them through, when suddenly the Aedui, whom Caesar had sent up by another route on the right to create a diversion, appeared on our right flank. The similarity of their arms to those of the enemy gave our soldiers a bad fright; for although they could see that the newcomers had their right shoulders uncovered – the sign always agreed upon to mark friendly troops – they imagined that this was a ruse employed by the enemy to trick them. At the same moment the centurion Fabius and the others who had climbed with him on to the rampart were surrounded and killed, and their bodies pitched down. Marcus Petronius, another centurion of the same legion, tried to break down the gate, but was overwhelmed by a host of assailants, and realizing that he was a doomed man – he was already covered with wounds – shouted to the men of his company who had followed him: 'I can't save myself and you. It's my fault you're in this tight corner, because I was so keen to distinguish myself. So at least I'll help you to get away with your lives. Now's your chance: look after yourselves.'

With these words he charged into the middle of the enemy, killed two of them and forced the rest a short way back from the gate. The men still tried to rescue him.

'It's no use,' he cried, 'trying to save me. I've lost too much blood and haven't any strength left. So get away while you have the chance and fall back to your legion.' So he went on fighting and a few moments later fell dead. But he had saved his men.

51. Harassed on every side, our men held their ground till they had lost forty-six centurions. When eventually they were driven back, the Gauls began to pursue relentlessly, but were checked by the 10th legion, which was posted in reserve on fairly level ground; and the 10th was in turn supported by the cohorts of the 13th under Sextius, which after leaving the small camp had moved forward to higher ground. As soon as they reached the plain, all the legions halted and re-formed facing the enemy, and Vercingetorix withdrew his men from the foot of the hill and led them within his entrenchments. Our losses that day amounted to nearly seven hundred.

52. The next day Caesar paraded the troops and reprimanded them for their rashness and impetuosity.[58] They had decided for themselves, he said, to advance farther and attack the town, neither halting when the retreat was sounded nor obeying the military tribunes and generals who tried to restrain them. He stressed the disadvantage of an unfavourable position, explaining the motives which had dictated his action at Avaricum, when, although he had caught the enemy without their general or their cavalry, he preferred to sacrifice a certain victory rather than incur even light casualties by fighting on unfavourable ground.

'Much as I admire the heroism that you showed,' he went on, 'in refusing to be daunted by a fortified camp, a high mountain, and a walled fortress, I cannot too strongly condemn your bad discipline and your presumption in thinking that you know better than your commander-in-chief how to win a victory or to foresee the results of an action. I want obedience and self-restraint from my soldiers, just as much as courage in the face of danger.'

53. He concluded his speech with words of encouragement, telling the men not to be upset by a reverse which was due to their unfavourable position and not to the enemy's fighting quality.

As he had not changed his mind regarding the advisability of a retirement, Caesar then led the legions out of camp and formed line of battle in a strong position. Vercingetorix, however, still remained within his entrenchments and would not come down into the plain; and after a cavalry skirmish which resulted in favour of the Romans Caesar marched the army back into camp. After offering battle again the next day he decided that he had done enough to humble the conceit of the Gauls and restore the confidence of his own troops, and he therefore set out for the country of the Aedui. Still the enemy did not follow; and on the third day Caesar reached the river Allier, repaired a broken-down bridge, and marched his army across.

4 Vercingetorix's defeat in open warfare (52 B.C.)

54. At the Allier the Aeduans Viridomarus and Eporedorix asked for an interview with Caesar and informed him that Litaviccus had gone with all the Gallic cavalry to try to seduce the Aedui from their allegiance; it was essential, they said, for them to get there before him in order to keep the tribe loyal. By this time Caesar had many proofs of the treachery of the Aedui, and felt sure that the result of letting these men go would be to make them revolt all the sooner. However, he thought it unwise to detain them, lest he should be accused of high-handed action or give an impression of being afraid. Before they went he briefly reminded them of his services to the Aedui – in what a feeble state they were when he received them into alliance, cooped up in their strongholds, stripped of their lands, deprived of all their allies, forced to pay tribute and submit to humiliating demands for hostages; and how he had not merely restored them to their previous position, but had raised them to a height of prosperity, prestige, and power that they had never reached before. Bidding them pass on this reminder to their countrymen he let them go.

55. Situated in a strategic position on the Loire was an Aeduan town called Noviodunum, to which Caesar had sent all his hostages from the various Gallic states, his stores of grain, public funds, a large part of his personal luggage and that of his troops, and numbers of horses that he had bought in Italy and Spain for use in the war. On reaching this town Eporedorix and Viridomarus heard the latest news about the Aedui – that Litaviccus had been received at Bibracte, one of their most important towns, and visited by the

chief magistrate Convictolitavis and a large number of councillors; and that an official embassy had been sent to Vercingetorix to conclude a treaty of peace and alliance. This was too good a chance, they thought, to be missed. Accordingly they massacred the garrison of Noviodunum and the merchants who lived there, shared the money and horses, had all the hostages taken to the magistrates at Bibracte, and carried away as much grain as they had time to stow into boats, the rest being thrown into the river or burnt. The town itself they thought they could not possibly hold, so they burnt it to prevent its being of use to the Romans. Then they set about collecting troops from the neighbourhood, placing detachments and pickets along the Loire, and making demonstrations here and there with their cavalry to intimidate the Romans. In this way they hoped either to starve them out or to force them by stress of famine to retire into the Province. They were greatly encouraged in this hope by the swollen state of the river – the result of melting snow – which made it to all appearance quite unfordable.

56. Caesar decided that he must act quickly. If he had to build bridges, a battle might be forced upon him; and in that case it would be better to fight before enemy reinforcements arrived. The only alternative was to alter his whole plan of campaign and retire to the Province, a course which some of his frightened officers thought unavoidable. But there were many reasons against it. It was undignified and humiliating; the route was a difficult one leading over the Cevennes; above all he was anxious about the legions under command of Labienus, who was separated from him. Accordingly he made a series of extraordinarily long marches, by day and night, and astonished everyone by appearing on the bank of the Loire. The cavalry found a ford good enough for an emergency – all that was needed for the men to be able to keep their shoulders and arms above water, so as to carry their shields and weapons. Cavalrymen waded in upstream to break the force of the current; and, as the shock of Caesar's appearance unnerved the enemy, the crossing was effected without loss. After provisioning the army with some grain and a quantity of cattle that were found in the neighbouring fields, he marched towards the country of the Senones.

57. Meanwhile Labienus,[59] leaving the draft recently arrived from Italy at Agedincum to protect the baggage, started with his four legions for Lutetia, a town of the Parisii situated on an island in the Seine. When the Gauls knew of his approach, large forces assembled from the neighbouring tribes and the chief command was given to an Aulercan named Camulogenus, who although enfeebled by age was called out of retirement to this post of honour on account of his unrivalled knowledge of warfare. Camulogenus noticed a long stretch of marsh which drained into the Seine and rendered a wide area almost impassable. Encamping near-by he prepared to prevent the Roman troops from crossing it.

58. Labienus first tried, under cover of a line of mantlets, to make a causeway across the marsh on a foundation of fascines and other material. Finding this too difficult, he silently quitted his camp some time after midnight and retraced his steps to Metlosedum, a town of the Senones situated like Lutetia on an island in the river. He seized some fifty boats, quickly lashed them together to form a bridge, and sent troops across to the island. Such of the inhabitants as were left in the town – many had been called up to the war – were terrified by this unexpected attack and surrendered the place without a fight. After repairing a bridge recently broken down by the enemy, Labienus crossed to the right bank of the river, marched downstream to Lutetia, and encamped near it. The enemy, informed of this by refugees from Metlosedum, sent orders to burn Lutetia and destroy its bridges; they then moved from their position by the marsh and encamped on the left bank opposite Labienus.

59. By this time people were saying that Caesar had retreated from Gergovia and rumours were circulating about the insurrection of the Aedui and the success of the general Gallic rising. Gauls who got into conversation with Roman soldiers said that Caesar had been prevented from continuing his march across the Loire and compelled by famine to return to the Province. The news of the Aeduan rebellion encouraged the Bellovaci, who had already been meditating revolt, to mobilize and make open preparations for war. Now that the situation was so much changed, Labienus saw that he must completely revise his plans; he no longer had any idea of making conquests or attacking, but was only concerned to get his

army safely back to Agedincum. On one side he was threatened by the Bellovaci, reputed the bravest fighters in Gaul; on the other, Camulogenus had a well-equipped army ready for action: and Labienus' own legions were separated from their reserves and their baggage by a great river. Confronted suddenly by such formidable difficulties, he realized that only resolute courage could save him.

60. Towards evening he assembled his officers. Urging them to execute his orders with energy and care, he placed a Roman knight in charge of each of the boats which he had brought from Metlosedum, and ordered them to move silently four miles downstream in the early part of the night and wait for him there. He detailed to guard the camp the five cohorts which he considered least reliable in action, and told the remaining five of the same legion to start upstream with all the luggage shortly after midnight, making as much commotion as possible. He also requisitioned some smaller boats, which he sent in the same direction at high speed, with loud splashing of the oars, and then himself moved quietly out of camp with the other three legions and marched downstream to the place where he had ordered the main flotilla to put in.

61. The enemy patrols posted all along the river were taken by surprise, because a sudden heavy storm concealed the approach of the legions, and both infantry and cavalry were quickly ferried across under the superintendence of the knights in charge of the boats. Just before dawn the enemy received several reports almost simultaneously – that there was an unusual commotion in the Roman camp, that a strong force was marching upstream, that the sound of oars was audible from the same direction, and that a little way downstream soldiers were being ferried across. This news made them think that the Romans were crossing at three different places and preparing for a general retreat in alarm at the revolt of the Aedui. They therefore divided their own troops into three sections. One section remained on guard opposite the Roman camp; a small force was dispatched towards Metlosedum with orders to advance upstream as far as the boats had gone; and the remainder were led against Labienus.

62. By dawn the whole of the three Roman legions had been taken across and were in sight of the enemy. Labienus urged them

to remember their long-standing tradition of courage and brilliant successes, and to imagine that Caesar, who had so often led them to victory, was present in person. He then gave the signal to attack. At the first onset the right wing, where the 7th legion was posted, drove back the enemy and put them to flight; on the left, where the 12th legion was, the enemy's front rank were killed or disabled by missiles, but the rest put up a determined resistance, and it was clear that not a single one of them had any thought of flight. Camulogenus was there in person encouraging his men. The issue still hung in the balance, when the 7th legion, whose military tribunes had received a report of what was happening on the left wing, appeared in the enemy's rear and charged. Even then not a single Gaul gave ground; all of them, including Camulogenus, were surrounded and killed. The detachment left on guard opposite Labienus' camp, on hearing that a battle was being fought, went to lend a hand and occupied a hill, but could not withstand the charge of the victorious Romans and joined their fleeing comrades. All who could not escape into woods or hills were killed by the cavalry. On the completion of this action Labienus returned to Agedincum, where he had left all the baggage, and then rejoined Caesar with his entire force.

63. The defection of the Aedui was the signal for a further extension of the war. They sent embassies into every part of Gaul and used all their influence, prestige, and money to induce other tribes to join them. The possession of the hostages whom Caesar had left in their keeping gave them another means of exerting pressure; by threatening to kill them they could intimidate tribes which hesitated. They asked Vercingetorix to visit them and arrange a plan of campaign, and when he came claimed the chief command for themselves. He refused their demand, and a pan-Gallic council was summoned at Bibracte. There was a full attendance of tribesmen from all parts. The matter was referred to their decision and they unanimously confirmed the appointment of Vercingetorix. The chief absentees were the Remi and Lingones, who stuck to their alliance with Rome, and the Treveri, who remained neutral throughout because they lived at a distance and were harassed by German attacks. It was a bitter disappointment to the Aedui to have their claim to leadership rejected. It was with

great reluctance that Eporedorix and Viridomarus – young men who regarded themselves as having a great future – took orders from Vercingetorix.

64. The various tribes were required to send hostages to Vercingetorix by a certain date, and the whole of the cavalry, numbering fifteen thousand, was ordered to concentrate immediately at Bibracte. He said that he would content himself with the infantry which he had in the previous campaign, and would not tempt fortune by fighting a pitched battle. With his great cavalry strength it would be quite easy to prevent the Romans from getting corn and forage.

'All you have to do,' he concluded, 'is to destroy your corn crops without hesitation and burn your granaries, knowing that this sacrifice will make you free men for ever and rulers over others.'

He then commanded the Aedui and the Segusiavi – a tribe living on the Provincial frontier – to supply ten thousand infantry, which together with eight hundred cavalry were placed under command of Eporedorix's brother and detailed to attack the Allobroges. At the same time, however, hoping that the memory of their recent defeat by Rome [61 B.C.] still rankled in the minds of the Allobroges, Vercingetorix tried to seduce them from their allegiance by sending secret agents and envoys, who offered bribes to their chiefs and promised the tribesmen that they should be made rulers of the whole Province. In another direction, the Gabali and the southernmost clans of the Arverni were sent to attack the Helvii, while the Ruteni and Cadurci were to devastate the country of the Volcae Arecomici.

65. To meet these various assaults, a force of militiamen amounting to twenty-two cohorts had been raised in the Province itself by the general Lucius Caesar and was posted all along the threatened frontier. The Helvii, who chose to offer battle to the invaders advancing across their borders, were defeated with heavy loss – their chief magistrate Gaius Valerius Domnotaurus, son of Valerius Caburus, being among the casualties – and were compelled to take shelter behind the walls of their strongholds. The Allobroges posted a closely linked chain of pickets along the Rhône and protected their frontier with great vigilance.

Meanwhile Caesar found a way of remedying his inferiority in cavalry. Since all the roads were blocked and no reinforcements could be got from the Province or from Italy, he sent across the Rhine to the German tribes which he had subdued in previous campaigns and obtained some of their cavalry, attended by the light infantrymen who always fought among them. As their horses were unsuitable for the service required of them, he mounted the Germans on horses requisitioned from the military tribunes and other Roman knights serving with him, and from the time-expired volunteers.

66. During all this time the Gauls were concentrating the troops which had been operating in the country of the Arverni and the cavalry levied from all over Gaul. A large number of cavalry had now been assembled; and while Caesar was marching through the south-eastern part of the Lingones' territory into that of the Sequani, so as to be in a better position for reinforcing the Provincial troops, Vercingetorix established himself in three camps about ten miles from the Romans, summoned his cavalry officers to a council, and addressed them.

'The hour of victory,' he said, 'has come. The Romans are fleeing to the Province and abandoning Gaul. But although this will assure our liberty for the moment, for future peace and security we need more than that; otherwise they will return in increased force and continue the war indefinitely. So let us attack them on the march while they are encumbered with their baggage. If the whole column of infantry halts to come to the rescue, they cannot continue their march; if – which I feel sure is more likely – they abandon the baggage and try to save their own skins, they will be stripped of the supplies without which they cannot live, and disgraced into the bargain. As for their cavalry, not a man of them will dare even to stir outside the column; you ought to know that as well as I do. To encourage your men I will draw up all my troops in front of the camps and overawe the enemy.'

The cavalrymen cried that they should all swear a solemn oath not to allow any man who had not ridden twice through the enemy's column to enter his home again or to see his wife, children or parents.

67. This proposal was approved and every man was duly sworn. Next day their cavalry was divided into three sections, two of

which made a demonstration on either flank of the Roman column
while the third barred the way of the vanguard. Caesar also divided
his cavalry into three sections and ordered them to advance against
the enemy. Simultaneous engagements took place all along the
column, which halted and formed a hollow square with the baggage
inside. If Caesar saw the cavalry in difficulties anywhere or
especially hard pressed, he moved up some of the infantry and
formed line of battle, which hindered the enemy's pursuit and
encouraged the cavalry by the assurance of support. At length the
German horse gained the top of some rising ground on the right,
dislodged some of the enemy, and chased them with heavy loss to
a river where Vercingetorix's infantry was posted. At this the rest
of his cavalry fled, afraid of being surrounded, and were cut down
in numbers all over the field. Three Aeduans of the highest rank
were brought to Caesar as prisoners: the cavalry commander Cotus,
who had been Convictolitavis' rival at the recent election; Cavarillus, who after Litaviccus deserted the Roman cause had been
placed in command of the Aeduan infantry; and Eporedorix,[60]
leader of the Aedui in their war with the Sequani before Caesar's
arrival in Gaul [70–65 B.C.].

5 Siege and capture of Alesia (52 B.C.)

68. After the rout of his cavalry Vercingetorix withdrew his troops
from their position in front of the camps and marched straight for
Alesia, a stronghold of the Mandubii, leaving orders for the heavy
baggage to be packed up immediately and brought after him.
Caesar, after removing the army's baggage with a guard of two
legions to the nearest hill, followed the enemy as long as daylight
lasted and killed some three thousand of their rearguard. The next
day he encamped near Alesia. The Gauls were terrified by the
defeat of their cavalry, the arm on which they placed the greatest
reliance. Accordingly, after reconnoitring the position of the town,
Caesar called on the soldiers to undertake the heavy task of
investing it with siege works.

69. It was clearly impregnable except by blockade; for it stood
at a high altitude on top of a hill washed by streams on the north

and south, and closely surrounded by other hills as high as itself on every side except the west, where a plain extended for some three miles. The whole of the slope below the town ramparts on the east was occupied by a camp crowded with Gallic troops, who had fortified it with a trench and a six-foot wall. The siege works that the Romans were starting to make had a circumference of ten miles. Eight camps were placed in strategic positions, linked together by fortifications along which twenty-three redoubts were built.[61] The redoubts were occupied in the daytime by pickets, to prevent a surprise attack at any point; at night strong garrisons bivouacked in them with sentries on duty.

70. During the construction of these works a hard-fought cavalry battle took place in the three-mile stretch of plain between the hills. Seeing his men in difficulties, Caesar reinforced them with the German cavalry and drew up the legions in front of their camps. Encouraged by their support the cavalry routed the enemy, whose flight was impeded by their own numbers. Hotly pursued by the Germans right up to the fortifications of Vercingetorix's camp, they got jammed in the narrow entrances and suffered heavy losses. Some let their horses go and tried to scramble over the trench and climb the wall. Caesar then ordered the legions posted in front of their camp ramparts to be moved forward a little, whereupon the Gauls inside the camp became as frightened as their fleeing cavalry and expecting an immediate attack shouted a call to arms. Some in their terror rushed right into the town, and Vercingetorix had the town gates shut for fear the camp should be left unguarded. Before retiring the Germans killed many of the fugitives and captured a number of horses.

71. Vercingetorix now decided to send out all his cavalry in the night, before the Roman entrenchments were completed. He bade them go every man to his own country and impress for service all the men of military age. He pointed out how much they owed him and urged them to consider his safety; after all he had done for the cause of national liberty they ought not to abandon him to the cruel vengeance of the enemy. Moreover, if they were slack in doing their duty, they would condemn eighty thousand picked men to perish with him. He had taken stock of the corn, he said, and by strict rationing would have enough for a month – even a little

longer, if the ration were reduced. With these instructions the cavalry was sent out in silence through a gap in the entrenchments shortly before midnight. Vercingetorix now ordered all the garrison, on pain of death, to surrender to him all the corn they had, and proceeded to dole it out a little at a time; the large quantity of livestock which had been brought in by the Mandubii was shared out individually at once. All the troops posted outside the town were taken inside. In this way Vercingetorix prepared to continue the struggle until the arrival of reinforcements.

72. On being informed of this by deserters and prisoners, Caesar started to construct more elaborate siege works. He dug a trench twenty feet wide, which, having perpendicular sides, was as broad at the bottom as at the top. The other works were kept some six hundred and fifty yards behind this trench, to protect them against surprise attacks; for as such a vast extent of ground had to be enclosed, and it was difficult to man the whole circuit, there would be a danger of the enemy's swooping down in force on the lines at night, or hurling javelins in the daytime when the men were tied down to their work. At this distance, therefore, Caesar dug two trenches of equal depth, each fifteen feet wide, and filled the inner one, where it crossed the low ground of the plain, with water diverted from the streams. Behind the trenches a palisaded rampart twelve feet high was erected, strengthened by a battlemented breastwork, with large forked branches projecting where it joined the rampart to hinder the enemy if they tried to climb over. Towers were placed at intervals of a hundred and thirty yards along the entire circuit of fortifications.

73. Parties had to be sent out constantly in search of timber and corn; and as this duty took them far afield, it seriously reduced the number of men available for the construction of the huge fortifications. Moreover, the Gauls tried many times to attack the works, making furious sorties from several of the town gates at once. Caesar decided, therefore, that he must strengthen them still further, to render them defensible by a smaller force. Accordingly tree trunks or very stout boughs were cut and their tops stripped of bark and sharpened; they were then fixed in long trenches dug five feet deep, with their lower ends made fast to one another to prevent their being pulled up and the branches projecting. There

were five rows in each trench, touching one another and interlaced, and anyone who went among them was likely to impale himself on the sharp points. The soldiers called them boundary posts. In front of them, arranged in diagonal rows forming quincunxes, were pits three feet deep, tapering gradually towards the bottom, in which were embedded smooth logs as thick as a man's thigh, with the ends sharpened and charred, and projecting only three inches above ground. To keep the logs firmly in position, earth was thrown into the pits and trodden down to a depth of one foot, the rest of the cavity being filled with twigs and brushwood to hide the trap. These were planted in groups, each containing eight rows three feet apart, and they were nicknamed lilies from their resemblance to that flower. In front of these again were blocks of wood a foot long with iron hooks fixed in them, called goads by the soldiers. These were sunk right into the ground and strewn thickly everywhere.

74. When these defences were completed, Caesar constructed a similar line of fortifications facing outwards instead of inwards. This line described a circuit of fourteen miles, running along the flattest ground that could be found, and its purpose was to hold off attacks from outside, so that, even if Vercingetorix's cavalry assembled a very large force, the troops defending the siege works could not be surrounded. To avoid the danger of having to send out foraging parties when the relieving force was near, every man was ordered to provide himself with a month's supply of corn and fodder.

75. Meanwhile the Gallic tribes convened a council of their leaders, who decided not to adopt Vercingetorix's plan of calling up everyone able to bear arms, as they were afraid that in such a vast mixed host they would be unable to control their contingents or keep them separate, or to organize an adequate supply of corn. They therefore demanded a specified number of men from each tribe as follows: Aedui (with their dependent tribes the Segusiavi, Ambivareti, Aulerci Brannovices, and Blannovii) – 35,000; Arverni (with their dependent tribes the Eleuteti, Cadurci, Gabali, and Vellavii) – 35,000; Sequani, Senones, Bituriges, Santoni, Ruteni, Carnutes – 12,000 each; Bellovaci, Lemovices – 10,000 each; Pictones, Turoni, Parisii, Helvetii – 8,000 each; Suessiones,

Ambiani, Mediomatrici, Petrocorii, Nervii, Morini, Nitiobroges, Aulerci Cenomani – 5,000 each; Atrebates – 4,000; Veliocasses, Aulerci Eburovices – 3,000 each; Rauraci, Boii – 1,000 each; Aremorican tribes (i.e., all the maritime tribes – Coriosolites, Redones, Ambibarii, Caleti, Osismi, Veneti, Lexovii, Venelli) – 20,000.

The Bellovaci did not send their full contingent, because they said they intended to fight the Romans on their own account and in their own way, and would not take orders from anyone. At the request of Commius, however, and in consideration of their friendship with him, they sent 2,000 men along with the other contingents.

76. In former years Commius had rendered Caesar loyal and useful service in Britain, as described above, and in return Caesar had ordered that his tribe should be immune from taxation and have its independence restored and had made Commius suzerain over the Morini. But the whole Gallic people were so united in their determination to liberate themselves and recover their former prestige that they allowed no favours or recollection of friendship to influence them, and all devoted their energies and resources to the prosecution of the war.

When eight thousand horse and about two hundred and fifty thousand infantry had been assembled in the country of the Aedui, a start was made to the task of reviewing and counting them and choosing officers. The chief command of this relieving army was entrusted to Commius the Atrebatian, the Aeduans Viridomarus and Eporedorix, and the Arvernian Vercassivellaunus, a cousin of Vercingetorix. With them were associated representatives of the various tribes, to act as an advisory committee for the conduct of the campaign. They all started for Alesia full of enthusiasm and confidence. Every single man believed that the mere sight of such an enormous host of infantry and cavalry would be enough to make the enemy turn tail, especially as he would be attacked on two fronts – for the besieged would sally out from the town at the same time as the relieving force came into view.

77. In Alesia, however, they knew nothing of these preparations; the time by which they had expected relief was past and their corn was exhausted. So they summoned an assembly and considered

what their fate was to be. Among the various speeches that were made – some advising capitulation, others recommending a sortie while they still had the strength – the speech of Critognatus, a noble Arvernian whose opinion commanded great respect, deserves to be recorded for its unparalleled cruelty and wickedness.

'I do not intend,' he said, 'to make any comment on the views of those who advise "capitulation" – the name they give to the most shameful submission to enslavement; in my opinion they ought not to be regarded as citizens or allowed in the assembly. I will concern myself only with those who advocate a sortie. You all approve their suggestion, as showing that we have not forgotten our traditional courage. But it is not courage, it is weakness, to be unable to endure a short period of privation. It is easier to find men who will voluntarily risk death than men who will bear suffering patiently. Even so, I would support their proposal – so much do I respect their authority – if it involved no loss beyond that of our own lives. But in making our decision we must consider all our fellow countrymen, whom we have called to our aid. If eighty thousand of us are killed in one battle, what heart do you suppose our relatives and kinsmen will have when they are compelled to fight almost over our corpses? Do not leave them to continue the struggle alone when for your sakes they have counted their own danger as nothing, and do not by folly and rashness, or by lack of resolution, ruin all Gaul and subject it to perpetual servitude. Because they have not come on the appointed day, do you doubt their loyalty or constancy to our cause? What? Do you suppose the Romans are working day after day on those outer fortifications to amuse themselves? Since our countrymen cannot get messengers through the cordon that is drawn round us, to assure you that they are coming soon, believe what the enemy are telling you by their actions: for it is the fear of their coming that keeps the Romans hard at work night and day.

'What counsel, then, have I to offer? I think we should do what our ancestors did in a war that was much less serious than this one [109–102 B.C.]. When they were forced into their strongholds by the Cimbri and Teutoni, and overcome like us by famine, instead of surrendering they kept themselves alive by eating the flesh of those who were too old or too young to fight.

Even if we had no precedent for such an action, I think that when our liberty is at stake it would be a noble example to set to our descendants. For this is a life and death struggle, quite unlike the war with the Cimbri, who, though they devastated Gaul and grievously afflicted her, did eventually evacuate our country and migrate elsewhere, and left us free men, to live on our own land under our own laws and in possession of our rights. The Romans, we know, have a very different purpose. Envy is the motive that inspires them. They know that we have won renown by our military strength, and so they mean to install themselves in our lands and towns and fasten the yoke of slavery on us for ever. That is how they have always treated conquered enemies. You do not know much, perhaps, of the condition of distant peoples; but you need only look at the part of Gaul on your own borders that has been made into a Roman province, with new laws and institutions imposed upon it, ground beneath the conqueror's iron heel in perpetual servitude.'

78. At the conclusion of the debate it was decided to send out of the town those whom age or infirmity incapacitated for fighting. Critognatus' proposal was to be adopted only as a last resort – if the reinforcements still failed to arrive and things got so bad that it was a choice between that and surrendering, or accepting dictated peace terms. So the Mandubian population, who had received the other Gauls into their town, were compelled to leave it with their wives and children. They came up to the Roman fortifications and with tears besought the soldiers to take them as slaves and relieve their hunger; but Caesar posted guards on the ramparts with orders to refuse them admission.[62]

79. Meanwhile Commius and the other commanders arrived before Alesia with the whole of their relief force and encamped on a hill outside the Roman lines, not more than a mile away. Next day they brought out their cavalry and occupied all the plain – three miles long, it will be remembered. Their infantry was moved away a short distance and posted on the slopes of the hill. As the town commanded a view over the plain, the besieged saw the troops who had come to their relief, and all crowding together in excitement rejoiced and congratulated one another on their deliverance. Then they brought out their forces, posted them in front

of the town, and filled the nearest trench with fascines and earth, ready for a sortie and all the perils it would entail.

80. Caesar placed the whole of his infantry along the two lines of entrenchments, so that in case of need every man could know his post and hold it. He then ordered out the cavalry to battle. The plain was visible from all the camps on the surrounding hilltops and the whole army was intently watching to see the result of the engagement. The Gauls had placed archers and light-armed infantrymen here and there among their cavalry, to support them if they had to give ground and to help them meet our cavalry charges. These took a number of our men by surprise and forced them to retire wounded from the battle. Feeling confident that their cavalry was winning, since it was obvious that our force was heavily outnumbered, the Gauls on every side – both the besieged and the relieving force – encouraged them with shouts and yells. As the action was taking place in full view of everyone, so that no gallant exploit and no act of cowardice could pass unnoticed, the thirst for glory and the fear of disgrace was an incentive to both sides. They had fought from midday till near sunset and the issue was still in doubt, when the German horse massed all their squadrons at one point, charged the Gauls, and hurled them back. When their cavalry broke and fled, the archers were surrounded and killed. The rest of our horsemen advanced from other points, pursued the fugitives right up to their camp, and gave them no chance of rallying. At this the Gauls who had come out of the town went back in, bitterly disappointed and now almost despairing of success.

81. After an interval of only one day, however, during which they prepared a great quantity of fascines, ladders, and grappling-hooks, the relieving army moved silently out of camp at midnight and advanced towards the entrenchments in the plain. Suddenly raising a shout to inform the besieged of their approach, they began to throw fascines into the trenches, drove the Romans from the rampart with arrows and stones discharged from slings or by hand, and employed every other method of assault.

Meanwhile, hearing the distant shouting, Vercingetorix sounded the trumpet and led his men out of the town. The Roman troops moved up to the posts previously allotted to them at the entrenchments and kept the Gauls at a distance with slingstones, bullets, large stones, and stakes which were placed ready at intervals along the rampart, while the artillery pelted them with missiles. It was too dark to see, and casualties were heavy on both sides. The generals Mark Antony and Gaius Trebonius, who had been detailed for the defence of this particular sector, reinforced the points where they knew the troops were hard pressed with men brought up from redoubts well behind the fighting line.

82. As long as the Gauls were at a distance from the entrenchments, the rain of javelins which they discharged gained them some advantage. But when they came nearer they suddenly found themselves pierced by the goads or tumbled into the pits and impaled themselves, while others were killed by heavy siege spears discharged from the rampart and towers. Their losses were everywhere heavy and when dawn came they had failed to penetrate the defences at any point. Afraid, therefore, of having their right flank turned by an attack from the camps on higher ground, they fell back upon their remaining troops. The besieged lost much time in bringing out the implements that Vercingetorix had prepared for the sortie and in filling up the first stretches of trench, and before they reached the main fortifications heard of the retreat of the relief force, so they returned into the town without effecting anything.

83. After this second costly repulse the Gauls held a council of war. By calling in men familiar with the ground they ascertained the positions of the higher camps and the nature of their defences. There was a hill on the north which had such a wide sweep that the Romans were unable to include it within the circuit of the siege works and were compelled to place the camp there on a slight slope, in what would ordinarily be considered a bad position. It was garrisoned by two legions under the generals Gaius Antistius Reginus and Gaius Caninius Rebilus. After sending out scouts to reconnoitre the ground, the enemy commanders selected from their whole force sixty thousand men belonging to the tribes with the highest reputation for courage, secretly decided on their objective and plan of action, and ordered them to begin an attack at noon under Vercassivellaunus the Arvernian, one of their four generals and a relative of Vercingetorix. Leaving camp in the early

evening, he almost completed his march before daybreak, and ordered his troops to rest under cover of the hill after their hard night's work. When he saw that it was getting on for midday, he marched towards the Roman camp referred to above, while at the same time the Gallic cavalry moved up to the fortifications in the plain and the rest of the army made a demonstration in front of their own camp.

84. On seeing these troop movements from the citadel of Alesia, Vercingetorix sallied out with the fascines, poles, sappers' huts, grappling-hooks, and other implements which he had prepared for the purpose. There was fighting simultaneously all over the field and the Gauls tried every expedient, concentrating on the weakest point of the defences. Distributed as they were along lines of such length, the Romans found it difficult to meet simultaneous attacks in many different places. They were unnerved, too, by the shouts they could hear behind them as they fought, which indicated that their lives were not in their own hands but depended on the bravery of others. It is nearly always invisible dangers that are most terrifying.

85. Caesar found a good observation point, from which he could follow the actions in every part of the field, and sent help where it was needed. Both sides realized that this was the time, above all others, for a supreme effort. The Gauls knew that unless they broke through the lines they were lost; the Romans, if they could hold their ground, looked forward to the end of all their hardships. The danger was greatest at the fortifications on the hill where, as said above, Vercassivellaunus had been sent. The unfavourable downward slope of the ground told heavily against the Romans. Some of the Gauls flung javelins, while others advanced to the attack with shields locked together above their heads, fresh troops continually relieving them when they were tired. All of them threw earth on to the fortifications, which enabled them to climb the rampart and covered the obstacles hidden in the ground.

86. At length, when Caesar saw that his men were weakening and running short of weapons, he sent Labienus to their relief with six cohorts, telling him to remain on the defensive if possible; but if he could not hold the camp by any other means, he must withdraw some cohorts from their positions and counter-attack.

Caesar himself visited other parts of the lines, urging the men to hold out: on that day, he said, on that very hour, depended the fruits of all their previous battles.

The besieged Gauls despaired at last of penetrating the huge fortifications in the plain and attempted to storm one of the steep ascents. Carrying there all the implements they had provided themselves with, they dislodged the defenders of the towers with a hail of missiles, filled the trenches with earth and fascines, and tore down the palisade and breastwork with their hooks.

87. Caesar first sent some cohorts to the rescue under young Brutus, then others under the general Gaius Fabius; finally, as the struggle grew fiercer, he led up a fresh detachment in person. These troops renewed the fight and succeeded in repulsing the attack.

Caesar now started for the sector to which he had sent Labienus, taking four cohorts from the nearest redoubt, and ordering a part of the cavalry to follow him; another detachment was to ride round the outer lines and attack the enemy in the rear. Labienus, when he found that neither ramparts nor trenches could check the Gauls' furious onslaught, had fortunately been able to collect eleven cohorts from the nearest posts, and at this moment sent to tell Caesar that he considered the time for decisive action was at hand. Caesar put on speed to get there in time for the fight.

88. The enemy knew that he was coming by the scarlet cloak which he always wore in action to mark his identity; and when they saw the cavalry squadrons and cohorts following him down the slopes, which were plainly visible from the heights on which they stood, they joined battle. Both sides raised a cheer, which was answered by the men on the rampart and all along the entrenchments. The Romans dropped their spears and fought with their swords. Suddenly the Gauls saw the cavalry in their rear and fresh cohorts coming up in front. They broke and fled, but found their retreat cut off by the cavalry and were mown down. Sedullus, chieftain and commander of the Lemovices, was killed, Vercassivellaunus was taken prisoner in the rout, seventy-four standards were brought in to Caesar, and only a few men of all the large army got back unhurt to their camp. When the Gauls in the town saw their countrymen being slaughtered in flight, they gave up hope

and recalled their troops from the entrenchments. The relieving forces immediately fled from their camps; and if the Romans had not been tired out after a long day's work, during which they had been repeatedly summoned to the relief of hard-pressed comrades, the enemy's army might have been annihilated. As it was, a large number were taken or killed by the cavalry, which was sent in pursuit and came up with their rear soon after midnight. The survivors dispersed to their homes.

89. The next day Vercingetorix addressed an assembly. 'I did not undertake the war,' he said, 'for private ends, but in the cause of national liberty. And since I must now accept my fate, I place myself at your disposal. Make amends to the Romans by killing me or surrender me alive as you think best.' A deputation was sent to refer the matter to Caesar, who ordered the arms to be handed over and the tribal chiefs brought out to him. He seated himself at the fortification in front of his camp, and there the chiefs were brought; Vercingetorix was delivered up,[63] and the arms laid down. Caesar set apart the Aeduan and Arvernian prisoners, in the hope that he could use them to regain the allegiance of their tribes; the rest he distributed as booty to the entire army, allotting one to every man.

90. He then went to the country of the Aedui and received their submission. Envoys from the Arverni waited upon him there, undertaking to obey any orders he gave, and were commanded to supply a large number of hostages. Some twenty thousand prisoners were restored to the Aedui and Arverni. Finally, the legions were distributed in winter quarters. Two legions and some cavalry were sent to the Sequani under the charge of Labienus, with Marcus Sempronius Rutilus under him; two were placed under Fabius and Basilus among the Remi, to protect them from injury at the hands of their neighbours the Bellovaci; Reginus was sent to the Ambivareti, Titus Sextius to the Bituriges, and Caninius to the Ruteni, each with one legion; and Cicero and Sulpicius Rufus were quartered in Aeduan territory at Chalon-sur-Saône and Mâcon, to collect grain. Caesar himself decided to winter at Bibracte. When the results of this year's campaign were reported in his dispatches, a thanksgiving of twenty days was celebrated in Rome.

BOOK VIII
THE FINAL REBELLION

1 Hirtius' preface[64]

Under constant pressure from you, Balbus, and since my regular refusal was beginning to look like a cover for laziness rather than a justified plea of the difficulty involved, I have undertaken this task – a very difficult one. I have written a continuation of our friend Caesar's commentaries on his achievements in Gaul, since his earlier writings do not link up with the later. His latest work, which leaves off at the events in Alexandria, I have completed up to the end of Caesar's life, though not to the end of civil dissension, for no end of that is in sight.

I hope my readers will realize how reluctantly I undertook writing, so that I may the more easily avoid the imputation of foolish arrogance in having thrust myself in the middle of Caesar's writings. It is an accepted fact that all the most strenuous literary efforts of others are surpassed by the elegance of these Commentaries. They were published to provide writers with information about such important events, but they have received such general approbation that future writers appear to have been forestalled, rather than provided with an opportunity. Yet we may feel greater admiration than the others, for they know how well and faultlessly he wrote, while we also know with what ease and speed he completed the work. Caesar not only had the gift of writing with consummate elegance, but also knew how most exactly to convey what his intentions were.

I myself did not, as it happens, even take part in the Alexandrian and African campaigns. Although they are in part known to me from conversation with Caesar, it is one thing to listen to accounts which captivate one with the novelty and remarkable nature of the events described, but quite another to listen with the aim of later putting them on record. However, I should not be surprised if,

while amassing reasons against my being compared with Caesar, I
should lay myself open to a charge of being conceited in supposing
that anyone should think I could be compared with him. Farewell.

2 Revolts of the Bituriges, Carnutes, and Bellovaci (52–51 B.C.)

1. The whole of Gaul was now conquered. Caesar had been
fighting almost continuously since the summer of the previous
year, and after such gruelling work wanted to recruit his soldiers'
strength by a winter's rest. But he heard that many of the tribes
were plotting together and concerting plans for a renewal of
hostilities. His informants pointed out the most probable explanation of this: the Gauls all realized that they could not resist the
Romans even with the largest possible army, if it was concentrated
in one place, but thought that if a number of tribes made
simultaneous attacks in different places, the Romans would not
have enough men or resources to meet them all in time. Any tribe
which had to suffer in consequence, it was argued, must be
prepared to accept its fate, if by delaying the enemy it could enable
the rest to assert their liberty.

2. Caesar did not want to let the Gauls be confirmed in this idea.
So leaving his quaestor Mark Antony in charge of his headquarters
at Bibracte, he set out with a cavalry escort on the 29th of
December[65] to join the 13th legion – quartered in the territory of
the Bituriges not far from the Aeduan frontier – and reinforced it
with the 11th, which was nearest to it. He left two cohorts from
each legion to guard the baggage and led the rest into the most
fertile part of the Bituriges' country. This tribe possessed a number
of towns and an extensive territory – too big for the single legion
quartered among them to be able to prevent them from plotting
and planning war.

3. Caesar's sudden march found them unprepared and scattered, tilling the fields without any thought of danger, and
naturally they were caught by the cavalry before they could take
refuge in the towns. They had not even the usual warning of a
hostile invasion – the sight of burning buildings; for Caesar had

commanded that nothing should be set on fire, in order to avoid giving the alarm, and to save the corn and hay, which he would need if he decided to advance far. The capture of thousands of prisoners threw the Bituriges into a panic, and those who managed to escape the first onset fled to the neighbouring tribes, either trusting to personal friends to take them in or hoping to be protected by the tribal authorities, since all alike were leagued together against the Romans. But they were disappointed; Caesar frustrated their design by making forced marches in every direction, which kept all the tribes so busy protecting themselves that they had no time to think about anyone else's safety. By this prompt action he confirmed the friendly tribes in their loyalty and frightened the waverers into accepting peace terms. When the Bituriges saw that his clemency offered them a chance of regaining his friendship, and that no punishment was inflicted on the neighbouring tribes which submitted and gave hostages, they availed themselves of the opportunity to follow the others' example.

4. As a reward to the soldiers for enduring such a hard campaign with the utmost patience and perseverance – marching through the short winter days over very bad roads in intolerable cold – Caesar promised each soldier a gratuity of two hundred sesterces in lieu of booty, and each centurion two thousand. He then sent the legions back to their winter quarters and returned to Bibracte after an absence of forty days.

While he was engaged there in hearing cases, envoys came from the Bituriges, complaining that the Carnutes had attacked them and asking for help. At this, although he had been only eighteen days at Bibracte, he summoned the 14th and 6th legions[66] – the two that were quartered, as said above, on the Saône to procure corn – and marched out to punish the Carnutes.

5. When they heard that a Roman army was coming, they took warning from the fate that had befallen other tribes: abandoning their villages and towns, where they were living in small buildings hastily constructed to meet the immediate need of winter shelter (for their recent defeat had involved the loss of many of their towns), they fled in all directions. Caesar did not want to expose his men to the rigours of the weather, which was particularly bad

just then, and therefore encamped at Cenabum, the capital of the
Carnutes. Some of the legionaries were lodged in houses belonging
to the Gauls, the rest were protected by shelters erected to cover
the tents and hastily thatched. The cavalry and auxiliary troops,
however, were sent out wherever the enemy was reported to have
gone – a policy justified by its results, for they generally returned
loaded with spoil. The Carnutes suffered from the severity of the
winter, and were greatly terrified; driven from their homes, they
dared not stay long anywhere and the woods did not give them
much shelter in such inclement weather. At length, after sustaining
very heavy losses, they scattered among the tribes on their borders.

6. At this season, when campaigning was so difficult, Caesar
thought it sufficient to prevent an attack by dispersing the enemy
forces that were assembling; and he was now reasonably certain
that no serious outbreak could occur there before the summer. So
putting the two legions he had with him in the charge of Trebonius,
he installed them in quarters at Cenabum, and turned to the next
matter requiring attention. Several deputations had come from the
Remi, warning him that the Bellovaci – the best fighters in the
whole of Gaul, surpassing even the rest of the Belgae – were
mobilizing in conjunction with their neighbours and concentrating
troops under their own leader Correus and Commius the Atrebatian. Their intention, it was said, was to make a concerted attack
on the Suessiones, who had been placed under the suzerainty of
the Remi. Caesar considered that both honour and prudence
required him to protect allies who had done Rome good service.
He therefore called out the 11th legion again, instructed Gaius
Fabius by letter to march his two legions into the territory of the
Suessiones, and sent to Labienus for one of the two under his
command. In this way, as far as the distribution of the winter
quarters and military necessity allowed, he called on the legions by
turns to share the labour of campaigning, while he himself never
rested.

7. When these troops were assembled he marched against the
Bellovaci, encamped in their territory, and sent squadrons of
cavalry in all directions to take some prisoners, from whom he
could discover the enemy's intentions. After executing his orders
the cavalry reported that only a few men were found in the houses

and that these had not stayed behind to till the fields (for the whole country had been completely evacuated), but had been sent back to act as spies. Caesar asked the prisoners where the main body of the Bellovaci was and what plans they had formed. They told him that all their men capable of bearing arms, as well as the Ambiani, Aulerci, Caleti, Veliocasses, and Atrebates, were encamped together on some high ground in a wood surrounded by a marsh and had conveyed all their property into more distant woods. Of the many chiefs who were in favour of rebellion, they said, the people paid most attention to Correus, because they knew that he loathed the very name of Rome. A few days before, Commius had left the camp to get help from the German tribes, who lived quite near by and had unlimited manpower. Finally they explained the plan that had been unanimously approved by the chiefs with the enthusiastic support of the people. If the report that Caesar was coming with only three legions proved to be true, they intended to offer battle, in order to avoid having to fight later on under harder and more unfavourable conditions, when the whole Roman army was in the field. If, however, he brought a larger force, they would remain in the position that they had chosen and by means of ambushes prevent the Romans from getting corn, forage (which at that time of year was scarce and could be found only here and there), and other supplies.

8. These facts were established by the testimony of a number of prisoners and the enemy's plan of campaign impressed Caesar as being well conceived and very different from the rash counsels which are characteristic of barbarian peoples. He therefore decided to do his best to bring them quickly to battle by making them think that they could afford to despise the force he was leading against them. Actually he had three veteran legions of exceptional valour – the 7th, 8th, and 9th – and also the 11th, a legion composed of picked men in the prime of life, who had now seen seven years' service and of whom he had the highest hopes, although they had not yet the same experience or reputation for courage as the others. Summoning his officers, he communicated to them all the information he had received and told them to encourage the men by passing it on to them. In the hope of enticing the enemy to fight by giving the impression that he had only three

legions, he made the three veteran legions march side by side in front, followed by the baggage train – which even when placed all together was quite small, as is usual in such expeditions – with the 11th legion bringing up the rear. In this way the enemy would be able to see only the number of legions they had declared themselves willing to encounter.

The column came into view earlier than the Gauls had expected. 9. They suddenly caught sight of it advancing with a firm step and formed almost into a hollow square as if for immediate action. In spite of the bold front they were reported to be showing, they did not quit the high ground – whether frightened at the prospect of an engagement, or taken aback by our sudden appearance, or waiting to see what we would do – but merely deployed in front of their camp. Caesar had intended to join battle; but he was surprised to see how strong their forces were and therefore encamped opposite them on the other side of a deep but not very wide valley. The Roman camp had a twelve-foot rampart with a breastwork of proportionate height, two trenches fifteen feet wide with perpendicular sides and three-storeyed towers at frequent intervals, joined together by floored galleries protected on the outside by wicker breastworks. Thus, in addition to the double trench, it could be guarded by two rows of defenders: one on the galleries, where they were less exposed on account of the height, and could therefore hurl their missiles with greater confidence and make them carry farther; the other on the actual rampart, where, although nearer the enemy, they were protected by the galleries from falling missiles. The gateways were fitted with doors and flanked with specially high towers.

10. These elaborate defences had two purposes. Caesar hoped that they would make the Gauls imagine that he was afraid, and so give them greater confidence. At the same time they would make the camp so strong that it could be defended by a small force, while the rest scoured the country in search of forage and corn.

Frequent skirmishes took place between small groups of men who ran forward into the marshy ground between the camps and sometimes the marsh was crossed, either by our Gallic and German auxiliaries, who then pursued the enemy vigorously, or by the enemy themselves, who in turn drove our men back some distance.

In the course of our daily foraging expeditions it inevitably happened – since the farms from which the hay was obtained were few and far between – that isolated parties were surrounded in places difficult to get out of; and although this only meant the loss of a few servants and animals, it raised foolish hopes in the minds of the Bellovaci, especially when Commius arrived back from his mission to the German tribes, mentioned above, with a squadron of horsemen. There were only five hundred of them, but the mere fact that German aid had come was enough to make these natives cock-a-hoop.

11. As the days went by, the enemy still stayed in their camp, which, protected as it was by the marsh and the strength of its position, obviously could not be stormed without a murderous struggle. To invest it, a larger force was needed. Accordingly, orders were sent to Trebonius to summon with all speed the 13th legion, which was wintering in the charge of Titus Sextius among the Bituriges, and having thus made up an army of three legions to join Caesar by forced marches. Meanwhile Caesar used the large number of cavalry which he had called up from the Remi, Lingones, and other tribes, to take turns in escorting the foraging parties and repelling any sudden attacks made upon them.

12. After doing this duty for some days they grew careless, as generally happens when a routine is continued for any length of time. The Bellovaci discovered where they posted themselves each day and placed an ambush of picked infantrymen in a spot screened by trees. Next day they sent some of their own cavalry there to decoy our men into the ambush, so that they could be surrounded and attacked. It happened to be the Remi who fell into the trap, as it was their turn of duty that day. Suddenly catching sight of the small party of enemy horsemen, and thinking themselves quite safe because of their superior numbers, they gave chase too eagerly and found themselves encircled by the infantrymen. Alarmed at this they retreated more precipitately than is customary in a cavalry action, with the loss of their commander Vertiscus, the chief magistrate of the tribe, who was almost too old to keep his saddle but, like a good Gaul, would not plead age as an excuse for declining the command and insisted on taking part in the fight. This success, involving the death of a principal magistrate and

general of the Remi, filled the enemy with pride and excitement, and our men were taught by their misfortune to reconnoitre more carefully before establishing their posts and to use more discretion in pursuing a retreating foe.

13. Fighting went on daily, within sight of both camps, at places where the marsh was fordable. In one of these encounters the whole of the light infantry which had been brought from Germany to fight among the cavalry went boldly over the marsh, killed the few Gauls who opposed them, and vigorously pursued all the rest. The enemy was panic-stricken. Not only those who were attacked at close quarters or wounded by missiles but even the reserves posted, as usual, at a distance, fled like cowards and, dislodged from every piece of high ground where they tried to make a stand, did not stop until they reached their camp. Some were too much ashamed to show their faces in camp and ran farther still. Their perilous experience filled the whole army of the Bellovaci with dismay; for these Gauls, whom any trifling success made so vainglorious, were just as easily frightened by the slightest reverse.

14. For several days they still remained in their camp. But when their leaders heard that Trebonius and his legions were close at hand, they were afraid of being blockaded as Vercingetorix was at Alesia, and therefore sent away by night all who were a hindrance – those who were too old or too weak to fight and those who had no arms – and all their heavy baggage. They were still busy forming up the disorderly train of frightened non-combatants (for Gauls always go with a long procession of wagons, even when they are supposed to be travelling light) when daylight overtook them, and they had to draw up a body of troops in front of the camp to prevent the Romans from pursuing the column and give it time to get some distance away. So long as these troops stood on the defensive Caesar did not think it prudent to attack them, as it would mean advancing up a steep hill; at the same time he wanted to move his legions far enough forward to threaten them and make it dangerous for them to leave their position. The marsh between the two camps was difficult to cross and would hinder a quick pursuit of the enemy. On the other side of it, however, was a hill almost touching that on which the Gauls' camp stood, being separated from it only by a small ravine. Accordingly he laid

causeways over the marsh, led the legions across, and hastened to reach a plateau on the hilltop, which was protected on two sides by steep slopes. After re-forming the troops there he advanced to the edge and drew up a battle line in a place where the closely packed enemy formations would be within range of his artillery.

15. Confident in the strength of their position, the Gauls were willing to fight if the Romans tried to climb the hill; but they dared not disperse their forces by sending detachments here and there, for fear of impairing their morale, and therefore stayed drawn up where they were. When Caesar saw that they would not budge he measured out ground for a camp, and keeping twenty cohorts ready for action set the rest to work at making the fortifications. When these were completed he drew up the infantry in front of them and placed pickets of cavalry in various spots with their horses ready bridled. The Bellovaci could not spend the night where they were – indeed they could not safely remain much longer. As they saw that the Romans were ready to pursue if they moved, they employed a ruse to get away. They had in the camp a large number of bundles of straw and twigs, which they had been using to sit on. These were passed along from hand to hand and placed in front of their battle line. Towards the evening the word was given to set fire to them all together, so that a curtain of flame suddenly hid their entire army from the Romans, and the natives seized the opportunity to run away as hard as they could.

16. Although the barrier of fire prevented Caesar from actually seeing them go, he guessed that its purpose was to cover their escape and therefore sent some cavalry in pursuit. He also moved the legions forward – with caution, because he feared a trap; the enemy's intention might be to hold their ground and inveigle him into a bad position. Most of the cavalrymen were afraid to enter the dense ring of smoke and fire, and those who were bold enough to attempt it found that they could scarcely see their own horses' heads. They too were suspicious of a trap and so left the enemy to retire unmolested. This retreat, dictated by fear but executed with the utmost ingenuity, enabled them to reach, without any loss, a very strong position barely ten miles farther on, where they encamped.

From there the Bellovaci kept sending out parties of horse and foot, which by laying ambushes here and there inflicted heavy casualties on the Roman foragers.

17. These attacks became more and more frequent. Eventually Caesar learnt from a prisoner that Correus had assembled a picked force of six thousand of his bravest infantrymen and a thousand cavalry, with which he intended to lay an ambush at a place where he expected the abundance of corn and hay would attract the Romans. Accordingly, the cavalry which always escorted the Roman foragers was sent there, with some light-armed auxiliary infantry dispersed among its ranks. Caesar himself led out an unusually strong legionary force, with which he approached as near the place as possible.

18. The Gauls had chosen for their ambush a plain not more than a square mile in extent, completely enclosed by almost impenetrable woods and a very deep river, and had surrounded it with a cordon. Our men knew what to expect and – being well armed and aware that the legions were coming up behind them – were ready to face any attack, so they rode on to the plain squadron by squadron. Correus thought this was his chance to strike. He came out of hiding, with a small force at first, and charged the nearest units. Our men met his onslaught resolutely and did not crowd together – a mistake frequently made in cavalry engagements through fright; in a tightly packed mass of horsemen losses are inevitable.

19. The squadrons took up separate positions and small groups of the men fought by turns, covering one another's flanks so that the Gauls could not surround them. While Correus' force was still engaged, the rest of the enemy cavalry came out of the woods. Hotly contested fights took place in various parts of the field and continued for a long while without decisive result, until the main body of the enemy's infantry gradually emerged from hiding in battle formation and forced our cavalry to retreat. The cavalry were quickly supported by the light infantry sent up with them in advance of the legions; the infantrymen dispersed themselves among the squadrons and fought with great steadiness. For some time the battle was even. Eventually it took the usual course of such engagements; the very fact that our troops had survived the initial shock without disaster, though ambushed and taken by

surprise, gave them an advantage. Meanwhile the legions were drawing near. Messengers kept arriving, and both sides heard simultaneously that the commander-in-chief was at hand with his troops prepared for action. At this our men fought with redoubled energy, sure of the legions' support in case the battle still dragged on, but determined to win without it if they could, so as to keep all the glory for themselves. The enemy's spirits were dashed and they tried to escape in every direction. This, however, was impossible, for they were trapped by the very same obstacles with which they had hoped to entrap the Romans. Demoralized by their defeat, however, and dismayed by the loss of more than half their number, they fled haphazardly towards the woods or the river, only to be slaughtered by pursuers following on their heels. But no misfortune could break Correus' resolutions. He would neither leave the battle nor take to the woods nor surrender when offered quarter, but fought on heroically, dealing out wounds right and left, until the victorious Romans were provoked by anger to shoot him down.

20. The battle was only just over when Caesar arrived with the legions. He expected that the news of such a disastrous defeat would make the Gauls abandon their camp, which was said to be only about eight miles from the scene of the carnage. Accordingly, although his passage was obstructed by the river, he got his army across and advanced. Meanwhile a handful of wounded fugitives, whom the woods had protected from destruction, arrived at the enemy's camp with the first news of the disaster. When they heard that everything had gone wrong, that Correus was dead, and their cavalry and the flower of their infantry lost, the Bellovaci and their allies made sure that the Romans must be marching to attack them. A mass meeting was hastily summoned by trumpet-calls and the soldiers insisted that envoys and hostages must be sent to Caesar.

21. When this was unanimously agreed to, Commius fled to the German tribes from whom he had borrowed reinforcements. The rest dispatched envoys on the spot and begged Caesar to be content with the punishment that they had undergone – a heavier one, they were sure, than a man of his clemency and humanity could ever inflict in cold blood, even upon a foe who had not suffered already. 'Our strength was broken,' they said, 'in the action against your cavalry. We lost many thousands of picked soldiers – indeed,

hardly any escaped to tell the tale of the massacre. However, we must be thankful for small mercies at such a time, and the battle has at least brought us one piece of good fortune: Correus, the popular agitator who was responsible for the war, has been killed. While he lived, our senate was always overruled by the ignorant proletariat.'

22. In reply to this appeal Caesar pointed out to the envoys that the Bellovaci had taken part in the general rising of the previous year and had persisted in their hostility more stubbornly than any of the other tribes, instead of being brought to reason by their surrender. It was very easy of course to lay the blame for their misdeeds at a dead man's door; but no man could be powerful enough, with only the feeble assistance of the populace, to start and carry on a war against the will of the tribal leaders and in face of opposition from the council and all patriotic citizens. However, he would be content with the punishment that they had already brought on themselves.

23. Returning to their countrymen at night, the envoys reported Caesar's reply and obtained the required number of hostages. The deputies of the other tribes, who had been waiting to see what success the Bellovaci had, now hastened to make their own submission, to supply the necessary hostages, and to comply with the demands made upon them. Only Commius kept away, being afraid to entrust his life to any man. For the year before, when Caesar was away holding the assizes in northern Italy, Labienus had discovered that Commius was intriguing with various tribes and plotting against Caesar, and decided that it would be no treachery to destroy such a traitor. It was useless to summon him to the camp; he would not have come, and the summons would have put him on his guard. So Labienus sent Volusenus with orders to stage a sham interview and have him put to death. Some centurions specially picked for the purpose went with him. At the interview Volusenus gave the pre-arranged signal by grasping Commius' hand, but the centurion who made the first sword thrust failed to dispatch him, only inflicting a severe head wound; either his nerve failed him because he was unused to such work, or Commius' friends were too quick for him. Both sides drew their weapons, but more with the object of getting safely away than of

fighting; for the Romans thought that Commius was mortally wounded, and the Gauls, realizing that they had been led into a trap, were afraid that more men might be concealed somewhere. After this experience Commius was said to have resolved never to come again into the presence of any Roman.

3 The last encounters; capture of Uxellodunum (51 B.C.)

24. Now that all the most warlike tribes had been conquered, there was no further prospect of organized resistance anywhere. But as many of the natives were leaving the towns and cultivated lands to avoid living under Roman rule as long as they could, Caesar resolved to send detachments into various parts of the country. He kept the 12th legion with him, and his quaestor Mark Antony. Gaius Fabius was sent with two legions and five cohorts to the extreme west of Gaul, because some of the tribes there were reported to be in arms, and the two legions which Caninius had in the district, being under strength, might not be able to hold them in check. Labienus was summoned to join Caesar, while the 15th legion, which had wintered under Labienus' command, was sent to northern Italy to protect the citizen colonies there from a repetition of the injury done to the people of Trieste the previous year, when a sudden raid by the barbarians took them by surprise.

Caesar himself set out to lay waste and plunder the territory of Ambiorix the Eburonian, who fled in terror and so could not be forced into submission. Caesar thought that the next best way of obtaining the satisfaction that his honour demanded was to strip the country of inhabitants, cattle, and buildings so thoroughly that any of the Eburones who had the good fortune to escape would loathe Ambiorix for bringing such calamities upon them and never allow him to return.

25. Detachments of legionary or auxiliary troops went all over the country, killing or capturing large numbers of the natives, burning the homesteads, and carrying off plunder, until it was completely devastated. Caesar then sent Labienus with two legions against the Treveri – a people who, living so near the German

border, were accustomed to fighting every day of their lives; they were nearly as fierce and uncivilized as the Germans themselves, and would never do as they were told unless compelled by armed force.

26. Meanwhile Caninius received letters and messages from Duratius – always a faithful ally of Rome, although a part of his fellow countrymen had revolted – telling him that a great crowd of the enemy had assembled in the country of the Pictones. He therefore set out for the town of Lemonum. On approaching it he obtained more exact information from prisoners. Duratius, they said, was besieged in the town by an army of many thousands under Dumnacus, commander of the Andes. Caninius dared not risk an engagement, as his legions were below their proper strength, and therefore took up a strong position and encamped. On learning of the legions' approach, Dumnacus turned his whole force round to face them and tried to storm the camp. After spending several days in this attempt, however, and losing a large number of men without being able to break the defences at any point, he returned to the siege of Lemonum.

27. Fabius received the submission of a number of tribes and took hostages from them as a guarantee. On the arrival of a dispatch from Caninius reporting what was happening among the Pictones, he set out to rescue Duratius. At this, Dumnacus decided that his position was hopeless; he could not withstand an attack from outside and at the same time keep an eye open for any threatening movement by the garrison of Lemonum. So he hastily retired; his only chance of safety, he thought, was to get his troops across the Loire, which was too wide to cross except by one of the bridges. Fabius had not yet come within sight of his enemy or effected a junction with Caninius, but the information he received from people acquainted with the district led him to expect that the frightened Gauls would take precisely the direction which they actually were taking; so he marched towards the same bridge as Dumnacus was making for. He sent his cavalry ahead of the legions, but told them to be careful not to go too far; they must be able, without tiring their horses, to get back to the camp which they were to share with the legions. These orders were duly carried out. The cavalry came up with the rear of Dumnacus' column and

attacked it. The fleeing Gauls were demoralized and hampered by the baggage that they were carrying; many of them were killed, and a quantity of booty was taken. After this success the cavalry made their way back to the camp.

28. The next night Fabius sent the cavalry out with orders to engage the enemy and delay their march until he came up. The cavalry commander, Quintus Atius Varus, a man of exceptional courage and intelligence, impressed upon his men the importance of following these instructions. On catching up with Dumnacus' column he placed some of his squadrons in convenient positions to act as reserves, and with the rest engaged the enemy's cavalry. The latter joined battle with unusual confidence; for the whole of the Gallic column halted, so that infantry could come to the support of their cavalry against ours. The fight was hotly contested. Our men regarded the enemy with contempt after beating them the day before, and, knowing that the legions were close behind, they were ashamed to give ground and wanted to finish the battle by themselves. So they struggled with desperate courage against the infantry. As for the enemy, their experience on the previous day led them to assume that our troops would not be reinforced, and they thought they had an opportunity of annihilating our cavalry.

29. As the struggle proved long and hard, Dumnacus drew up his infantry in regular line of battle, so that they could give protection to each squadron of cavalry as need arose. Suddenly the serried ranks of our legions came into view. The sight gave the enemy such a shock that cavalry and infantry alike fled helter-skelter with loud cries of terror, leaving the baggage train in complete confusion. Our cavalry were now rewarded for their heroic efforts to overcome the enemy's resistance. Beside themselves with joy at their success, they rode forward everywhere with rousing cheers, encircled the retreating Gauls, and killed them without ceasing until their horses were exhausted and their right arms tired. More than twelve thousand were slaughtered – some still with their weapons in their hands, while others had thrown them down in their fear – and the whole baggage train was captured.

30. After the rout of the Gallic army news was brought that Drappes, a Senonian, and Lucterius, a Cadurcan, were marching

towards the Province with a small force – some two thousand at most – collected from the fugitives. Drappes had been raiding the Roman baggage and supply convoys, ever since the beginning of Vercingetorix's rebellion, with a band of desperadoes assembled from all quarters, including slaves to whom he had promised their liberty, outlaws from various tribes, and bandits. Lucterius, as mentioned above, had already attempted to invade the Province in the opening stage of the rebellion. Caninius hastened in pursuit of them with two legions, thinking that it would be a serious disgrace if any damage were done to the Province, or its inhabitants alarmed, by the depredations of these brigands.

31. Fabius, who by this time had joined Caninius, started with the rest of the army for the territories of the Carnutes and the other tribes which had suffered such heavy losses in the battle with Dumnacus. After their recent defeat, he thought, they would be more inclined to submission; but if they were allowed any respite Dumnacus might induce them to fight again. As things turned out, Fabius was remarkably successful in bringing them quickly to heel. The Carnutes, who though frequently hard put to it had not asked for terms before, now offered hostages and surrendered; and the Aremorican tribes, who live on the Atlantic coast in the extreme west, followed their example, submitting to Fabius' demands directly he appeared with his army. Dumnacus was driven into exile and forced to go skulking alone from place to place until he reached the remotest corner of Gaul.

32. When Drappes and Lucterius heard that Caninius was close behind them, they realized that it would be certain destruction to enter the Province with a pursuing army at their heels, and that it was no longer possible for them to wander about the country as they pleased committing acts of brigandage. So they halted in the territory of the Cadurci, Lucterius' fellow countrymen. He had great power over the tribe in the days before the defeat of Vercingetorix, and was still an influential agitator among the ignorant natives. With his own and Drappes' troops he now occupied Uxellodunum, a town of great natural strength which had previously been a dependency of his, and prevailed on its inhabitants to join him.

33. Caninius went at once to the place to reconnoitre. The town

was protected on every side by precipitous rocks, which would be difficult for men carrying arms to scale, even if they met with no resistance. On the other hand, it would not be easy for the Gauls to evacuate it by stealth. He could see that they had a large quantity of heavy baggage, which could not be got away without being open to attack both by his cavalry and by the legions. He formed his troops into three divisions and pitched three camps on very high ground, from which he began to build entrenchments round the town as fast as he could with the limited number of men available.

34. The townspeople, haunted by the recollection of the tragic events at Alesia, now began to fear a similar fate if they were besieged; Lucterius in particular, who had been through the former siege, kept warning them that they must arrange for a supply of food. The leaders decided unanimously to leave a part of their troops in the town and go out themselves with a lightly equipped force to get in grain. The next night, leaving two thousand armed men inside, Drappes and Lucterius started out with the rest. In a few days they got a large quantity of grain from the country of the Cadurci, partly by voluntary contribution from the inhabitants, partly by forcible requisition. They also made occasional night attacks on Caninius' fortified posts, in view of which he decided not to complete the line of entrenchments for the time being; for he saw that he would be compelled either to leave a part of it unguarded or, by distributing his men among a large number of strong points, to make the individual posts dangerously weak.

35. Eventually Drappes and Lucterius took up a position about ten miles from the town, intending to carry in their big store of corn a little at a time. They divided the superintendence of this work between them: Drappes stayed to protect the camp with a part of the troops, while Lucterius led the convoy of packhorses close up to the town. He then placed pickets at various points, and shortly before daybreak attempted to smuggle in the corn by following narrow tracks through the woods. But the noise attracted the attention of the sentries on duty at the Roman camp, and scouts were sent out to see what was happening. Directly he received their report, Caninius summoned the cohorts which were ready armed in the nearest posts and charged the convoy just as day was breaking. Taken by surprise, the Gauls scattered in alarm to seek

the protection of their pickets. As soon as the Romans caught sight
of men with weapons in their hands they attacked with redoubled
fury, giving no quarter to anyone. Lucterius got away with a
handful of men, but could not make his way back to the camp.

36. After this success Caninius learnt from several prisoners,
whom he questioned separately in order to corroborate their
statements, that a part of the enemy's forces was encamped with
Drappes about twelve miles from the scene of the action. Now that
one of their two leaders had been forced to take flight, it ought to
be easy, he thought, to surprise and overawe the rest of them; it
was a lucky chance that none of Lucterius' men, as far as was
known, had escaped back to the camp to inform Drappes of their
defeat. In any case, Caninius saw no danger in attempting a
surprise attack. He therefore sent ahead all his cavalry and the
German infantry, who were very fleet of foot. Then he divided one
legion between the three camps and led out the other, lightly
equipped for action. As he came near the enemy, the scouts sent
on in front brought word that according to the usual Gallic custom
Drappes had left the high ground and placed his camp on a river
bank, and that the Germans and the cavalry had swooped down on
it without any warning and attacked. Caninius at once led the
infantry forward, drawn up in battle order with their weapons in
their hands, and at a given signal they quickly occupied all the
surrounding high ground. On seeing the legions' standards the
Germans and the cavalry pressed their attack very strongly. The
legionaries charged at once from every side, killed or captured all
the Gauls, and took a quantity of booty. Drappes himself was
among the prisoners.

37. The Romans thus achieved complete success, almost without
casualties. Having got rid of his enemy in the open, Caninius
returned to the siege of Uxellodunum. Hitherto he had been afraid
to complete the investment of the town and distribute his troops
among a large number of guard posts. Now he gave orders to push
on with the work everywhere, and the next day Fabius' army
returned from its expedition against the Carnutes and took over a
sector of the siege works.

38. In the meantime Caesar had left Antony with fifteen cohorts
in the territory of the Bellovaci to prevent the Belgae from forming

any fresh plans for revolt, and himself visited the tribes in western Gaul. From some he demanded additional hostages, but his main concern was to reassure them and allay their fears. The Carnutes were particularly alarmed because they knew they had been guilty of shedding the first blood at the beginning of the great rebellion, as shown above. In order to relieve the tribe as a whole from further anxiety, Caesar called on them to deliver up for punishment Gutuater, the person chiefly responsible for the outrage and the principal warmonger. This man went in such fear of his life that he did not let even his fellow citizens know his whereabouts; but they all made diligent search for him and quickly brought him to the Roman camp. Though Caesar was always averse to harsh punishments, he was forced to execute him in order to satisfy the soldiers, who crowded round and charged Gutuater with responsibility for all the perils and losses they had suffered in the fighting. Accordingly he was flogged to death and his head cut off.

39. While in the country of the Carnutes Caesar received several dispatches in close succession from Caninius, telling him what had happened to Drappes and Lucterius, and with what determination the defenders of Uxellodunum were holding out. Although their numbers were insignificant, Caesar thought they ought to be severely punished for their obstinacy; otherwise, all the Gauls might suppose that their failure to defeat the Romans was due not to any lack of strength, but to a lack of perseverance, and other tribes which were advantageously situated might follow the example set at Uxellodunum and make a bid for freedom. They all knew that his command was due to expire after one more summer, so that if they could hold out for that time they would have nothing more to fear. Accordingly, leaving his general Quintus Calenus with two legions to follow at normal marching pace, he advanced at top speed with all the cavalry to join Caninius.

40. His arrival at Uxellodunum was a surprise to everyone. The town was now completely invested, and the Romans were committed to prosecuting the siege at all costs. As he learnt from deserters that the garrison had a large stock of provisions, he decided to try cutting off their water supply. A river flowed along the deep valley that almost surrounded the mountain on which the town stood. There was no way of diverting the water, on account of its position;

it ran so low down at the mountain foot that it was impracticable to dig channels which would drain it off in any direction. But the way down to it from the town was so steep and difficult that any opposition on the Romans' part would make it impossible for the defenders to get to the water without the risk of being killed or wounded, or to return safely up the precipitous slope. Accordingly Caesar posted archers and slingers at various points to prevent them from approaching the river, and even trained artillery upon some of the easiest ways down.

41. All the besieged, when they needed water, now had to go to one particular spot right at the foot of the town wall, where a copious spring gushed out. This was on the side of the town which, for a space of about three hundred feet, was not encircled by the river. All our men were anxious to find a way of keeping the enemy away from this spring, but only Caesar saw how it could be done. Opposite the place he advanced a line of mantlets up the slope and began to build a terrace. This involved not only much labour but continual fighting; for the enemy ran down and threw missiles from above at a safe distance, so that our men's determined efforts to ascend the slope cost them many casualties. In spite of this they pushed forward the mantlets and surmounted the difficulties of the terrain by working hard at their task. At the same time they dug mines towards the spring and the rills which fed it; this work involved no danger, since it could be done without the Gauls' suspecting it. The terrace was raised to a height of sixty feet, and a tower of ten storeys placed upon it, not with the object of reaching the level of the walls, which no siege works could possibly have done, but in order to dominate the spring. Artillery was then mounted in the tower and trained on the approach to the spring; and it became so dangerous to go there for water that before long not only the cattle and packhorses but also the large population of the town were tormented by thirst.

42. The besieged were dismayed by this calamity. Filling barrels with tallow, pitch, and pieces of lath, they set them on fire and rolled them down on our works, delivering fierce attacks at the same time, so that our soldiers would be forced to protect themselves and unable to extinguish the flames. The mantlets and terrace were immediately set ablaze, because anything thrown

down the slope could not miss them, and they were easily ignited by the burning material that lodged upon them. Our men had to fight in a situation of great danger, with the ground against them, but they faced all their difficulties with splendid courage. In their elevated position they were in full view of the rest of the army and both sides were cheering loudly. Thus every man, in order to prove his mettle before so many witnesses, tried to make himself as conspicuous as he could in risking injury from wounds or burns.

43. Observing that heavy losses were being sustained, Caesar ordered the cohorts to clamber up the rocks wherever it was practicable, and by raising shouts to give the impression that they were getting a footing on the rampart at various points. By this means the garrison – who could only guess what was happening on other sides of the town – were frightened into recalling their troops from the attack on our works and sending them to man the walls. Relieved from the necessity of fighting, our soldiers soon extinguished the flames in some places, and isolated the parts which were still burning. The townsmen, however, still resisted obstinately and held out even when numbers had died of thirst, until in the end our mines tapped the rivulets which supplied the spring and diverted them. The sudden drying up of this supply, which had never failed them before, reduced the Gauls to such despair that they did not realize that it was due to the cunning of their enemy, but thought it was the will of supernatural powers and, yielding to necessity, surrendered.

44. Caesar saw that his work in Gaul could never be brought to a successful conclusion if similar revolts were allowed to break out constantly in different parts of the country; and his clemency was so well known that no one would think him a cruel man if for once he took severe measures.[67] So he decided to deter all others by making an example of the defenders of Uxellodunum. All who had borne arms had their hands cut off and were then let go, so that everyone might see what punishment was meted out to evildoers. Drappes, on being captured, as previously said, by Caninius, had starved himself to death, either because he could not endure the humiliation of being kept in chains or because he feared a still heavier punishment. Lucterius, after his escape from the encounter outside Uxellodunum, had kept continually on the move, because

he thought it dangerous to stay long anywhere after earning Caesar's implacable hatred. He was thus compelled to entrust his life to one man after another and at length came into the power of an Arvernian called Epasnactus, who, being an enthusiastic pro-Roman, without a moment's hesitation put him in chains and took him to Caesar.

45. Meanwhile Labienus fought a successful cavalry action in the country of the Treveri, inflicting severe casualties upon them and their German allies, who were always ready to help anyone against the Romans. He also captured the chiefs of the Treveri and with them the only Aeduan chief who was still in arms – Surus, a man of illustrious birth and distinguished courage.

46. The situation was now everywhere satisfactory. In several years' campaigns nearly all Gaul had been thoroughly conquered. As Caesar had not personally visited Aquitania, however, although it had been partially subdued by Publius Crassus,[68] he set out with two legions to spend the last part of the summer there. He conducted the campaign with his usual speed and success; all the Aquitanian tribes sent envoys and gave hostages. After that he started for Narbonne with an escort of cavalry, leaving his generals to install the army in winter quarters.[69] Four legions were stationed in Belgic territory under the generals Antony, Trebonius, and Publius Vatinius; two in the country of the Aedui, the most influential tribe in Gaul; two among the Turoni on the frontier of the Carnutes, to hold all the west up to the Atlantic seaboard; the remaining two in the country of the Lemovices, not far from the Arvernian border. In this way no part of Gaul was left without troops. Caesar stayed a few days in the Province, passing quickly from one to another of the assize towns, settling political disputes and bestowing rewards where they were deserved. He had good opportunities of learning what attitude each man had adopted in the general revolt, which the loyal aid rendered by the Province had enabled him to withstand. On the completion of this business he rejoined the legions quartered among the Belgae and spent the winter at Nemetocenna.

47. There he heard how Commius the Atrebatian came to blows with a party of our cavalry. Antony had reached his winter quarters and the Atrebates were quiet; but Commius, ever since he was

wounded at his meeting with Volusenus, as related above, had always been ready to act as an agitator and ringleader in any intrigues or warlike plots that might be hatched among his fellow tribesmen. As the Atrebates were at present submitting to Roman control, he organized a band of horsemen and supported himself and his followers by brigandage, intercepting by means of raids several convoys destined for the Roman camp.

48. Volusenus, who was attached to Antony's legion for the winter as cavalry commander, was detailed to pursue Commius' horsemen – a task for which his outstanding courage fitted him, and which he undertook all the more willingly because he detested Commius. So he laid ambushes in various places and made a number of successful attacks on the horsemen. At length, in a particularly fierce encounter, he and a few of his men made a determined effort to catch Commius himself by pursuing him closely. Commius galloped off and drew them some distance away. Then, in his hatred of Volusenus, he suddenly appealed to his followers to help him avenge the wound which had been so treacherously inflicted on him, and turning his horse round rode forward alone and daringly charged his enemy. The others followed his example and Volusenus' handful of men were forced to fly with the Gauls in pursuit. Putting spurs to his horse Commius rode close up behind Volusenus and with his lance couched made a hard thrust clean through his thigh. Seeing their commander wounded, our men drew rein without a moment's hesitation, wheeled round, and repulsed their pursuers. A number of the Gauls were knocked down and wounded by the violence of the charge and either trampled under the horses' feet in the pursuit or taken prisoner – a fate which Commius escaped by the swiftness of his horse. Thus our horsemen had the best of the fight; but Volusenus was carried back to camp with a wound so severe that it looked as if it might prove fatal. Either Commius was satisfied with his revenge, or else he had lost too many of his followers to be able to pursue the quarrels farther; in any case, he sent to Antony and offered hostages as a guarantee that he would live where he was bidden and do as he was told. His only request was that as a concession to the fear which haunted him he should not be required to come into the presence of any Roman. Antony decided that his fears were

justified and therefore granted his petition and accepted the
hostages.

I know that Caesar wrote one book of the Commentaries for
each year. I did not consider that I ought to do this, because the
following year, the consulship of Lucius Paulus and Gaius Marcellus (50 B.C.), contained no major campaigns in Gaul. However, so
that no one may be unaware of where Caesar and his army were at
that time, I have decided to append a brief account to this
Commentary.

49. During the winter which he spent in Belgic Gaul Caesar
made it his single aim to keep the tribes loyal and to see that none
had any pretext for revolt or any hope of profiting by it. The last
thing he wanted was to have to fight a campaign immediately
before his departure; for it would mean leaving Gaul in a state of
rebellion when the time came to withdraw his army and all the
tribes would be only too willing to take up arms when they could
do so without immediate risk. So he made their condition of
subjection more tolerable by addressing the tribal governments in
complimentary terms, refraining from the imposition of any fresh
burdens, and bestowing rich presents upon the principal citizens.
By these means it was easy to induce a people exhausted by so
many defeats to live at peace.[70]

4 Civil war impends

50. After the stay in winter quarters was over Caesar, contrary to
his usual practice, went to Italy, proceeding by forced marches, to
make a personal canvass of the towns and colonies whose support
he had solicited for his quaestor, Mark Antony, in his candidacy
for the priesthood. He was glad to lend his influence as Antony,
whom he had sent ahead a little previously, to pursue his election
campaign, was his close friend. He was also keen to counter the
small faction of influential men who wanted to secure Antony's
defeat in order to undermine Caesar's own influence when he
returned from his province. The news that Antony had been made
augur reached him when he was still on the way to Italy.
Nevertheless, he felt that he had still just as much reason to visit

the towns and colonies, both to thank them for turning out in large numbers to support Antony and also to canvass for his own candidacy for office in the following year. His opponents, he knew, were insolently boasting that Lucius Lentulus and Gaius Marcellus had been made consuls for the purpose of depriving Caesar of all official standing and prestige, and Servius Galba had been robbed of the consulship, despite his far greater popularity and larger number of votes, because he was closely connected with Caesar both as a friend and as a general.

51. The towns and colonies welcomed Caesar's arrival with incredible displays of honour and affection. This was the first time he visited them after that great war against the whole of Gaul. Every possible decoration that could be devised was used to dress up the gates, the route, every place he would go. The whole population, children and all, turned out to meet him, victims were sacrificed everywhere, and main squares and temples were crammed with banqueting couches, anticipating, as it were, the joyfulness to come when he celebrated his keenly awaited triumph. The wealthy put on a great show, the poorer displayed their enthusiasm.

52. Caesar hurried through the Cisalpine province and very quickly returned to the army at Nemetocenna. He summoned all the legions from winter quarters to the territory of the Treveri and there held a review of the army. He put Labienus in charge of Cisalpine Gaul, to further the latter's candidature for the consulship. He himself made only as many marches as he thought sufficient to promote the health of the legions by moving them about, although frequent reports reached him that his enemies were attempting to suborn Labienus and that a small group was plotting to use a senatorial decree to deprive him of some part of his army. However, he did not believe the stories about Labienus, nor could he be induced to take any action to prevent a senatorial decree. His view was that if the senators were left free to decide his cause would easily prevail.

Gaius Curio, tribune of the plebs, who had undertaken to look after Caesar's interest and position, had often proposed to the Senate that if anyone felt alarm at Caesar's military might, and since, especially, Pompey's dominance, backed by arms, engendered no small fear at Rome, both should give up their commands and disband their armies. If this was done, he said, the state would be free and independent. He went beyond proposing, and actually began to proceed to a senatorial vote; but the consuls and Pompey's friends intervened, and so by delaying tactics prevented action being taken.

53. This was a clear indication of the attitude of the Senate as a whole and agreed with its earlier behaviour; for in the previous year Marcellus, in an assault on Caesar's position, raised prematurely in the Senate, in contravention of the Licinian-Pompeian law, the question of Caesar's provinces. There was a debate. When Marcellus, whose attempts to build up his own political standing rested entirely on stirring up feeling against Caesar, proceeded to a vote, a crowded Senate rejected his motion. This did not discourage Caesar's enemies, but merely stimulated them to cultivate their connections so as to be able to force the Senate to fall in with their wishes.

54. Then a senatorial decree was passed ordering Pompey and Caesar each to contribute one legion to the Parthian campaign. This clearly meant that one of them lost two legions, for Pompey contributed, as though from his own complement, the 1st legion, which was levied in Caesar's province and which he had sent to Caesar. However, though Caesar was in no doubt about the intentions of his opponents, he returned the legion to Pompey and from his own forces he ordered the 15th legion, quartered in Cisalpine Gaul, to be handed over in accordance with the Senate's decree. To replace it he sent the 13th legion into Italy to man the garrisons from which the 15th was being withdrawn. He allotted his army to winter quarters. Trebonius was posted with four legions in Belgium, and Fabius among the Aedui, also with four legions. Caesar thought the best means of securing Gaul was to station forces among the Belgae, the bravest people, and the Aedui, the most influential. He himself went to Italy.

55. On arrival, he learned that through the agency of the consul Marcellus the two legions he had returned, which under the senatorial decree were due to be taken to the Parthian campaign, had been handed over to Pompey and retained in Italy. Though this action made it perfectly plain what was planned against Caesar,

he nevertheless thought that he should put up with everything, so long as some hope remained of reaching a settlement by constitutional means rather than resorting to war.

NOTES

1. (I.2) The large Celtic tribe of the Helvetii had been for nearly half a century under constant pressure from the Germans, and was now confined within the area of modern Switzerland. It was perhaps the fear of fresh German attacks, after Ariovistus' entry into Gaul, that determined them to seek a new home in western France.

2. (I.6) The route leading between the Jura and the Rhône is the Pas de l'Ecluse, through which the road from Geneva to Lyons passes.

3. (I.7) The 'yoke' was made of two spears fixed upright, with a third fastened horizontally across them at such a height that the defeated soldiers, in filing under it, were obliged to stoop in token of submission.

4. (I.10) Since the route through the territory of the Sequani lay outside the Roman Province, Caesar had, strictly speaking, no right to interfere further. But the danger of which he speaks may have been a real one (although the territory of the Santoni was some 130 miles from the frontier of the Province), and there was precedent for such preventive action on the part of provincial governors.

5. (I.18) It suits Caesar's purpose to represent Dumnorix as merely an ambitious adventurer; but the facts suggest that he was really the leader of a popular party which opposed, in the national interest, the pro-Roman policy of the Aeduan nobles.

6. (I.24) A phalanx was a closely packed mass of troops, formed up in considerable depth and – at any rate in the original form used by the Macedonians – armed with very long pikes, so as to present to an enemy an impenetrable thicket of spearpoints. When this formation was adopted by the Gauls and Germans, the men in the front rank held their shields overlapping one another in front of their bodies.

7. (I.25) It was the custom in ancient warfare to attack, if possible, the right flank of enemy troops, because on that side they could not easily protect themselves with their shields.

8. (I.40) The slave war referred to was fought in 73–71 B.C. A Thracian gladiator named Spartacus raised a large force and defeated several Roman armies. He was eventually crushed by Crassus, the future triumvir.

9. (I.43) The plain in which Caesar and Ariovistus were encamped was the plain of Alsace.

10. (I.53) According to the manuscripts of Caesar's text the Rhine was

'some five miles' away from the battlefield. But although the site of the battle cannot be certainly identified, none of the possible sites is less than twelve miles from the Rhine. Perhaps the numeral should be XV instead of V.

11. (I.54) The winter quarters of the legions in the country of the Sequani were presumably at Besançon. The fact that Caesar did not withdraw them to the Province for the winter made it clear for the first time that he intended to attempt the conquest of Gaul. Apart from his personal ambition, it might be urged that the only way of preventing renewed German invasions was to hold the Rhine frontier.

12. (II.2) The two new legions raised in the winter of 58 B.C. were the 13th and 14th. This addition brought Caesar's army up to eight legions, at which strength it remained until 54 B.C.

13. (II.4) The estimate supplied by the Remi of the Belgic forces was no doubt exaggerated, but even so they must have greatly outnumbered the Romans.

14. (II.7) Numidians were generally employed by the Romans as cavalry, but a later passage in this book (II.24) shows that Caesar used them as light infantry.

15. (II.29) The town defended by the Atuatuci was either at Namur or at Mont Falhize, about midway between Namur and Liège.

16. (II.35) On the strength, no doubt, of Caesar's optimistic dispatches to the Senate, it seems to have been thought at Rome that the conquest of Gaul was virtually completed.

17. (III.1) The route which Galba's expedition was intended to open was through the Great St Bernard pass. Its failure was due to the inadequate size of his force.

18. (III.7) After spending most of the winter in Illyria and northern Italy, in early April Caesar had secret conferences first with Crassus at Ravenna and, a few days later, with Pompey at Lucca, before returning to Gaul. Pompey and Crassus became consuls for 55 B.C. and sponsored a law extending Caesar's command for a further five years; the Senate had already, in May 56, formally granted him the right to appoint ten generals and agreed to take responsibility for paying the four legions he had raised on his own initiative (I.10, II.1).

There is reason to suppose that as early as 57 B.C. Caesar was planning an expedition to Britain, and it may have been the knowledge of this that provoked the Veneti to revolt. They were the strongest of the maritime tribes of Gaul and carried on a considerable trade with Britain.

19. (III.16) Caesar's pretext for his savage treatment of the surrendered Veneti is a poor one. The Romans detained by them and their neighbours

were not ambassadors but requisition officers. What Caesar really wanted to teach the Gauls was that it was dangerous to rebel against him.

20. (III.20) Caesar says (III.11) that he wanted to prevent the Aquitanians from sending help to the rebels in Celtic Gaul. As it is improbable that there was any real likelihood of their doing so, his attack on them seems to have been an act of unprovoked aggression. Publius Crassus' conduct of the operation was brilliantly successful.

21. (III.28) Although Caesar says that he set out to attack both the Morini and the Menapii, the narrative that follows, taken in conjunction with that describing the operations of the next year in this area (IV.37–8), shows that he originally invaded only the territory of the Morini, who controlled the Channel ports nearest Britain.

22. (IV.10) The Meuse does not rise in the Vosges, but on the plateau of Langres. This plateau is in the country of the Lingones; the Vosges are not.

In saying that the Meuse flows into the Rhine, Caesar (or the geographer from whom his information is derived) evidently means that it flows into the Waal, which joins the Rhine not far from Arnhem. The Meuse now meets the Waal only about forty miles from the sea; but the two rivers approach very near each other at the point indicated by Caesar, and may then have been connected by a channel.

23. (IV.13) This episode was discreditable to Caesar. The arrest of the German envoys who came to explain their alleged breach of the truce – which may not have been serious or deliberate – was justly criticized as an infraction of the rule of international law to which Caesar himself had so recently appealed in the case of the Veneti (III.9). His enemy Cato actually proposed that Caesar should be disowned and surrendered to the Germans; but this was no doubt only a political move, and no notice was taken of it.

24. (IV.15) The rendering 'they reached the confluence of the Moselle and the Rhine' depends on an emendation of the text, in which the rivers mentioned are the *Meuse* and the Rhine. That would indicate that the battlefield was in Holland somewhere near the River Waal, in which case the Germans must have retreated a long way north before the engagement. If the emendation is right, they must have advanced south-east through the Ardennes.

25. (IV.17) Caesar's bridge was probably near Coblenz.

26. (IV.19) In spite of the elaborate preparations made for this invasion of Germany it may be that, as Caesar suggests, it was not intended as anything more than a punitive raid and a demonstration of strength. The multiple justifications put forward (IV.16) for undertaking the raid, as in the case also of Britain (IV.20), reflect the fact that Caesar was technically

exceeding his powers in campaigning outside his provinces – the more blatantly so, the further he went – and so running the risk of prosecution.

27. (IV.20) Although there was much intercourse between Gaul and Britain, the military aid which Caesar says the Gauls received from the Britons cannot have been the real reason for his invasion. Such assistance could hardly have been of much importance, and in any case the Romans were now in control of the Channel. Probably an important motive was to secure the glory of leading an army to victory on a distant and unknown island, the wealth of which was reputed to be much greater than it really was. The first expedition, which lasted only about three weeks, was intended merely to reconnoitre the country with a view to a more serious invasion the next year.

28. (IV.22) Caesar sailed with the infantry from Boulogne. The cavalry sailed from Ambleteuse, six miles north of Boulogne. The British coast was first reached near Dover. The landing took place between Deal and Walmer Castle.

29. (IV.25) A silver eagle mounted on a pole was the legionary standard.

30. (IV.33) The British war chariots had two wheels and were drawn by two horses. Remains of chariots have been found in British graves. Many more have been found in France; but evidently the mainland Gauls, before the time of Caesar's conquest, had abandoned them in favour of cavalry.

31. (V.5) The ships built in the country of the Meldi (the neighbourhood of Meaux) sailed first down the Marne, then down the Seine. On being driven back by a contrary wind they doubtless returned to the mouth of the Seine.

32. (V.8) The second invasion of Britain was an ambitious undertaking. The size of the forces employed suggests that Caesar planned to conquer and occupy at any rate the southern part of the country. In that case, the failure of the enterprise must be counted as a serious reverse for him and for the Roman arms.

The landing must have been made somewhere between Sandwich and Deal. The cavalry fight apparently took place on the banks of the River Stour, not far from Canterbury.

33. (V.12) The civilization of Britain had many features – including Druidism – in common with that of Gaul, but was less highly developed. Monarchy was still the usual form of government.

To say that tin is found 'inland' is an odd way of referring to the famous tin mines of Cornwall, which had been exploited for centuries by Carthaginians and Gauls. Caesar – or the authority upon whom he is relying – apparently did not know what part of the country it came from. He is also mistaken in implying that copper was not mined in Britain and that the beech did not grow there. The iron found 'near the coast' is that obtained from the ancient mines in Sussex.

34. (V.13) It will be obvious to English readers that the coasts of Britain are incorrectly oriented in Caesar's description, and their length overestimated. The idea that northern Spain lay to the west of Britain, with Ireland between them, resulted from misconceptions shared by most ancient geographers. According to their belief, (1) the coast of Gaul stretched south-west in an approximately straight line from the Rhine to the Pyrenees; (2) the south coast of Britain was roughly parallel to it; (3) the Pyrenees ran north and south; (4) the north coast of Spain ran not west but north-west from the Pyrenees and was much nearer Britain than it really is.

Caesar here calls the Isle of Man 'Mona', although in other ancient writers the name is always applied to Anglesey.

35. (V.22) Cassivellaunus' kingdom was in Middlesex and Hertfordshire. His stronghold was formerly thought to have been Verulamium, near St Albans; but although Verulamium was certainly the chief town of his son and successor Tasciovanus, it is probable that Cassivellaunus' fortress was at Wheathampstead, about five miles north-north-east of St Albans.

As no troops were left behind in Britain the Romans retained no real hold upon it. The possession of British hostages may have secured the payment of tribute for the time being; but even that no doubt ceased after Caesar's departure from Gaul.

36. (V.24) The ill-fated legion placed under Sabinus and Cotta was the 14th. It is not known what legion or legions the five cohorts belonged to.

37. (V.30) It is surprising to find Sabinus walking so recklessly into the trap set for him by Ambiorix; for in his campaign against the Venelli in 56 B.C. (II.17) he nearly lost his chance of victory by excessive caution, and then saved the situation by employing a similar trick himself.

38. (V.37) Sabinus' blunder had cost the lives of at least six thousand legionaries. It is said that when Caesar heard the news he let his hair and beard grow in token of mourning, and continued so until the defeat was avenged. The scene of the catastrophe is not mentioned in his account, but a later passage (VI.37) shows that it was at Atuatuca, in Belgium.

39. (V.38) Caesar claimed that the Nervii were 'almost annihilated' by their defeat in 57 B.C., and the survivors of that defeat said that scarcely five hundred men capable of bearing arms remained (II.28). The following narrative shows that these statements were exaggerations, though doubtless many of those who took part in the attack on Cicero's camp had reached military age since 57 B.C.

The site of Cicero's camp cannot be identified, but it must have been somewhere on or near the Sambre and cannot have been less than some eighty miles distant from Samarobriva (Amiens), where Caesar was.

40. (V.47) The narrative shows that Caesar had one legion when he set out from Samarobriva to relieve Cicero. This must have been the legion which was wintering (no doubt at Samarobriva) under Trebonius.

41. (V.53) For the first time Caesar spent the winter in Gaul. The three legions with which he went into winter quarters at Samarobriva were (1) Crassus' legion, which Caesar had left at Samarobriva when he set out thence to relieve Cicero; (2) Trebonius' legion, which Caesar had taken with him to Cicero's camp; (3) Cicero's legion.

42. (VI.1) From 57 to 54 B.C. Caesar had eight legions. The losses under Sabinus were perhaps not much more than the full complement of one legion, which would leave seven. Of the two new legions now enrolled in northern Italy (in the winter of 54 B.C.), one took the number of the 14th, destroyed under Sabinus; the other was numbered the 15th. The legion borrowed from Pompey was the 1st, though apparently Caesar renumbered it afterwards (see note on VIII.5). This reinforcement brought the number of his legions up to ten.

Pompey held proconsular command as nominal governor of Spain. In his consulship of 55 B.C. he had been invested with special powers which enabled him to levy troops even in provinces under the control of other governors.

43. (VI.11) There are several instances in Caesar's narrative of faction-fighting between members of the same family – e.g. Diviciacus and his brother Dumnorix (I.18ff.), Indutiomarus and his son-in-law Cingetorix (V.3–4, VI.8), Vercingetorix and his uncle Gobannitio (VII.4).

44. (VI.13) The rich and powerful corporation of the Druids does not appear to have played any part as a body in the national resistance to the Romans, though some individuals among them, such as Diviciacus the Aeduan, exercised considerable political power.

45. (VI.15) The Gallic knights were noblemen. Most of the Celtic tribes – though few of the Belgic – had by Caesar's time abandoned monarchy and were generally ruled by oligarchies of these noblemen, who acted as magistrates and members of the tribal councils, and surrounded themselves like feudal barons with hosts of serfs and retainers.

46. (VI.18) Father Dis was the god of death and king of the dark underworld. Hence the importance of night in the Gauls' reckoning of time.

47. (VI.27) The 'ox shaped like a deer' is apparently the reindeer; but in reality it has two antlers. The idea that the elk had no joints in its legs and slept against trees is of course a fairy-tale. As for the alleged method of catching the animal, it is hard to believe that Caesar took such a traveller's tale seriously.

48. (VI.29) This incursion into Germany had achieved as little as the

former one. Perhaps to distract his readers' attention from its insignificant results, Caesar inserted at this point a long digression (VI. 11–28) on the customs and institutions of Gaul and Germany.

49. (VI.33) The Scheldt does not flow into the Meuse, but there is some reason for thinking that these rivers did at one time communicate with each other near their mouths.

50. (VI.39) The two thousand cavalry of the Sugambri must have been accompanied, according to the German custom (I.48, VII.65), by a similar number of infantry, since they regarded with contempt a Roman force which must have considerably exceeded two thousand.

51. (VI.42) Caesar treats Quintus Cicero very tenderly whenever he refers to him in the *Gallic War*, wishing to gratify his brother Marcus Cicero, whose friendship was useful to Caesar. In the present passage he lets him off with a reprimand much less severe than he deserved and mentions all the extenuating circumstances he can think of. Cicero had certainly been incautious and disobedient.

52. (VI.44) The 'ancient Roman manner' of execution was by scourging and beheading. By thus setting himself up as a judge over the Gauls, Caesar is quite openly treating them as the inhabitants of a conquered province.

53. (VII.8) Caesar's unexpected march across the Cevennes in midwinter disorganized Vercingetorix's strategical plan, which was to start a widespread revolt in central and western Gaul before Caesar could rejoin his army after his usual winter visit to northern Italy, and at the same time to threaten an invasion of the Province.

54. (VII.15) Vercingetorix saw now that it was useless either to fight pitched battles or to try holding one fortress after another, and decided on the one strategy that might have been successful – to starve the Roman army by means of a 'scorched earth' policy. But his followers could not see that, to be effective, the work of destruction must be persisted in ruthlessly, and he had no means of compelling them.

55. (VII.36) Excavations carried out in 1861–5 on the instructions of the Emperor Napoleon III revealed remains of the two Roman camps and the double trench connecting them.

56. (VII.40) Caesar had six legions at Gergovia (VII.34). Two of these were placed in the small camp on the hill when it was first occupied (VII.36); but the major part of this garrison was evidently withdrawn later, since in the final stage of the siege the small camp had a garrison only some cohorts strong (VII.49, 51). So Caesar could take approximately four legions to deal with the Aedui and leave two with Fabius to guard the main camp.

57. (VII.47) It is difficult to believe Caesar's statement that his only objective in this battle was the capture of three half-empty Gallic camps. It

seems much more likely that he hoped to take the town by a surprise attack and sounded the recall only when he saw that this could not be done.

58. (VII.52) This was the only defeat that Caesar himself suffered at the hands of the Gauls. Both he and his troops were to blame – Caesar, for sounding a vital trumpet signal in a place where it was inaudible to most of those whom it was intended to reach; the soldiers, for disobeying the orders of the generals and military tribunes on the spot.

59. (VII.57) Labienus had been sent with four legions against the Parisii and Senones soon after the fall of Avaricum (VII.34).

60. (VII.67) The Eporedorix who had led the Aedui against the Sequani was evidently a different person from the Aeduan of that name mentioned several times earlier in this chapter.

61. (VII.69) The sites of the eight Roman camps and of five out of the twenty-three redoubts were discovered by Napoleon III's excavations.

62. (VII.78) The story of the starving Mandubii is made terribly dramatic by what it does *not* say. Of course Caesar had not enough food to relieve them without the risk of running short himself. According to a later historian, he hoped they would be re-admitted to the town and so hasten the time when it must surrender; but they were left outside to die of starvation.

63. (VII.89) So ended the brief but brilliant career of a great patriot. Caesar pays a fine tribute to the qualities of leadership which enabled Vercingetorix to strengthen his hold upon his followers and re-animate them in the hour of defeat (VII. 29–30), but either could not or would not protect him from the fate which Roman custom demanded for a vanquished barbarian. Six years after his capture Vercingetorix was exhibited at Rome in Caesar's triumph and then executed.

64. (VIII. Preface) This final book is the work of Caesar's friend Aulus Hirtius.

65. (VIII.2) Caesar knew that many of the Gallic patriots still refused to accept their defeat as final and he was anxious to finish off the war at the earliest possible moment. He therefore remained in Gaul and actually spent a large part of the winter in active campaigning. The campaign against the Bituriges started on the 29th of December, 52 B.C., according to the current Roman calendar. But the calendar was in advance of the true seasons, and the date was really about four weeks earlier.

66. (VIII.4) This is the first mention of the 6th legion. There is reason for thinking that Caesar had assigned this number to the legion borrowed from Pompey in the winter of 54 B.C. (VI.1 and n.), which was called the 1st at the time when Caesar took it over.

67. (VIII.44) The unanimous testimony of his contemporaries shows that Caesar had the reputation of a merciful man, and in the civil war he

certainly treated his defeated enemies with remarkable generosity. But in dealing with barbarians the tradition of Roman warfare knew no mercy, and in the particular case of Uxellodunum there was the additional excuse that the garrison was largely composed of criminals and penniless adventurers who were a continual menace to the peace of Gaul. Such terrorism, too, was common amongst the Gauls themselves; Vercingetorix thought nothing of punishing lukewarm supporters of the national cause by mutilation or death at the stake.

68. (VIII.46) Crassus' campaign in Aquitania took place in 56 B.C. (III.20ff.).

69. (VIII.46) The legions now distributed in winter quarters totalled ten, and the 15th had already been sent to northern Italy (VIII.24). So at this time Caesar had eleven in all, whereas he had only ten in the campaign of 52 B.C. The additional legion was probably the 5th, which he is known to have raised about this time in Transalpine Gaul. It was quite exceptional in this period for a legion to be recruited outside Italy, i.e. from non-citizens.

70. (VIII.49) Caesar's conciliatory treatment of Gaul as a whole, following on his frightful punishment of the last obstinate rebels, had the desired effect. It was a long time before the Gauls gave much further trouble.

APPENDIX I
THE TEXT

Handford's translation normally follows the Teubner Text of A. Klotz. Differences from the readings of the Oxford Classical Text of Renatus Du Pontet are listed below.

O.C.T. READING	READING ADOPTED

BOOK I

16.2	quod Gallia . . . posita est	*delete*
19.3	Procillus	Troucillus
24.3	[ita uti supra]; sed	*delete*
	collocari, ac	collocavit, ita uti supra se
	compleri, et	compleret
27.4	nocte intermissa, circiter	*delete*
28.3	Latovicos, in	Latovicos, Rauracos, in
44.11	[sed hoste]	*delete*
47.2	poterant	potuerant
51.2	Sedusios	Eudusios
53.1	quinque	quindecim
54.1	Ubii	ubi

BOOK II

1.1	Gallia [in hibernis]	Gallia, legionesque erant collocatae in hibernis
	ita uti supra demonstravimus	*delete*
3.2	Andecomborium	Andecombogium
4.9	Menapios VII	Menapios novem
4.9	*et sqq.* Aduatucos	Atuatucos
4.10	Caeroesos	Caerosos
6.2	portas succendunt	propius succedunt
10.4	convenire[nt]	convenire
19.2	†quod hostis†	quod hostibus
19.5	†porrecta	prospectus
20.1	signum tuba dandum	*delete*

22.1	ut ante demonstravimus	*delete*
25.1	deserto	desertos
27.2	pugnant quo	pugnandi studio
30.2	pedum in circuitu quindecim	pedum XII in circuitu quinque
30.4	hominibus	omnibus
	in†muros sese†	in muro se posse
34.1	*et sqq.* Curiosolitas, Esubios	Coriosolitas, Essuvios

BOOK III

1.6	[ad hiemandum]	*delete*
7.4	Silio	Sillio
8.2	Sili atque Velani	Silli atque Velani, et si quos intercipere potuerunt
9.3	cognito	cognito Romanorum consilio de
12.1	his	*delete*
13.6	scopulis	copulis
20.2	*et sqq.* Sontiatum	Sotiatium
20.3	valebant, in itinere	valebant, praemisso in itinere
21.1	tamen	tandem
22.1	*et sqq.* Adiatunnus	Adiatuanus
27.1	Garumni, Sibuzates	Garunni, Sibulates

BOOK IV

1.1	*et sqq.* Tencteri	Tenctheri
1.10	haberent	habeant
	lavantur	laventur
3.3	†paulo quam sunt eiusdem generis et ceteris	paulo sunt quam eiusdem generis ceteri
10.3	Nantuatium . . . Mediomatricum	Nemetum . . . Mediomatricorum
23.2	administratum, ipse	administratum, aestibus marinis naves in continentem reiectae sunt. ipse
25.6	ex† proximis primis † navibus	ex proximis navibus
35.1	de quo ante dictum est	*delete*

BOOK V

19.1	ut supra demonstravimus	*delete*
19.2	omnibus viis	omnes viis notis
20.1	*et sqq.* Trinobantes	Trinovantes

22.1	[quod . . . demonstravimus]	*delete*
22.3	Atrebatem	*delete*
24.3	†Belgis†	Belgio
25.3	†inimicis	inimici
	et eis	*delete*
28.4	quantasvis magnas	quantasvis Gallorum magnas
31.5	augeatur	augetur
42.1	IX	X
42.4	[p̄. xv]	*delete*
49.2	repetit	repperit
49.8	valles	vallem

BOOK VI

1.2	consules	consul
2.1	ut docuimus	*delete*
11.4	itaque	idque
21.4	alii . . . alii	ali . . . ali
22.2	qui †cum † una	quique una
23.9	quaque	quacumque
40.4	docuimus	*delete*
43.2	incendebantur, praeda	incendebantur, pecora interficiebantur, praeda

BOOK VII

3.1	Cotuato	Gutuatro
3.2	ubique	ubi quae
8.4	ne [ve] ab hostibus diripiantur	neu se ab hostibus diripi patiatur
14.4	diligi	deleri
14.10	aestimare	aestimari debere
27.2	extra castra	*delete*
35.1	utrimque	utrique
	e regione castris castra	e regione castrorum Caesaris castra
38.4	multos	omnes
45.2	impedimentorum	iumentorum
45.7	qui	ne
47.1	legionique decimae, quacum erat †concionatus† signa constituit	legionisque decimae quacum erat continuo signa constiterunt
48.1	ut supra demonstravimus	*delete*

50.2	†pacatum†	pactum
53.2	minus in	minus [intra munitiones maneret neque] in
54.3	copiis	sociis
56.2	ut commutato	ne commutato
	ut ne metu quidem	ut non nemo metu quidem
58.3	*et sqq.* Metiosedum	Metlosedum
62.10	die III	*delete*
65.2	Donnotauro	Domnotauro
65.5	[sed et]	*delete*
69.7	posita	posita octona, quae inter se munitionibus coniungebantur
70.2	ne qua . . . fiat	*delete*
72.4	pedes	passus
74.1	†eius discessu†	equitum accessu
75.2	†Ambluaretis†	Ambivaretis
	† Senonibus†	Suessionibus
	†Lexoviis†	*delete*
75.3	Nitiobriges	Nitiobroges
75.4	bina; XXX	∞∞; XX
75.5	†Lemovices†	Lexovii
84.5	salute	virtute
87.5	XL	XI
88.4	Sedulius	Sedullus
	Arvernus	*delete*
90.6	Ambibaretos	Ambivaretos

APPENDIX I THE TEXT

BOOK VIII

5.2	dimiserant	amiserant
10.4	nitebantur	inflabantur
12.6	inflabantur	inflantur
15.1	possent	auderent
15.5	ut consueverant	ubi consederant
18.1	silvis undique aut impeditissimo flurine	silvis impeditissimis aut flumine altissimo
19.7	amissa	amissa quo fors tulerat
24.4	†incolae illorum†	illorum
27.2	et Romanum	*delete*
29.4	eo	*delete*
36.1	longe	*delete*
38.5	accepta	a Gutuatro accepta
48.4	per fidem	perfidia
48.7	†ac si†	ac sic
52.5	†iusserunt†	intercesserunt

APPENDIX II
THE ROMAN ARMY

Apart from an unknown number of auxiliary troops (Gallic and Numidian light infantry, Cretan archers, and slingers from the Balearic Isles), the forces which Caesar commanded in Gaul consisted of a number of legions varying between six and eleven and a cavalry force composed entirely of foreigners. The bulk of the cavalry, which at one time numbered at least five thousand (IV.12), were Gauls requisitioned from friendly or conquered tribes. On the conclusion of a campaign most of them were sent home and a new force raised the next year. In the campaign of 52 B.C. Caesar had some squadrons of German cavalry, with light infantry trained to fight among its ranks (VII.65).

The legions were supposed to consist entirely of men possessing Roman citizenship; but when troops were urgently needed no doubt many exceptions were made, and towards the end of the war Caesar enrolled a whole legion in the province of Transalpine Gaul. The rest of the legions which he raised in the Gallic war were recruited in northern Italy. The legionaries were volunteers serving for pay and signed on for a definite term of service. At some point during his Gallic campaign Caesar raised legionary pay, probably to the level standard for all legions by A.D. 14, i.e. ten *asses* per day. In Caesar's time the legionaries were recruited mainly by the commanders who required them. They took an oath of loyalty directly to him and were often paid out of booty or funds raised by him. This bad system made the men dependent on, and hence loyal to, their commander rather than the state.

The nominal strength of a legion was six thousand, divided into ten cohorts of six hundred each – the most important tactical units. Each cohort contained three maniples of two hundred each and each maniple two centuries of one hundred each. However, legions were often considerably under their nominal strength. The legion had at this date no permanent commander. The generals (*legati*) serving under Caesar were men of senatorial rank appointed by the Senate on his recommendation. He had five at the start of the war, and eventually ten. Their duties were assigned to them at Caesar's discretion and included taking command of legions in battle, on the march or in winter quarters, procuring supplies, superintending shipbuilding, raising fresh levies, and so on. Some of them may have been without much military experience. Each legion had six military tribunes (nominated, and perhaps actually appointed, by the commander-in-chief) who were often young aspirants to public office and were sometimes chosen merely on personal or political grounds. They manoeuvred their legions in action under the direction of a general (II.26, VII.47) and sometimes acted on their own initiative (VII.63). No doubt they also discharged routine administrative duties. Perhaps more important than the military tribunes on the actual battlefield – certainly mentioned and praised much more often by Caesar – were the centurions, ex-rankers promoted for bravery and powers of leadership to the command of the centuries. Of the sixty centurions in a legion the six belonging to the first cohort (referred to in this translation as 'first grade centurions') held posts of special responsibility and were summoned with the generals and military tribunes to councils of war. Their duties on occasion must have been at least as important as those of a company commander in a modern army. The most responsible post of all was held by the chief centurion of the legion i.e. the centurion of the first century of the first cohort.

The legionaries wore a woollen tunic, a leather coat protected by metal bands, long puttees, and a cloak or blanket for protection from cold or rain. Their armour consisted of a helmet (slung over the chest when they were on the march), a large rectangular shield of wood covered with leather, greaves, and probably a leather cuirass. Their weapons were pointed two-edged swords and heavy throwing-spears. The latter were sometimes nearly seven feet long; between the tempered point and the handle was a shank made of soft iron, which bent when the spear pierced an enemy's shield, so that it could not easily be pulled out and was useless for throwing back (I.25).

The kit that the soldiers had to carry on the march included, besides their rations, cooking-vessels, and so on, the tools required for the constructional work on which they were constantly engaged – a spade, hatchet, and saw. The heavy baggage contained the military stores – including pieces of artillery, material for making mantlets, and other apparatus – as well as personal property belonging not only to the officers but apparently to the common soldiers also (V.33). For carrying it a large number of horses or mules was needed and no doubt wagons, though these are not mentioned in the *Gallic War*. The non-combatants included the animal drivers, officers' servants, sutlers, and dealers who sold goods to the sutlers and bought booty from the soldiers.

Siege operations are described several times in the *Gallic War*. These usually involved the use of artillery, either catapults or machines resembling huge crossbows. These were used to discharge stones or feathered javelins against the defenders and derived their power from the recoil of tightly twisted gut or horsehair springs. Mantlets, stout wooden sheds usually some sixteen feet long and eight wide, mounted on wheels, were used, placed end to end in a line, to form a covered way for the protection of soldiers bringing up materials for the construction of a siege terrace. This consisted of logs piled in layers, enclosing a core of earth and rubble. It was begun at some distance from the wall of the place under siege and gradually advanced towards it, the length of the terrace being usually at right angles to the wall. Wooden towers several storeys high were erected on the terrace and artillery and snipers placed in them. Battering-rams were brought up under cover and used directly against walls or gates. For prolonged investment, a system of trenches and ramparts was used – that at Alesia was unusually elaborate (VII.72–3).

APPENDIX III

CHRONOLOGICAL OUTLINE
OF THE CAREER OF CAESAR

B.C 100   (traditional date) Born.

81–78   On Governors' staffs in Asia and Cilicia.

81   Envoy to King Nicomedes of Bithynia.

73   Elected to college of priests.

68   Quaestor in Spain.

65   Aedile.

63   Elected head of college of priests (*pontifex maximus*).

62   Praetor.

61   Governor of Further Spain.

60   First triumvirate formed.

59   Consul.

58–49   Governor of Cisalpine Gaul, Transalpine Gaul, and Illyricum. Conquest of Gallia Comata.

49   Dictator.

48   Dictator and consul.

47   Dictator.

46   Dictator and consul. Quadruple triumph.

45   Dictator and consul. Triumph.

44   Dictator and consul; declared dictator in perpetuity. 15 March – assassinated.

GLOSSARY OF
PERSONS AND PLACES

ACCO (VI.4, 44): a leader of the Senones.

ADIATUANUS (III.22): king of the Sotiates.

ADMAGETOBRIGA (I.31): the site of a battle between Ariovistus and the Gauls (61 B.C.) in the territory of the Sequani.

AEDUI (Introd.; I.10 *et passim*; II.5, 10, 14, 15; V.6, 7, 54; VII *passim*; VIII.45, 46, 54): a large tribe living in central France, between the Loire and the Saône.

Lucius AEMILIUS (I.23): a cavalry commander.

Lucius AEMILIUS Paulus (VIII.48): consul 50 B.C.

AGEDINCUM (VI.44; VII.10, 57, 59, 62): a town of the Senones, about sixty-five miles south-east of Paris, on the site of Sens.

AISNE (Axona) (II.5, 9): a river of northern France flowing from the Argonne Forest into the Oise.

ALESIA (VII.68–84; VIII.14, 34): a stronghold of the Mandubii on the plateau of Mont Auxois, about thirty miles north-west of Dijon; modern Alise Ste Reine.

ALLIER (Elaver) (VII.34, 35, 53): a river of southern central France flowing into the Loire.

ALLOBROGES (I.6, 10; II.14, 28, 44; III.1, 6; VII.64, 65): a powerful tribe whose territory lay between the Rhône, the Isère, and the lake of Geneva, and formed the northernmost part of the Roman province of Transalpine Gaul.

ALPS (I.10; III.1, 2, 7; IV.10): a mountain range running from the Franco-Italian border into Yugoslavia.

AMBARRI (I.11, 14): allies and kinsmen of the Aedui.

AMBIANI (II.4, 15; VII.75; VIII.7): a Belgic tribe living on the Somme in the neighbourhood of Samarobriva (modern Amiens).

AMBIBARII (VII.75): a tribe living near the Atlantic seaboard.

AMBILIATI (III.9): allies of the Veneti.

AMBIORIX (V.24–41; VI.2–9, 29–43; VIII.24, 25): joint ruler of the Eburones with Catuvolcus.

AMBIVARETI (VII.75, 90): a dependent tribe of the Aedui.

AMBIVARITI (IV.9): a tribe living near the Meuse.

ANARTES (VI.25): a tribe living near the Danube.

ANCALITES (V.21): a tribe living in south-east Britain.

ANDECOMBOGIUS (II.3): a leader of the Remi.

ANDES (II.35; III.7; VII.4; VIII.26): a tribe living north of the lower Loire, in Anjou.

Gaius ANTISTIUS Reginus (VI.1; VII.83, 90): one of Caesar's generals.

Mark ANTONY (Marcus Antonius) (Introd.; VII.81; VIII.2, 24, 38, 46–50): born 82 B.C. One of Caesar's generals in Gaul 52 B.C.; quaestor 51 B.C.; tribune at Rome 49 B.C.; controlled Italy as Caesar's deputy for a time after Pharsalus; consul 44 B.C. After Caesar's death formed, with Marcus Aemilius Lepidus and Octavian, the 'Second Triumvirate', which controlled the Roman world. After Lepidus was forced out, estrangement between Octavian and Antony developed into civil war, in which Antony had the support of Cleopatra. Defeated at Actium 31 B.C.; committed suicide the following year.

Lucius APPULEIUS Saturninus (Introd.): tribune 103 B.C., 100 B.C. and tribune-elect for 99 B.C. Associated with Marius. He forced through a series of demagogic revolutionary measures by violent means. Marius, as consul, was requested by the Senate to restore order; he besieged Saturninus and his supporters on the Capitol and imprisoned them, but was unable to save Saturninus from the mob, who pelted him to death (Dec. 10, 100 B.C.).

AQUILEIA (Introd.; I.10): a town in Cisalpine Gaul, at the head of the Adriatic.

AQUITANI (I.1; III.21): a group of tribes living in south-west France (Aquitania).

AQUITANIA (I.1; III.11, 20–27; VII.31; VIII.46): south-west France, between the River Garonne and the Pyrenees.

ARDENNES (V.3; VI.29, 31, 33): a dense forest in south-east Belgium, extending into France and Luxembourg.

ARECOMICI *see* VOLCAE.

AREMORICAN TRIBES (Introd.; V.53; VII.75; VIII.31): a group of tribes living in Normandy and Brittany.

ARIOVISTUS (Introd.; I.31–53; IV.16; V.29, 55; VI.12): king of the German tribe of the Suebi.

Marcus ARISTIUS (VII.42, 43): a military tribune.

Gaius ARPINEIUS (V.27, 28): a Roman knight.

ARVERNI (Introd.; I.31, 45; VII.3, 5–9, 34–8, 64–90; VIII.46): a powerful tribe living in south central France, in the district of the Auvergne mountains.

Quintus ATIUS Varus (VIII.28): a cavalry commander.

Titus ATIUS Labienus (I.10, 21, 22, 54; II.1, 11, 26; III.11; IV.38; V.8, 11, 23, 24, 27, 37, 46–58; VI.5, 7, 8, 33; VII.34, 56–62, 86, 87, 90; VIII.6, 23, 24, 25, 45, 52): the ablest of Caesar's generals in the Gallic

War; fought against Caesar in the Civil War and died in the final campaign (45 B.C.).

ATLANTIC OCEAN (Oceanus): (I.1; II.34; III.7, 9, 13; IV.29; VII.4, 75; VIII.31, 46).

ATREBATES (II.4, 16, 23; IV.21; V.46; VII.75; VIII.7, 47): a Belgic tribe living in northern France in the neighbourhood of Arras.

Quintus ATRIUS (V.9, 10): a Roman officer.

ATUATUCA (VI.32, 35): a fortress in the territory of the Eburones (not, despite its name, belonging to the Atuatuci); perhaps Tongres in east Belgium, twelve miles north-north-west of Liège.

ATUATUCI (II.4, 16, 29, 30; V.27, 38, 39, 56; VI.2, 33): a tribe living in south-east Belgium, principally on the left bank of the Meuse.

AULERCI (II.34; III.17, 29; VII.4, 75; VIII.7): a group of tribes living between the lower Seine and the lower Loire.

AULERCI BRANNOVICES (VII.75): a tribe in the above group.

AULERCI CENOMANI (VII.75): a tribe in the above group.

AULERCI EBUROVICES (III.17; VII.75): a tribe in the above group; allies of the Venelli.

Lucius AURUNCULEIUS Cotta (II.11; IV.22, 38; V.24–37, 52; VI.32, 37): one of Caesar's generals.

AUSCI (III.27): one of the Aquitanian tribes.

AVARICUM (Bourges) (VII.13–18, 29–32, 47, 52): the chief town of the Bituriges, sixty miles south-east of Orleans.

BACENIS (VI.10): a forest in northern Bavaria.

BACULUS see Sextius.

BALBUS see Cornelius.

BALEARIC slingers (II.7): specialized auxiliaries from the Balearic Islands (modern Majorca and Minorca).

Titus BALVENTIUS (V.35): a chief centurion.

BASILUS see Minucius.

BATAVIANS (IV.10): a tribe living on an island between the Waal and the Meuse.

BELGAE, BELGIC (Introd.; I.1; II.1–6, 14–19; III.7, 11; IV.38; V.12, 24, 25; VIII.6, 38, 46, 49, 54): one of the main divisions of the Gallic tribes, inhabiting northern France, Belgium, southern Holland, and the part of Germany lying west of the Rhine.

BELLOVACI (II.4, 5, 10, 13, 14; V.46; VII.59, 75, 90; VIII.6, 7, 12–23, 38): a powerful Belgic tribe, inhabiting, however, a comparatively small area in northern France, the district around Beauvais.

BESANÇON (Vesontio) (Introd.; I.38, 39): the largest town of the Sequani.

BIBRACTE (I.23; VII.55, 63, 90; VIII.2, 4): the chief town of the Aedui, on Mont Beuvray (twelve miles west of Autun).

BIBRAX (II.6): a town of the Remi, north of the Aisne, between Laon and Rheims.

BIBROCI (V.21): a tribe of south-east Britain.

BIGERRIONES (III.27): one of the Aquitanian tribes.

BITURIGES (I.18; VII.5, 8–15, 21, 29, 75, 90; VIII.2, 3, 4, 11): a tribe living in west central France, in the neighbourhood of Avaricum (Bourges).

BLANNOVII (VII.75): a dependent tribe of the Aedui.

BODUOGNATUS (II.23): commander-in-chief of the Nervii.

BOII (I.5, 25, 28, 29; VII.9, 10, 17, 75): a Celtic tribe which migrated westwards with the Helvetii and was afterwards settled in central France, probably between the Loire and the Allier.

BRANNOVICES see Aulerci Brannovices.

BRATUSPANTIUM (II.13): a stronghold of the bellovaci, probably between Amiens and Beauvais.

BRITAIN (Britannia): (II.4, 14; III.8, 9; IV.20–30, 37, 38; V.2, 4–6, 8–23; VI.13; VII.76).

BRITONS (Britanni): (IV.21, 24–36; V.11, 12, 14, 22).

BRUTUS see Junius.

CABURUS see Valerius.

CADURCI (VII.4, 64, 75; VIII.32, 34): a tribe inhabiting a district in south-west France roughly corresponding to the Department of the Lot.

CAEROSI (II.4): a German tribe.

CAESAR see Julius.

CALENUS see Fufius.

CALETI (II.4; VII.75; VIII.7): a tribe living in north-east France.

Lucius CALPURNIUS Piso (I.12): consul 112 B.C.; killed in battle with the Helvetii 107 B.C.

Lucius CALPURNIUS Piso (I.6, 12): consul 58 B.C.; grandson of the above, and father of Caesar's wife Calpurnia.

CAMULOGENUS (VII.57, 59, 62): a leader belonging to the tribe of the Aulerci.

Gaius CANINIUS Rebilus (Introd.; VII.83, 90; VIII.24–39, 44): one of Caesar's generals; in Gaul 52 B.C., Italy 49 B.C., Africa, with Curio, 48 B.C.; besieged Thapsus 46 B.C.; in Spain 45 B.C.; notorious for consulship lasting a single day (end of 45 B.C.).

CANTABRI (III.26): a tribe living on the north coast of Spain.

CARCASSONNE (Carcaso) (III.20): a town in south-eastern France.

CARNUTES (II.35; V.25, 29, 56; VI.2, 3, 4, 13, 44; VII.2, 3, 11, 75;

VIII.4, 5, 31, 38, 46): a tribe living south-west of Paris between the Seine and the Loire.

CARVILIUS (V.22): a Kentish king.

CASSI (V.21): a tribe living in south-east Britain.

Lucius CASSIUS (I.7, 12): consul 107 B.C.; killed by the Tigurini.

CASSIVELLAUNUS (V.11, 18–22): leader of the Britons against Caesar's second invasion.

CASTICUS (I.3): a leader of the Sequani.

CATAMANTALOEDIS (I.3): a former king of the Sequani, father of Casticus.

CATILINE see Sergius.

CATO see Porcius.

CATURIGES (I.10): an Alpine tribe.

CATUVOLCUS (V.24, 26; VI.31): joint king of the Eburones with Ambiorix.

CAVARILLUS (VII.67): an Aeduan nobleman.

CAVARINUS (V.54; VI.5): king of the Senones.

CELTILLUS (VII.4): father of Vercingetorix.

CENABUM (VII.3, 11, 14, 17, 28; VIII.5, 6): a town of the Carnutes on the site of Orleans.

CENIMAGNI (V.21): a tribe living in south-east Britain.

CENOMANI see Aulerci Cenomani.

CEUTRONES (i) (I.10): an Alpine tribe; (ii) (V.39): a tribe ruled by the Nervii.

CEVENNES (Cevenna) (VII.8, 56): a mountain range in southern France west of the Rhône.

CHÂLON-SUR-SÂONE (Cabillonum) (VII.42, 90): a town in Aeduan territory.

CHERUSCI (VI.10): a German tribe, probably living between the Elbe and the Weser.

CICERO see Tullius.

CIMBERIUS (I.37): leader, with his brother Nasua, of the Suebi.

CIMBRI (Introd.; I.33, 40; II.4, 29; VII.77): a nomadic German tribe.

CINGETORIX (i) (V.3, 4, 56, 57; VI.8): a chief of the Treveri, rival of his father-in-law; (ii) (V.22): one of four kings of Kent.

CISALPINE PROVINCE (Introd.; VII.1, VIII.52, 54): the province of Cisalpine Gaul (i.e. Gaul on the Italian side of the Alps), northern Italy between the Alps and the Apennines.

Gaius CLAUDIUS Marcellus (i) (Introd.; VIII.48, 55): consul 50 B.C.; probably died before Pharsalus; (ii) (VIII.50): consul 49 B.C.; cousin of (i).

Appius CLAUDIUS Pulcher (V.1): consul 54 B.C.

Publius CLODIUS Pulcher (VII.1): brother of Appius; tribune of the plebs 58 B.C., murdered 52 B.C.

COCOSATES (III.27): one of the Aquitanian tribes.

COMMIUS (IV.21, 27, 35; V.22; VI.6; VII.75, 76, 79; VIII.6, 7, 10, 21, 23, 47, 48): King of the Atrebates.

CONCONNETODUMNUS (VII.3): the leader of the Carnutes.

CONDRUSI (II.4; IV.6; VI.32): a tribe of German origin.

Publius CONSIDIUS (I.21, 22): a Roman officer.

CONVICTOLITAVIS (VII.32, 33, 37, 39, 42, 55, 67): a magistrate of the Aedui.

CORIOSOLITES (II.34; III.7, 11; VII.75): a tribe living near the Atlantic seaboard.

Lucius CORNELIUS Balbus (VIII.Preface): a Roman knight, Spanish in origin; Caesar's friend, on his staff in Gaul, and agent at Rome during the Gallic campaigns and later during the Civil War; consul 40 B.C.

Lucius CORNELIUS Lentulus Crus (VIII.50): consul 49 B.C.; a violent opponent of Caesar; killed in Egypt soon after Pompey's murder.

Lucius CORNELIUS Sulla Felix (I.21): dictator 82–80 B.C.; died 78 B.C.

CORREUS (VIII.6, 7, 17–21): a leader of the Bellovaci.

COTTA see Aurunculeius.

COTUS (VII.32, 33, 39, 67): an Aeduan nobleman and commander of cavalry.

CRASSUS see Licinius.

CRETE (II.7): Mediterranean island, whose archers were noted.

CRITOGNATUS (VII.77–8): an Arvernian nobleman.

CURIO see Scribonius.

DACIANS (VI.25): a tribe living in modern Rumania.

DANUBE (Danuvius) (VI.25): a river flowing from southern Germany to the Black Sea.

DECETIA (VII.33): a town of the Aedui on the Loire, on the site of Decize, about twenty miles south-east of Nevers.

DIABLINTES (III.9): allies of the Veneti.

DIVICIACUS (i) (II.4): a king of the Suessiones about 100 B.C.; (ii) (I.3, 16–20, 31, 32, 41; II.5, 10, 14, 15; VI.12; VII.39): a pro-Roman Aeduan, brother of Dumnorix.

DIVICO (I.13, 14): a leader of the Helvetii.

Lucius DOMITIUS Ahenobarbus (Introd.): consul 54 B.C.; opponent of Caesar in the Civil War; failed to hold Corfinium and Massilia; commanded the left wing at Pharsalus; killed after the battle. His grandfather's victories had led to the formation of the Transalpine province.

DOUBS (Dubis) (I.38): a river of eastern France, tributary of the Saône.

DRAPPES (VIII.30, 32, 35, 36, 39, 44): a leader of the Senones.

DRUIDS (VI.13–14, 16): Gallic religious and judicial authorities.

DUMNACUS (VIII.26–31): a leader of the Andes.

DUMNORIX (Introd.; I.3, 9, 18–20; V.6, 7): an anti-Roman Aeduan, brother of Diviciacus (ii).

DURATIUS (VIII.26, 27): a pro-Roman leader of the Pictones.

DUROCORTORUM (VI.44): a town of the Remi, on the site of Rheims.

DURUS see Laberius.

EBURONES (II.4; IV.6; V.24, 28, 29, 39, 47, 58; VI.5, 31–5): a Belgic tribe inhabiting a large area west of the lower Rhine, on both banks of the Meuse, including part of east Belgium and a strip of West Germany.

EBUROVICES see Aulerci Eburovices.

ELEUTETI (VII.75): a dependent tribe of the Arverni.

ELUSATES (III.27): an Aquitanian tribe.

EPASNACTUS (VIII.44): a pro-Roman Arvernian.

EPOREDORIX (i) (VII.67): a former leader of the Aedui; (ii) (VII.38–40, 54, 55, 63, 64, 76): a young Aeduan noble supposedly killed by the Romans.

ERATOSTHENES (VI.24): a Greek scholar of the third century B.C., head of the library at Alexandria; a man of great and varied learning, especially in mathematics and geography. He calculated the circumference of the earth to within some 200 miles of the correct figure.

ESSUVII (II.34; III.7; V.24): a tribe living near the Atlantic seaboard.

EUDUSII (I.51): a German tribe.

Gaius FABIUS (V.24, 46, 47, 53; VI.6; VII.40, 41, 87, 90; VIII.6, 24, 27, 28, 31, 37, 54): one of Caesar's generals.

Lucius FABIUS (VII.47, 50): centurion of the 8th legion.

Quintus FABIUS Maximus (I.45): consul 121 B.C.

FLACCUS see Valerius.

Quintus FUFIUS Calenus (VIII.39): one of Caesar's generals; governed Greece after Pharsalus; consul 47 B.C.; supported Antony after the death of Caesar; governed Narbonensis 41 B.C.; died 40 B.C.

Gaius FUFIUS Cita (VII.3): a Roman of equestrian rank killed at Cenabum.

GABALI (VII.7, 64, 75): a tribe neighbouring the Arverni.

Aulus GABINIUS (I.6): consul 58 B.C.

GALBA (II.4, 13): king of the Suessiones.

GALBA see Sulpicius.

GALLUS see Trebius.

GARONNE (Garumna) (I.1): a river of south-west France flowing to join the Dordogne.

GARUNNI (III.27): one of the Aquitanian tribes.

GATES (III.27): one of the Aquitanian tribes.

GAULS (I.1): one of the three main tribal groups in Gaul, living between the Garonne and the Marne and Seine; called Celts by the Romans.

GEIDUMNI (V.39): a tribe ruled by the Nervii.

GENEVA (Genava) (I.6, 7): frontier town of the Allobroges.

GENEVA, Lake (lacus Lemannus) (I.2, 8; III.1): one of the boundaries of Helvetic territory.

GERGOVIA (VII.4, 34–45, 59): a stronghold of the Arverni on a plateau 1,200 feet high at the north end of the Auvergne mountains, about four miles south of Clermont-Ferrand.

GOBANNITIO (VII.4): uncle of Vercingetorix.

GORGOBINA (VII.9): a town of the Boii in central France, near Nevers.

GRACCHI (Introd.): the brothers Tiberius Sempronius Gracchus and Gaius Sempronius Gracchus, tribunes respectively in 133 B.C. and 123–122 B.C., whose attempts to introduce radical policies of reform by legislating directly through the popular assemblies, by-passing Senate, resulted in their deaths by violence.

GRAIOCELI (I.10): an Alpine tribe.

GRUDII (V.39): a tribe ruled by the Nervii.

GUTUATER (VII.3; VIII.38): ringleader of revolt among the Carnutes.

HARUDES (I.31, 37, 51): a German tribe living probably in the neighbourhood of Hamburg.

HELVETII (Introd.; I.1-30, 40; IV.10; VI.25; VII.75): a Gallic tribe living in modern Switzerland.

HELVII (VII.7, 8, 64, 65): a tribe living in the province of Transalpine Gaul at the north end of the Cevennes.

HERCYNIAN FOREST (VI.24, 25): a huge tract of forest in Central Europe, said to extend from the source of the Danube to Bohemia.

Aulus HIRTIUS (Introd.): on Caesar's staff in Gaul from c. 54 B.C.; served in the East and Spain during the Civil War; praetor 46 B.C., Governor of Transalpine Gaul 45 B.C., consul 43 B.C.; killed at Mutina in that year. He wrote the eighth book of *The Conquest of Gaul* and, some think, also *The Alexandrian War*.

ICCIUS (II.3, 6, 7): a leader of the Remi.

ILLYRIA, ILLYRICUM (Introd.; II.35; III.7; V.1): a district on the east of the Adriatic, attached to Cisalpine Gaul.

INDUTIOMARUS (V.3, 4, 26, 53-8; VI.2, 8): a chief of the Treveri, rival of his son-in-law Cingetorix.

ISLE OF MAN (V.13): called by Caesar *Mona*, although in other ancient writers the name is always applied to Anglesey.

ITALY *see* Northern Italy.

ITIUS *see* Portus.

Lucius JULIUS Caesar (VII.65): a relative of Gaius Julius Caesar; consul 64 B.C.; one of Caesar's generals in the later Gallic campaigns.

Quintus JUNIUS (V.27, 28): a Spaniard employed by Caesar as an emissary.

Decimus JUNIUS Brutus (III.11, 14; VII.9, 87): commanded the fleet against the Veneti 56 B.C.; commanded the fleet at Massilia in the Civil War 49 B.C.; Governor of Transalpine Gaul 48–46 B.C.; one of the ringleaders in Caesar's assassination 44 B.C.; pro-consul of Cisalpine Gaul 44–43 B.C.; killed on Antony's orders 43 B.C.

Marcus JUNIUS Silanus (VI.1): one of Caesar's generals.

JURA (I.2, 6, 8): mountains along the border of France and Switzerland.

KENT (Cantium) (V.13, 14, 22): an area of south-east Britain.

Quintus LABERIUS Durus (V.15): a military tribune killed in Britain.

LABIENUS *see* Atius.

LATOVICI (I.5, 28, 29): an Alpine tribe.

LEGIONS: 1st (VIII.54); 6th (VIII.4); 7th (II.23, 26; III.7; IV.32; V.9; VII.62; VIII.8); 8th (II.23; VII.47; VIII.8); 9th (II.23; VIII.8); 10th (I.40–42; II.21, 23, 25, 26; VII.47, 51); 11th (II.23; VIII.2, 6, 8); 12th (II.23, 25; III.1; VII.62; VIII.24); 13th (V.53; VII.51; VIII.2, 11, 43); 14th (VI.32; VIII.4); 15th (VIII.24, 54).

LEMONUM (VIII.26): a town of the Pictones on the site of Poitiers.

LEMOVICES (VII.4, 75, 88; VIII.46): a tribe occupying the province of Limousin, west of the Auvergne mountains.

LENTULUS *see* Cornelius.

LEPONTII (IV.10): an Alpine tribe.

LEUCI (I.40): a tribe living between the Meuse and the Moselle.

LEVACI (V.39): a tribe ruled by the Nervii.

LEXOVII (III.9, 11, 17, 29; VII.75): a tribe occupying the coast of Normandy in the neighbourhood of Caen and Lisieux.

Marcus LICINIUS Crassus (i) (Introd.; I.21; IV.1; VIII.53): consul 70 B.C. and 55 B.C.; member of the 'first triumvirate'; killed in battle against the Parthians 53 B.C.; (ii) (V.24, 46, 47; VI.6): elder son of the triumvir; quaestor 54 B.C., served in Gaul 54–53 B.C.; governed Cisalpine Gaul 49 B.C.

Publius LICINIUS Crassus (I.52; II.34; III.7–11, 20–27; VIII.46): younger son of the triumvir; one of Caesar's officers during the earlier campaigns in Gaul; possibly Quaestor 55 B.C.; served with his father on the Parthian campaign 53 B.C. and was killed.

GLOSSARY OF PERSONS AND PLACES

LINGONES (I.26, 40; IV.10; VI.44; VII.9, 63, 66; VIII.11): a tribe living in central France in the neighbourhood of Langres and Dijon.

LISCUS (I.16–18): an Aeduan magistrate.

LITAVICCUS (VII.37–43, 54, 55, 67): an Aeduan nobleman.

LOIRE (Liger) (III.9; VII.5, 11, 55, 56; VIII.27): a river of central France flowing into the Bay of Biscay.

Quintus LUCANIUS (V.35): a centurion.

LUCTERIUS (VII.5, 7, 8; VIII.30–35, 39, 44): a leader of the Cadurci.

LUGOTORIX (V.22): a Kentish nobleman.

LUTETIA (VI.3; VII.57, 58): a town of the Parisii, the nucleus of Paris, situated on the Ile de la Cité in the Seine.

MÂCON (Matioco) (VII.90): a town in Aeduan territory.

MANDUBII (VII.68, 71, 78): a tribe living in central France, north-west of Dijon.

MANDUBRACIUS (V.20, 22): a chief of the Trinovantes.

Lucius MANLIUS (III.20): Governor of Transalpine Gaul 78 B.C.; took part in the war against Sertorius in Spain and was forced to retreat into Aquitania, where the natives attacked and defeated him.

MARCELLUS see Claudius.

MARCOMANNI (I.51): a German tribe.

Gaius MARIUS (Introd.; I.40): a democratic leader, uncle by marriage of Caesar, seven times consul between 107 and 86 B.C.; defeated the Teutoni and the Cimbri 102–101 B.C.; responsible for the reorganization of the Roman army, converting it from a citizen levy into a professional army.

MARNE (Matrona) (I.1): a river of north-east France flowing into the Seine.

MAXIMUS see Fabius.

MEDIOMATRICI (IV.10; VII.75): an Alpine tribe.

MELDI (V.5): a tribe living on the Marne near Meaux (twenty-five miles east of Paris).

MENAPII (Introd.; II.4; III.9, 28; IV.4, 22, 38; VI.2, 5, 6, 9, 33): a Belgic tribe living mainly in south Holland.

MESSALLA see Valerius.

Marcus METIUS (I.47, 53): an envoy sent by Caesar to Ariovistus.

METLOSEDUM (VII.58, 60, 61): a town of the Senones standing on an island in the Seine, near the site of Melun (twenty-five miles south-south-east of Paris).

MEUSE (Mosa) (IV.9, 10, 12, 16; V.24; VI.33): a river of north-east France flowing into the North sea.

Lucius MINUCIUS Basilus (VI.29, 30; VII.90): a cavalry commander, possibly ranking as general; praetor 45 B.C.

MITHRIDATES (Introd.): 'the great', King of Pontus. His aggressive expansionist policy led to three wars with Rome (88–64 B.C.). He was finally defeated by Pompey and committed suicide in 63 B.C.

MORINI (Introd.; II.4; III.9, 28; IV.21, 22, 37, 38; V.24; VII.75, 76): a tribe living on the coast of Belgium and northern France approximately between Zeebrugge and Boulogne.

MORITASGUS (V.54): brother of Cavarinus, King of the Senones.

MOSELLE (Mosella) (IV.15): a river of eastern France flowing into the Rhine.

Lucius MUNATIUS Plancus (V.24, 25): one of Caesar's generals; pro-consul in Transalpine Gaul 44–43 B.C.; founded colonies at Augst and Lyons; consul 42 B.C.; initially supported Antony in the Civil War, then transferred to Octavian; censor 22 B.C.

NAMMEIUS (I.7): an envoy of the Helvetii.

NAMNETES (III.9): tribal allies of the Veneti.

NANTUATES (III.1, 6): a tribe living in south-west Switzerland on the upper Rhône, in the neighbourhood of St Maurice.

NARBONNE (Narbo Martius) (III.20; VII.7; VIII.46): a Roman citizen colony in the Province, which was later called Narbonensis after it.

NASUA (I.37): the leader, with his brother Cimberius, of the Suebi.

NEMETES (I.51; IV.10; VI.25): a German tribe.

NEMETOCENNA (VIII.46, 52): a town of the Atrebates on the site of Arras.

NERVII (Introd.; II.4, 15–32; V.24, 38–48, 56, 58; VI.2, 3, 29; VII.75): a Belgic tribe living east of the Scheldt in central Belgium.

NITIOBROGES (VII.7, 31, 46, 75): a tribe living in south-west France between the rivers Dordogne and Garonne.

NOREIA (I.5): a town in the Austrian province of Styria, on the site of Neumarkt.

NORTHERN ITALY (Introd.; I.54; II.35; V.1; VI.1, 44; VIII.23, 24), also simply 'Italy' (I.24; II.1, 2; III.1; V.1, 2, 29; VI.32; VII.1, 6, 7, 55; VIII.50, 54): the province of Cisalpine Gaul.

NOVIODUNUM (i) (VII.55): a town of the Aedui on the Loire, probably on the site of Nevers; (ii) (VII.12, 14): a town of the Bituriges in central France, probably near the site of Neuvy-sur-Barangeon (eighteen miles north-north-west of Bourges); (iii) (II.12): a fortress of the Suessiones, just over two miles north-west of Soissons.

NUMIDIANS (II.7, 10, 24): natives of Numidia (Algiers) serving as auxiliary troops, especially archers and slingers.

OCELUM (I.10): a town on the north-west border of Italy, probably Avigliana on the south bank of the Dora Riparia (about eighteen miles west of Turin).

OCTODURUS (III.1): a town of the Veragri situated near Martigny in south-west Switzerland.

OLLOVICO (VII.31): the father of Teutomatus, King of the Nitiobroges.

ORCYNIA (VI.24): Greek name for the Hercynian Forest.

ORGETORIX (Introd.; I.2-4, 9, 26): a Helvetian nobleman.

OSISMI (II.34; III.9; VII.75): a tribe living in Brittany in the neighbour-hood of Brest.

PAEMANI (II.4): a German tribe.

PARISII (VI.3; VII.4, 34, 57, 75): a tribe living in the neighbourhood of Lutetia, a town on the site of Paris.

PAULUS *see* Aemilius.

Quintus PEDIUS (II.2, 11): one of Caesar's generals, and a relative; aedile 54 B.C.; in Caesar's army in Civil War; triumphed 45 B.C., suffect consul 43 B.C.

PETROCORII (VII.75): a tribe in Aquitania, in the neighbourhood of the modern Périgueux.

Marcus PETRONIUS (VII.50): a centurion of the 8th legion.

Lucius PETROSIDIUS (V.37): a standard bearer.

PICTONES (III.11; VII.4, 75; VIII.26, 27): a tribe living on the west coast of France, on the south bank of the Loire. The town of Lemonum (i.e. Poitiers) was in their territory.

PIRUSTAE (V.1): a tribe living on the border with Illyricum.

PISO (IV.12): a nobleman of the Aquitani.

PISO *see* Calpurnius, Pupius.

PLANCUS *see* Munatius.

PLEUMOXII (V.39): a tribe ruled by the Nervii.

PO (Padus) (V.24): a river of northern Italy.

Gnaeus POMPEIUS (V.36): an interpreter employed by Sabinus.

POMPEY (Gnaeus Pompeius Magnus) (Introd.; IV.1; VI.1; VII.6; VIII.52-5): consul 70 B.C., 55 B.C., 52 B.C.; member with Caesar of the 'first triumvirate'; after his defeat by Caesar at Pharsalus in the Civil War (48 B.C.), he withdrew to Egypt, where he was murdered.

Marcus PORCIUS Cato (Introd.): supported Cicero's measures against the Catilinarians; his opposition to the requests of Caesar, Crassus, and Pompey instrumental in bringing about the formation of the 'first triumvirate'; constant opponent thereafter; advocated Pompey's consul-ship in 52 B.C.; supported Pompey in Civil War, while trying to avert bloodshed; in command at Utica during the final campaign in Africa; committed suicide after Thapsus.

PORTUS ITIUS (V.2, 5): probably the harbour of Boulogne (possibly Wissant, eleven miles north of Boulogne).

PRAECONINUS *see* Valerius.

PROCILLUS *see* Valerius.

PROVINCE, the (I.8, 14, 15, 33, 44, 53; II.29; III.2, 6, 9, 20; VII.7, 55, 56, 59, 64, 65, 66; VIII.30, 32, 46); the Roman Province (Introd.; I.2, 6, 10, 28, 33; II.29; VI.24; VII.77); the Province of Gaul (I.19); the Transalpine province (Introd.; VII.6): Transalpine Gaul, formed into a province by Rome in 121 B.C., comprising the French Mediterranean coast, the lower Rhône valley, and part of the western Alps.

PTIANII (III.27): an Aquitanian tribe.

Titus PULLO (V.44): a centurion.

Marcus PUPIUS Piso (I.2, 35): consul 61 B.C.

PYRENEES (I.1): mountains forming the border between modern France and Spain.

QUADRATUS *see* Volusenus.

RAURACI (I.5, 28, 29; VI.25; VII.75): a tribe taking part in the migrations of the Helvetii.

REBILUS *see* Caninius.

REDONES (II.34; VII.75): a tribe living on the Atlantic seaboard.

REGINUS *see* Antistius.

REMI (II.3–7, 9, 12; III.11; V.3, 24, 53–6; VI.4, 12, 44; VII.63, 90; VIII.6, 11, 12): a powerful Belgic tribe living on both sides of the Aisne, in the neighbourhood of Rheims.

RHINE (Rhenus) (I.1, 2, 5, 27, 28, 31–7, 43, 44, 53, 54; II.3, 4, 29, 35; III.11; IV.1, 3–6, 10, 14–19; V.3, 24, 27, 29, 49, 55; VI.9, 24, 29, 32, 35, 41, 42; VII.65; VIII.13): a river dividing Germany from Belgic and Gallic territory.

RHÔNE (Rhodanus) (I.1, 2, 6, 8, 10–12, 33; III.1; VII.65): a river rising in Switzerland and flowing into the Mediterranean at the Gulf of Lyons.

Lucius ROSCIUS (V.24, 53): one of Caesar's generals; quaestor in Gaul 54 B.C.; praetor 49 B.C.; Caesarian in the Civil War; died 43 B.C.

RUFUS *see* Sulpicius.

RUTENI (I.45; VII.5, 7, 64, 75, 90): a tribe living in southern France.

RUTILUS *see* Sempronius.

SABINUS *see* Titurius.

SAMAROBRIVA (Amiens) (V.24, 47, 53): a town seventy-four miles north of Paris.

SAMBRE (Sabis) (II.16, 18): a tributary of the Meuse.

SANTONI (I.10, 11; III.11; VII.75): a tribe of western France living near the River Charente in the neighbourhood of modern Saintes.

SAÔNE (Arar) (I.12, 13, 16; VII.90; VIII.4): a river of eastern France.

SATURNINUS *see* Appuleius.

SCHELDT (Scaldis) (VI.33): a river in Belgic territory.

Gaius SCRIBONIUS Curio (Introd.; VIII.52): a young Roman nobleman whose support Caesar gained by payment of his debts; tribune of the plebs 50 B.C.; killed with his army in Africa 49 B.C.

SEDULLUS (VII.88): chieftain of the Lemovices.

SEDUNI (III.1, 2, 7): a tribe living in south-west Switzerland on the upper Rhône, in the neighbourhood of modern Sion.

SEGNI (VI.32): a tribe of Germanic origin.

SEGONTIACI (V.21): a tribe of south-east England.

SEGOVAX (V.22): a Kentish king.

SEGUSIAVI (I.10; VII.64, 75): a dependent tribe of the Aedui, living on the west bank of the Rhône, just over the Provincial frontier (around modern Lyons).

SEINE (Sequana) (I.1; VII.57, 58): a river of northern France flowing into the Channel.

Marcus SEMPRONIUS Rutilus (VII.90): one of Caesar's officers.

SENONES (II.2; V.54, 56; VI.2–5, 44; VII.4, 11, 34, 56, 58, 75): a tribe living south-east of Paris in the neighbourhood of Agedincum (modern Sens).

SEQUANI (I.1–12, 19, 31–5, 38, 40, 44, 48, 54; IV.10; VI.12; VII.66, 67, 75, 90): a tribe living in eastern France between the River Saône and the Vosges and Jura mountains.

Lucius SERGIUS Catilina (Introd.): agent of Sulla before and during his dictatorship. After his provincial command in Africa he was tried and acquitted on a charge of misgovernment, and the trial prevented his candidacy to be consul in 65 B.C. He stood unsuccessfully twice, the first time, simultaneously with Cicero, probably with Crassus' support and the second time on a programme of agrarian reform and debt relief. In 63 B.C. he organized a conspiracy for a coup d'état, which was detected and suppressed by Cicero. He was killed in a battle with the government's forces.

Quintus SERTORIUS (III.23): appointed Governor of Hither Spain 83 B.C.; maintained himself there as a rebel until 73 B.C.; assassinated.

Titus SEXTIUS (VI.1; VII.49, 51, 90; VIII.11): one of Caesar's generals.

Publius SEXTIUS Baculus (II.25; III.5; VI.38): chief centurion of the 12th legion.

SIBULATES (III.27): an Aquitanian tribe.

SILANUS *see* Junius.

Titus SILLIUS (III.7, 8): one of Caesar's officers, of equestrian status.

SOTIATES (III.20, 21): a tribe living in Aquitania.

SUEBI (I.37, 51, 54; IV.1, 3, 4, 7, 8, 16, 19; VI.9, 10, 29): a powerful German people who had for about a century before Caesar's time been gradually expanding south-westwards from their home in northern Germany.

SUESSIONES (II.3, 4, 12, 13; VII.75; VIII.6): a Belgic tribe living in the Department of the Aisne, in the neighbourhood of Soissons.

SUGAMBRI (IV.16, 18, 19; VI.35): a German tribe living on the east bank of the Rhine between the rivers Ruhr and Sieg.

SULLA *see* Cornelius.

Servius SULPICIUS Galba (III.1–6; VIII.50): one of Caesar's generals.

Publius SULPICIUS Rufus (IV.22; VII.90): one of Caesar's generals.

SURUS (VIII.45): an Aeduan chief.

TARBELLI (III.27): an Aquitanian tribe.

TARUSATES (III.23, 27): an Aquitanian tribe.

TASGETIUS (V.25, 29): a nobleman of the Carnutes.

TAXIMAGULUS (V.22): a Kentish king.

TECTOSAGES *see* Volcae.

TENCTHERI (IV.1, 4, 16, 18; V.55; VI.35): a German tribe.

Titus TERRASIDIUS (III.7, 8): an officer of equestrian rank.

TEUTOMATUS (VII.31, 46): King of the Nitiobroges.

TEUTONI (Introd.; I.33, 40; II.4, 29; VII.77): a nomadic German tribe.

THAMES (Tamesis) (V.11, 18): a river of south-east Britain.

TIGURINI (I.12): one of four clans of the Helvetii.

Quintus TITURIUS Sabinus (II.5, 9, 10; III.11, 17–19, IV.22, 38; V.24, 26–33, 36–41, 47, 52, 53; VI.1, 32, 37): one of Caesar's generals.

TOLOSATES (I.10; VII.7): a tribe living in the Province, in the neighbourhood of Tolosa (Toulouse).

TOULOUSE (Tolosa) (III.20): a town in south-west France.

TRANSALPINE GAUL *see* province, the.

Marcus TREBIUS Gallus (III.7, 8): one of Caesar's officers of equestrian rank.

Gaius TREBONIUS (i) (V.17, 24; VI.33; VII.11, 81; VIII.6, 11, 14, 46, 54): tribune 55 B.C.; proposer of the law assigning Syria to Crassus and Spain to Pompey; then one of Caesar's generals in Gaul; governed Further Spain 47–46 B.C.; suffect consul 45 B.C.; in the assassination conspiracy 44 B.C.; governed Asia 43 B.C.; put to death by Dolabella at Smyrna 42 B.C.; (ii) (VI.40): an officer of equestrian rank.

TREVERI (I.37; II.24; III.11; IV.6, 10; V. 2–4, 24, 47, 53, 55, 58; VI.2–9, 29, 32, 44; VII.63; VIII.25, 45, 52): a tribe living west of the Rhine in south-east Belgium, Luxembourg, and part of Rhenish Prussia; the town of Treves preserves their name.

TRIBOCI (I.51; IV.10): a German tribe.

TRIESTE (Tergeste) (VIII.24): a town at the north end of the Adriatic.

TRINOVANTES (V.20–22): a tribe living in Essex; their chief town was Camulodunum, on the site of Colchester.

TROUCILLUS see Valerius.

TULINGI (I.5, 25, 26, 28, 29): a tribe living to the north-east of the Helvetii.

Marcus TULLIUS Cicero (Introd.): the famous orator, brother of Quintus. Consul 63 B.C.; exiled 58 B.C. but recalled the following year and supported the triumvirs thereafter; opted for Pompey at the outbreak of the Civil War, but took no active part; pardoned by Caesar; after the latter's death, strongly opposed Mark Antony, who had him proscribed; killed 43 B.C.

Quintus TULLIUS Cicero (V.24, 27, 38–41, 45, 48, 49, 52, 53; VI.32, 36; VII.90): younger brother of Marcus Tullius Cicero (see Introd.) the orator. Served under Caesar 54–52 B.C., but on Pompey's side in the Civil War; put to death, like his brother, by Antony 43 B.C.

TULLUS see Volcacius.

TURONI (II.35; VII.4, 75; VIII.46): a tribe living on the banks of the Loire.

UBII (IV.3, 8, 11, 16, 19; VI.9, 10, 29): a German tribe living on the east bank of the Rhine between the rivers Sieg and Main.

USIPETES (IV.1, 4, 16, 18; VI.35): a German tribe which invaded Gaul in 55 B.C.

UXELLODUNUM (VIII.32, 37, 39, 40, 44): a stronghold of the Cadurci in south-west France, probably the hill called Puy d'Issolu, near Vayrac in the Department of the Lot.

Gaius VALERIUS Caburus (I.47; VII.65): a prominent man of the Helvii, granted Roman citizenship in 83 B.C.; father of C. Valerius Procillus and C. Valerius Domnotaurus.

Gaius VALERIUS Domnotaurus (VII.65): son of C. Valerius Caburus.

Gaius VALERIUS Flaccus (I.47): governor of the province of Transalpine Gaul in 83 B.C.

Marcus VALERIUS Messalla (I.2, 23); consul 61 B.C.

Lucius VALERIUS Praeconinus (III.20): a Roman general defeated in Aquitania in 78 B.C.

Gaius VALERIUS Procillus (I.47, 53): son of Gaius Valerius Caburus.

Gaius VALERIUS Troucillus (I.19): a Gallic interpreter.

VALETIACUS (VII.32): a magistrate of the Aedui.

VANGIONES (I.51): a German tribe.

VARUS see Atius.

Publius VATINIUS (VIII.46): a man with a chequered career. Prosecuted after being quaestor in 63 B.C. on a charge of extortion; notorious for his depredations as an officer in Further Spain 62 B.C.; tribune in 59 B.C. and supported Caesar; elected praetor for 55 B.C. by bribery; prosecuted 54 B.C., and defended by Cicero; Caesar's general in Gaul 51 B.C.; defended Brundisium in the Civil War; consul for a few months in 47 B.C.; commanded the army in Illyricum from 45 B.C.; triumphed at the end of 43 B.C., though his army had already deserted.

Quintus VELANIUS (III.7, 8): an officer of equestrian rank.

VELIOCASSES (II.4; VII.75; VIII.7): a Belgic tribe living along the lower Seine.

VELLAUNODUNUM (VII.11, 14): a town of the Senones in central France, probably Montargis, between Orleans and Sens.

VELLAVII (VII.75): a dependent tribe of the Arverni.

VENELLI (II.34; III.11, 17; VII.75): a tribe living on the coast of Normandy in the neighbourhood of Cherbourg.

VENETI (II.34; III.7–11, 16–18; VII.75): a tribe living in the Department of the Morbihan in Brittany.

VENETIA (III.9): territory of the Veneti.

VERAGRI (III.1, 2): a tribe living in south-west Switzerland on the upper Rhône, near Martigny.

VERBIGENI (I.27): a clan of the Helvetii.

VERCASSIVELLAUNUS (VII.76, 83, 85, 88): a leader of the Arverni, cousin to Vercingetorix.

VERCINGETORIX (VII.4, 8, 9, 12–21, 26–89): an Arvernian; commander-in-chief in the revolt of 52 B.C.

VERTICO (V.45, 49): a Nervian deserter employed by Cicero during the siege of his camp.

VERTISCUS (VIII.12): a chief magistrate and cavalry commander of the Remi.

VERUCLOETIUS (I.7): an envoy of the Helvetii.

VIENNE (Vienna) (VII.9): a town on the Rhône.

VIRIDOMARUS (VII.38–40): a young Aeduan noble supposedly killed by the Romans.

VIRIDOVIX (III.17, 18): a leader of the Venelli.

VIROMANDUI (II.4, 16, 23): a tribe living on the upper Somme near St Quentin.

VOCATES (III.23, 27): a tribe of Aquitania.

VOCCIO (I.53): King of Noricum, brother-in-law of Ariovistus.

VOCONTII (I.10): a tribe living in the Province.

Gaius VOLCACIUS Tullus (VI.29): a Roman officer of equestrian rank.

VOLCAE ARECOMICI (VII.7, 64): a tribe living in the Province near the Pyrenees.

VOLCAE TECTOSAGES (VI.24): a Gallic tribe which migrated into Germany.

Gaius VOLUSENUS Quadratus (III.5; IV.21, 23; VI.41; VIII.23, 48): a military tribune; commander of Caesar's cavalry in the later campaigns.

Lucius VORENUS (V.44): a centurion.

VOSGES (IV.10): a range of mountains in north-east France.

WAAL (Vacalus) (IV.10): a river, the southern branch of the lower Rhine.

INDEX TO MAPS

NORTHERN GAUL

100 miles
50
0

SUGAMBRI
UBII
MENAPII
EBURONES
TREVERI
MORINI
NERVII
ATUATUCI
SEQUANI
Besançon
B E L G A E
LINGONES
Alesia
ATREBATES
Samarobriva
REMI
Bibracte
Portus
Itius
BELLOVACI
SUESSIONES
CALETI
Lutetia
PARISII
Agedincum
SENONES
LEXOVII
CARNUTES
Avaricum
BRITANNIA
ANDES
BITURIGES
VENELLI
CORIOSOLITES
PICTONES
OSISMI
VENETI

SOUTHERN GAUL

0   50   100 miles

HELVETII

ALLOBROGES

AEDUI

BOII

HELVII

Massilia

BITURIGES

Gergovia

ARVERNI

LEMOVICES

THE PROVINCE

VOLCAE
ARECOMICI

Narbo

PICTONES

Lemonum

Uxellodunum

TOLOSATES

SANTONI

AQUITANI

Pyrenees

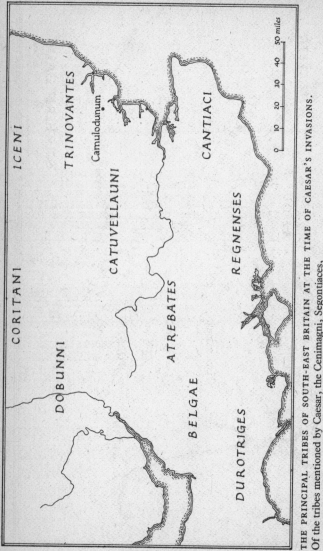

THE PRINCIPAL TRIBES OF SOUTH-EAST BRITAIN AT THE TIME OF CAESAR'S INVASIONS.
Of the tribes mentioned by Caesar, the Cenimagni, Segontiaces,
Ancalites, Bibroci, and Cassi remain known to us only as names.

THE SIEGE OF ALESIA

A Infantry Camps
B Cavalry Camps
++++ 20-foot Ditches

0   1 mile

Circumvallation
Contravallation
Gallic Wall
ALESIA
R. Ose
R. Oserain
R. Brenne
Gallic Relief Army

MORE ABOUT PENGUINS
AND PELICANS

For further information about books available from Penguins please write to Dept EP, Penguin Books Ltd, Harmondsworth, Middlesex UB7 0DA.

In the U.S.A.: For a complete list of books available from Penguins in the United States write to Dept CS, Penguin Books, 625 Madison Avenue, New York, New York 10022.

In Canada: For a complete list of books available from Penguins in Canada write to Penguin Books Canada Ltd, 2801 John Street, Markham, Ontario L3R 1B4.

In Australia: For a complete list of books available from Penguins in Australia write to the Marketing Department, Penguin Books Australia Ltd, P.O. Box 257, Ringwood, Victoria 3134.

In New Zealand: For a complete list of books available from Penguins in New Zealand write to the Marketing Department, Penguin Books (N.Z.) Ltd, P.O. Box 4019, Auckland 10.